TEACHING OF MATHEMATICS I

TEACHING OF
MATHEMATICS I

Arul Jothi
M.Sc., M.Ed.
Principal, Arcot Sri Mahalakshmi Women's Teacher Training Institute,
Villapakkam, Vellore Dist.-632521 T.N.

Dr. D.L. Balaji
B.Com., M.A., M.Phil., D.Lit.
Correspondent, Arcot Sri Mahalakshmi Educational Institutions,
Villapakkam, Vellore Dist.-632521 T.N.

Er. Nishit Mathur
C Level (Computers), B.Tech. (Electronics)
Former Associate & Consultant,
Doon International University

CENTRUM PRESS
NEW DELHI-110002 (INDIA)

CENTRUM PRESS
H.O.: 4360/4, Ansari Road, Daryaganj,
New Delhi-110 002 (India)
Ph.: 23278000, 23261597

B.O.: No. 1015, Ist Main Road, BSK IIIrd Stage
IIIrd Phase, IIIrd Block,
Bangalore - 560 085 (India)
Tel.: 080-41723429
Visit us at: www.centrumpress.com

Teaching of Mathematics I

First Edition, 2009

PRINTED IN INDIA

Printed at Mehra Offset Press, Delhi

Contents

Preface

The Mathematics book for B.Ed. students is written, with an intention to help students in their careers in the area of Mathematics. The purpose of the book is to present a reasonably comprehensive account of sampling theory as it has been developed for use in sample surveys, with sufficient illustrations to show how the theory is applied in practice, and with a supply of exercises to be worked by the student.

The main feature of this book is the use of the Concrete > Pictorial > Abstract approach. The students are provided with the necessary learning experiences beginning with the concrete and pictorial stages, followed by the abstract stage to enable them to learn mathematics meaningfully. This approach encourages active thinking process, communication of mathematical ideas and problem solving. This helps develop the foundation students will need for more advanced mathematics.

Practice exercises are designed to provide the students with further practice after they have done the relevant workbook exercises. Review exercises are provided for cumulative reviews of concepts and skills. All the practice exercises and review exercises are optional exercises.

The book contains more material than can be required for B.Ed. students However, the sections have been prepared so that many of them can be omitted, or condensed to a brief statement of the results, without detriment to later parts of the book. There are, for instance, numerous discussions of special topics, which attempt to answer questions that have been raised by alert sampling practitioners but which are not essential to a firm understanding of the fundamentals of the subject.

Author

Unit I

Nature, Characteristics and Development of Mathematics

MEANING OF MATHEMATICS

Mathematics is commonly defined as the study of patterns of structure, change, and space; more informally, one might say it is the study of 'figures and numbers'. In the formalist view, it is the investigation of axiomatically defined abstract structures using logic and mathematical notation; other views are described in Philosophy of mathematics.

The specific structures that are investigated by mathematicians often have their origin in the natural sciences, most commonly in physics, but mathematicians also define and investigate structures for reasons purely internal to mathematics, because the structures may provide, for instance, a unifying generalization for several sub fields, or a helpful tool for common calculations. Finally, many mathematicians study the areas they do for purely aesthetic reasons, viewing mathematics as an art form rather than as a practical or applied science.

Mathematics is often abbreviated to math in North America and maths in other English-speaking countries.

OVERVIEW AND HISTORY OF MATHEMATICS

The word "mathematics" comes from the Greek μάθημα (máthema) which means "science, knowledge or learning"; μαθηματικός (mathematikós) means "fond of learning".

The major disciplines within mathematics arose out of the

need to do calculations in commerce, to measure land and to predict astronomical events. These three needs can be roughly related to the broad subdivision of mathematics into the study of structure, space and change.

The study of structure starts with numbers, firstly the familiar natural numbers and integers and their arithmetical operations, which are recorded in elementary algebra. The deeper properties of whole numbers are studied in number theory. The investigation of methods to solve equations leads to the field of abstract algebra, which, among other things, studies rings and fields, structures that generalize the properties possessed by the familiar numbers. The physically important concept of vector, generalized to vector spaces and studied in linear algebra, belongs to the two branches of structure and space.

The study of space originates with geometry, first the Euclidean geometry and trigonometry of familiar three-dimensional space, but later also generalized to non-Euclidean geometries which play a central role in general relativity. Several long standing questions about ruler and compass constructions were finally settled by Galois theory. The modern fields of differential geometry and algebraic geometry generalize geometry in different directions: differential geometry emphasizes the concepts of functions, fibre bundles, derivatives, smoothness and direction, while in algebraic geometry geometrical objects are described as solution sets of polynomial equations. Group theory investigates the concept of symmetry abstractly and provides a link between the studies of space and structure. Topology connects the study of space and the study of change by focusing on the concept of continuity.

Understanding and describing change in measurable quantities is the common theme of the natural sciences, and calculus was developed as a most useful tool for doing just that. The central concept used to describe a changing variable is that of a function. Many problems lead quite naturally to relations between a quantity and its rate of change, and the methods to solve these are studied in the field of differential equations. The numbers used to represent continuous quantities are the real numbers, and the detailed study of their properties and the properties of real-valued functions is known as real analysis. For several reasons, it is convenient to generalize to the complex numbers which are studied in complex analysis. Functional analysis focuses attention on (typically infinite-dimensional) spaces of functions, laying the groundwork for quantum mechanics among many other things. Many phenomena in nature can be described by dynamical systems and chaos theory deals with the fact that many of these systems exhibit unpredictable yet deterministic behaviour.

In order to clarify and investigate the foundations of mathematics, the fields of set theory, mathematical logic and model theory were developed.

When computers were first conceived, several essential theoretical concepts were shaped by mathematicians, leading to the fields of computability theory, computational complexity theory, information theory and algorithmic information theory. Many of these questions are now investigated in theoretical computer science. Discrete mathematics is the common name for those fields of mathematics useful in computer science.

An important field in applied mathematics is statistics, which uses probability theory as a tool and allows the description, analysis and prediction of phenomena and is used in all sciences. Numerical analysis investigates the methods of efficiently solving various mathematical problems numerically on computers and takes rounding errors into account.

Mathematics

Deductive study of numbers, geometry, and various abstract constructs, or structures; the latter often "abstract" the features common to several models derived from the empirical, or applied, sciences, although many emerge from purely mathematical or logical considerations. Mathematics is very broadly divided into foundations, algebra, analysis, geometry, and applied mathematics, which includes theoretical computer science.

The term foundations is used to refer to the formulation and analysis of the language, axioms, and logical methods on which all of mathematics rests (see logic; symbolic logic). The scope and complexity of modern mathematics requires a very fine analysis of the formal language in which meaningful mathematical statements may be formulated and perhaps be proved true or false. Most apparent mathematical contradictions have been shown to derive from an imprecise and inconsistent use of language. A basic task is to furnish a set of axioms effectively free of contradictions and at the same time rich enough to constitute a deductive source for all of modern mathematics. The modern axiom schemes proposed for this purpose are all couched within the theory of sets, originated by Georg Cantor, which now constitutes a universal mathematical language.

Algebra

Historically, algebra is the study of solutions of one or several algebraic equations, involving the polynomial functions of one or several variables. The case where all the polynomials have degree one (systems of linear equations) leads to linear algebra. The case of a single equation, in which one studies the roots of one polynomial, leads to field theory and to the so-called Galois theory. The general case of several equations of high degree leads to algebraic geometry, so named because the sets of solutions of such systems are often studied by geometric methods.

Geometry

The shape, size, and other properties of figures and the nature of space are in the province of geometry. Euclidean geometry is concerned with the axiomatic study of polygons, conic sections, spheres, polyhedra, and related geometric objects in two and three dimensions—in particular, with the relations of congruence and of similarity between such objects. The unsuccessful attempt to prove the "parallel postulate" from the other axioms of Euclid led in the 19th cent. to the discovery of two different types of non-Euclidean geometry.

DEVELOPMENT OF MATHEMATICS

The earliest records of mathematics show it arising in response to practical needs in agriculture, business, and industry. In Egypt and Mesopotamia, where evidence dates from the 2d and 3d millennia b.c., it was used for surveying and mensuration; estimates of the value of pi are found in both locations. There is some evidence of similar developments in India and China during this same period, but few records have survived. This early mathematics is generally empirical, arrived at by trial and error as the best available means for obtaining results, with no proofs given. However, it is now known that the Babylonians were aware of the necessity of proofs prior to the Greeks, who had been presumed the originators of this important step

CHARACTERISTICS OF MATHEMATICS

Some typical characteristics of mathematics anxiety, or "mathophobia," are poor performance, misunderstandings, and dislike of math. Children may exhibit feelings in insecurity, as well as fears of failure, punishment, ridicule, or stigmatizing labels. Children with math anxiety may also have a negative attitude or negative emotional reaction to math.

The best strategy to use in order to overcome math anxiety is prevention or early detection. There are different techniques teachers can use in order curb early signs of math anxiety. Teachers should emphasize meaning and understanding rather than memorization. Students need to understand that failure in a problem does not indicate an inability to be successful in math. Mistakes are a natural process of problem solving. Teachers need to provide students with experiences that they will be successful in, in order to promote a more positive attitude. Teachers should show enjoyment for math and project a positive attitude. These learning bridges or strategies are good ways to help prevent the early development of math anxiety.

ABSTRACTIONS, PROOFS, APPLICATIONS

With even a superficial knowledge of mathematics, it is easy to recognize certain characteristic features: its abstractness, its precision, its logical rigor, the indisputable character of its conclusions, and finally, the exceptionally broad range of its applications.

The abstractness of mathematics is easy to see. We operate with abstract numbers without worrying about how to relate them in each case to concrete objects. In school we study the abstract multiplication table, that is, a table for multiplying one abstract number by another, not a number of boys by a number of apples, or a number of apples by the price of an apple.

Similarly in geometry we consider, for example, straight lines and not stretched threads, the concept of a geometric line being obtained by abstraction from all other properties, excepting only extension in one direction. More generally, the concept of a geometric figure is the result of abstraction from all the properties of actual objects except their spatial form and dimensions.

Abstractions of this sort are characteristic for the whole of mathematics. The concept of a whole number and of a geometric figure are only two of the earliest and most elementary of its concepts. They have been followed by a mass of others, too numerous to describe, extending to such abstractions as complex numbers, functions, integrals, differentials, functionals, n-dimensional, and even infinite-dimensional spaces, and so forth. These abstractions, piled up as it were on one another, have reached such a degree of generalization that they apparently lose all connection with daily life and the "ordinary mortal" understands nothing about them beyond the mere fact that "all this is incomprehensible."

In reality, of course, the case is not so at all. Although the concept of n-dimensional space is no doubt extremely abstract, yet it does have a completely real content, which is not very difficult to understand. In the present book it will be our task to emphasize and clarify the concrete content of such abstract concepts as those mentioned earlier, so that the reader may convince himself that they are all connected with actual life, both in their origin and in their applications.

But abstraction is not the exclusive property of mathematics; it is characteristic of every science, even of all mental activity in general. Consequently, the abstractness of mathematical concepts does not in itself give a complete description of the peculiar character of mathematics.

The abstractions of mathematics are distinguished by three features. In the first place, they deal above all else with quantitative relations and spatial forms, abstracting them from all other properties of objects. Second, they occur in a sequence of increasing degrees of abstraction, going very much further in this direction than the abstractions of other sciences. We will illustrate these two features in detail later, using as examples the fundamental notions of number and figure. Finally, and this is obvious, mathematics as such moves almost wholly in the field of abstract concepts and their interrelations. While the natural scientist turns constantly to experiment for proof of his assertions, the mathematician employs only argument and computation.

It is true that mathematicians also make constant use, to assist them in the discovery of their theorems and methods, of models and physical analogues, and they have recourse to various completely concrete examples. These examples serve as the actual source of the theory and as a means of discovering its theorems, but no theorem definitely belongs to mathematics until it has been rigorously proved by a logical argument.

If a geometer, reporting a newly discovered theorem, were to demonstrate it by means of models and to confine himself to such a demonstration, no mathematician would admit that the theorem had been proved. The demand for a proof of a theorem is well known in high school geometry, but it pervades the whole of mathematics. We could measure the angles at the base of a thousand isosceles triangles with extreme accuracy, but such a procedure would never provide us with a mathematical proof of the theorem that the angles at the base of an isosceles triangle are equal. Mathematics demands that this result be deduced from the fundamental concepts of geometry, which at the present time, in view of the fact that geometry is nowadays developed on a rigorous basis, are precisely formulated in the axioms. And so it is in every case. To prove a theorem means for the mathematician to deduce it by a logical argument from the fundamental properties of the concepts occurring in that theorem. In this way, not only the concepts but also the methods of mathematics are abstract and theoretical.

The results of mathematics are distinguished by a high degree of logical rigor, and a mathematical argument is conducted with such scrupulousness as to make it incontestable and completely convincing to anyone who understands it. The scrupulousness and cogency of mathematical proofs are already well known in a high school course. Mathematical truths are in fact the prototype of the completely incontestable. Not for nothing do people say "as clear as two and two are four." Here the relation "two and two are four" is introduced as the very image of the irrefutable and- incontestable.

But the rigour of mathematics is not absolute; it is in a process of continual development; the principles of mathematics have not congealed once and for all but have a life of their own and may even be the subject of scientific quarrels.

In the final analysis the vitality of mathematics arises from the fact that its concepts and results, for all their abstractness, originate, as we shall see, in the actual world and find widely varied application in the other sciences, in engineering, and in all the practical affairs of daily life; to realise this is the most important prerequisite for understanding mathematics.

The exceptional breadth of its applications is another characteristic feature of mathematics.

In the first place we make constant use, almost every hour, in industry and in private and social life, of the most varied concepts and results of mathematics, without thinking about them at all; for example, we use arithmetic to compute. our expenses or geometry to calculate the floor area of an apartment. Of course, the rules here are very simple, but we should remember that in some period of antiquity they represented the most advanced mathematical achievements of the age.

Second, modern technology would be impossible without mathematics. There is probably not a single technical process which can be carried through without more or less complicated calculations; and mathematics plays a very important role in the development of new branches of technology.

Finally, it is true that every science, to a greater or lesser degree, makes essential use of mathematics. The "exact sciences," mechanics, astronomy, physics, and to a great extent chemistry, express their laws, as every schoolboy knows, by means of formulas and make extensive use of mathematical apparatus in developing their theories. The progress of these sciences would have been completely impossible without mathematics. For this reason the requirements of mechanics, astronomy, and physics have always exercised a direct and decisive influence on the development of mathematics.

In other sciences mathematics plays a smaller role, but here too it finds important applications. Of course, in the study of such complicated phenomena as occur in biology and sociology, the mathematical method cannot play the same role as, let us say, in physics. In all cases, but especially where the phenomena are most complicated, we must bear in mind, if we are not to lose our way in meaningless play with formulas, that the application of mathematics is significant only if the concrete phenomena have already been made the subject of a profound theory. In one way or another, mathematics is applied in almost every science, from mechanics to political economy.

Let us recall some particularly brilliant applications of mathematics in the exact sciences and in technology.

The planet Neptune, one of the most distant in the Solar System, was discovered in the year 1846 on the basis of mathematical calculations. By analyzing certain irregularities in the motion of Uranus, the, astronomers Adams and Le Verrier came to the conclusion that these irregularities were caused by the gravitational attraction of another planet. Le Verrier calculated on the basis of the laws of mechanics exactly where this planet must be, and an observer to whom he communicated his results caught sight of it in his telescope in the exact position indicated by Le Verrier. This discovery was a triumph not only for mechanics and astronomy, and in particular for the system of Copernicus, but also for the powers of mathematical calculation.

Another example, no less impressive, was the discovery of electromagnetic waves. The Scottish physicist Maxwell, by generalizing the laws of electromagnetic phenomena as established by experiment, was able to express these laws in the form of equations. From these equations he deduced, by purely mathematical methods, that electromagnetic waves could exist and that they must be propagated with the speed of light.

On the basis of this result, he proposed the electromagnetic theory of light, which was later developed and deepened in every direction. Moreover, Maxwell's results led to the search for electromagnetic waves of purely electrical origin, arising for example from an oscillating charge. These waves were actually discovered by Hertz. Shortly afterwards, A S Popov, by discovering means for exciting, transmitting, and receiving electromagnetic oscillations made them available for a wide range of applications and thereby laid the foundations for the whole technology of radio. In the discovery of radio, now the common possession of everyone, an important role was played by the results of a purely mathematical deduction.

So from observation, as for example of the deflection of a magnetic needle by an electric current, science proceeds to generalization, to a theory of the phenomena, and to formulation of laws and to mathematical expression of them. From these laws come new deductions, and finally, the theory is embodied in practice, which in its turn provides powerful new impulses for the development of the theory.

It is particularly remarkable that even the most abstract constructions of mathematics, arising within that science itself, without any immediate motivation from the natural sciences or from technology, nevertheless have fruitful applications. For example, imaginary numbers first came to light in algebra, and for a long time their significance in the actual world remained uncomprehended, a circumstance indicated by their very name.

But when about 1800 a geometrical interpretation was given to them, imaginary numbers became firmly established in mathematics, giving rise to the extensive theory of functions of a complex variable, i.e., of a variable of the form x + y"-1. This theory of "imaginary" functions of an "imaginary" variable proved itself to be far from imaginary, but rather a very practical means of solving technological problems. Thus, the fundamental results of N E Zhukovskii concerning the lift on the wing of an airplane are proved by means of this theory. The same theory is useful, for example, in the solution of problems concerning the oozing of water under a dam, problems whose importance is obvious during the present period of construction of huge hydroelectric stations.

Another example, equally impressive, is provided by non-Euclidean geometry, which arose from the efforts, extending for 2000 years from the time of Euclid, to prove the parallel axiom, a problem of purely mathematical interest. N I Lobachevsky himself, the founder of the new geometry, was careful to label his geometry "imaginary," since he could not see any meaning for it in the actual world, although he was confident that such a meaning would eventually be found. The results of his geometry appeared to the majority of mathematicians to be not only "imaginary" but even unimaginable and absurd.

Nevertheless, his ideas laid the foundation for a new development of geometry, namely the creation of theories of various non-Euclidean spaces; and these ideas subsequently became the basis of the general theory of relativity, in which the mathematical apparatus consists of a form of non-Euclidean geometry of four-dimensional space. Thus the abstract constructions of mathematics, which at the very least seemed incomprehensible, proved themselves a powerful instrument for the development of one of the most important theories of physics. Similarly, in the present-day theory of atomic phenomena, in the so-called quantum mechanics, essential use is made of many extremely abstract mathematical concepts and theories, as for example the concept of infinite-dimensional space.

There is no need to give any further examples, since we have already shown with sufficient emphasis that mathematics finds widespread application in everyday life and in technology and science; in the exact sciences and in the great problems of technology, applications are found even for those theories which arise within mathematics itself. This is, one of the characteristic peculiarities of mathematics, along with its abstractness and the rigor and conclusiveness of its results.

NATURE OF MATHEMATICS

In discussing these special features of mathematics we have been far from explaining its essence; rather we have merely pointed out its external marks. Our task now is to explain the essential nature of these characteristic features. For this purpose it will be necessary to answer, at the very least, the following questions:

What do these abstract mathematical concepts reflect? In other words, what is the actual subject matter of mathematics?

Why do the abstract results of mathematics appear so convincing, and its initial concepts so obvious? In other words, on what foundation do the methods of mathematics rest?

Why, in spite of all its abstractness, does mathematics find such wide application and does not turn out to be merely idle play with abstractions? In other words, how is the significance of mathematics to be explained?

Finally, what forces lead to the further development of mathematics, allowing it to unite abstractness with breadth of application? What is the basis for its continuing growth?

In answering these questions we will form a general picture of the content of mathematics, of its methods, and of its significance and its development; that is, we will understand its essence.

Idealists and metaphysicists not only fall into confusion in their attempts to answer these basic questions but they go so far as to distort mathematics completely, turning it literally inside out. Thus, seeing the extreme abstractness and cogency of mathematical results, the idealist imagines that mathematics issues from pure thought.

In reality, mathematics offers not the slightest support for idealism or metaphysics. We will convince ourselves of this as we attempt, in general outline, to answer the listed questions about the essence of mathematics. For a preliminary clarification of these questions, it is sufficient to examine the foundations of arithmetic and elementary geometry, to which we now turn.

LOGICAL SEQUENCE IN MATHEMATICS

The problem is predicting the next term of a partially specified sequence. The user shall input the rst few terms of a mathematical sequence. The expert system will rst try to understand the pattern and using the found pattern it would predict the next term. The domains from which the user can choose terms are the following: The domain of integers and the domain of strings over a nite alphabet. This report also discusses the extention of the prototype to include other domains like the rational numbers. It must be noted that there are quite dierent kinds of rules for these dierent do- mains. Whereas we have some arithmetic operators preened over numbers that implicitly store the pattern in the sequence of numbers, for strings its identifying the changes in the strings.

INTEGER SEQUENCES

Integer sequences are the most commonly seen sequences. The main idea of the approach used in identifying the integer sequences is that we can perform certain operations on the terms of the given sequence and form new integer sequences such that once the next term of the new sequence is known, the next term of the original sequence can be determined fairly easily. For integer sequences, its the addition, subtraction and multiplication operators that play the major role in xing up the function f. So, in order to discover the function f, we need to perform various operations on the integers that are the first few given terms of the sequence.

For example, consider the sequence 3; 7; 11; 15; . ... The way this sequence is understood is by taking the dierence between adjacent terms of the sequence. Doing this we get another sequence namely, 4; 4; 4; .... This sequence can be trivially identied as the constant sequence. But the new sequence thus constructed may not always be so simple. So essentially we have formed another problem from the original problem.

We can recursively solve the problem for the new sequence. Consider another example, 2; 2; 4; 16; 256; .... This time construct a new sequence by dividing a term by its predecessor. We get 1; 2; 4; 8. Applying the same principle to this sequence yields 2; 2; 2. Again this can be easily identied as the constant sequence. In case simple transformations like the ones discussed above fail, we go into more complicated methods. Algorithm Identify-Integer-Sequence

1. If the sequence can be identified to be a sub-sequence of a sequence in the database of integer sequences, then its trivially solved.
2. If the sequence is seen to be a sub-sequence of some sequence in its context, then it is solved.
3. If the sequence has all of its terms equal, then it is a constant sequence.
4. *Method 1:* Construct a new sequence S with the difference of adjacent terms in the sequence S as its terms. Put sequence S in the context of sequence S_1. Recursively call.

Identify-Integer-Sequence(S_1). In case the sequence S_1 is successfully identified and its next term is found to be s_1, then the next term of sequence S is s_1 plus the last term of S.

5. In case the process of identification of sequence S1 fails, continue with the next method.
5. *Method 2:* If each term in the given sequence divides the next term, construct a new sequence S_1 with the quotient of adjacent terms in the sequence S as its

terms. Put sequence S in the context of sequence S_1. Recursively call Identify-Integer-Sequence(S_1). In case the sequence S_1 is successfully identified and its next term is found to be s_1, then the next term of sequence S is s1 multiplied by the last term of S. In case the process of identification of sequence S fails, continue with the next method.

6. *Method 3:* If each term in the given sequence divides the previous term, construct a new sequence S_1 with the quotient of adjacent terms (term divided by the next term) in the sequence S as its terms. Put sequence S in the context of sequence S_1. Recursively call Identify-Integer-Sequence(S_1). In case the sequence S1 is successfully identified and its next term is found to be s_1, then the next term of sequence S is the last term of S divided by s_1. In case the process of identification of sequence S_1 fails, continue with the next method.
7. *Method 4:* If the number of terms in S is substantially large, (which in this case is 5), then divide the sequence S into 2 sub-sequences S_1 and S_2, where S_1 contains all the odd terms of sequence S and S_2 contains all the even terms. Again recursively identify the next terms of the sequences S_1 and S_2 after having put S in their context. If both S_1 and S_2 are identified, then S is trivially identified. If either one fails, then this method fails. Move on to the next method.
8. *Method 5:* Get a formula (almost fourth degree polynomial in n) that best describes the last given term in the sequence S as a function of n. If that formula explains all the other terms of the sequence too, then it can be used to generate the next term of sequence S.
9. If all the above methods fail, then fail. In case any of the sequences is identified, its result is propogated back to the original sequence at the top level 6.

The methods are tried in the order in which they are enumerated above. The choice for the specific order was based on experience and knowledge of the domain. It is also clear that the prototype can be easily expanded to include more methods by adding them down in the above ordering. That way the system continues to do what it does presently and also more depending on the power of the new methods.

One good method for future consideration would be improving the last method for identifying the integer sequences. Currently it does not do much but it can be easily improved. The main idea is to generate a function that has the minimum number of non-zero coefficients. Mathematically, this problem involves solving some system of linear equations the above mentioned constraint.

This was not done in this project because of limited amount of time. Other methods for identification of integer sequences are not difficult to envisage. One such method would be to convert the integer sequence into a string solution by mapping 0 to a, 1 to b, 2 to c and so on. Subsequently the methods for identifying the string sequences can be used on this new sequence. Finally, the results can be converted back. Any new method added over the existing structure would actually enhence the power of the system many-folds because of the inherent recursive way the methods are used.

For example, method 1 may be used on the original sequence S to form a new sequence S1. Method 4 may then be applied to S to form S_2. S_2 may be nally solved by some other method (which can be the new method also!) As an example of the application of the above procedure, consider the following sample sequence, 1; 2; 1; 2; 2; 4; 3; 6; 5; 10; 8; 16; ...

Method 1, method 2 and method 3 fail on this. Applying method 4, we get two sub-sequences,

S_1 = 1; 1; 2; 3; 5; 8; ...S2 = 2; 2; 4; 6; 10; 16; ...

Now, we can apply method 1 on the sequence S1 to get,

S_3 = 0; 1; 1; 2; 3; ...7

which is seen to be a sub-sequence of the sequence S in the context. Hence, the next term of sequence S_3 is 5. So, the next term of S_1 is 8 + 5 which is 13. Similar reasoning leads to an answer of 26 for the second sequence S_2. This solves the original sequence S.

EXPLANATION FOR INTEGER SEQUENCES

The method used for generating explanations is based on the ideas in [6] and [7]. The part of the programmeme that identifies a particular sequence is responsible for generating explanations for the solution of that sequence. All explanations are template based. Since the method used for identifying integer sequences is recursive in nature, so we get different explanations for each level.

For example, consider the sequence S = (2; 3; 5; 9; 17). Applying method 1 to this sequence we create the new sequence S_1 = (1; 2; 4; 8). Applying method 1 again on S_1 gives S_2 = (1; 2; 4). Now step 1 of the above algorithm identifies the sequence S2 to be a sub-sequence of sequence S which happens to be in the context of sequence S_2. So, next term of S_2 is 8 because 8 occurs after (1; 2; 4) in S_1. Therefore next term of S_1 is 8 + 8 = 16. Therefore the next term of S is 17 + 16 = 33.

The explanation generated by the programmeme is similar to what has been described above and is shown below!

Input the first few terms of the sequence: 2 3 5 9 17 Input sequence is (2 3 5 9 17) ***** 33 is the next term At level 3: Sequence (1 2 4) is observed to be a sub-sequence of the sequence at level 2. This is a recursively defined sequence. Since the term after (1 2 4) in sequence (1 2 4 8) is 8, therefore the next term is 8. At level 2: Sequence (1 2 4 8) has the property that each element can be obtained from the previous one by adding numbers from the sequence (1 2 4). Since the next term of sequence (1 2 4) is 8, therefore the next term of sequence (1 2 4 8) is 16.

At level 1: Sequence (2 3 5 9 17) has the property that each element can be obtained from the previous one by adding numbers from the sequence (1 2 4 8). Since the next term of sequence (1 2 4 8) is 16, therefore the next term of sequence (2 3 5 9 17) is 33. Each sub-sequence created by any method is considered to be at a level one below the level of the original sequence. Each level generates explanation for why the next term for that level is the one displayed.

The programmeme fails to identify sequences in which the function f describing the nth term of the sequence, is not a simple closed form mathematical function. Getting general methods for these sequences is difficult. Examples of such sequences are

1. 2; 3; 5; 7; 11; ... where $f(n)$ = nth prime number.
2. 3; 1; 4; 1; 5; 9; ... where $f(n)$ = nth digit in the decimal expansion of.

Clearly, there are no methods to identify sequences like these! The programme also fails for integer super-exponential sequences. For example, consider S = (2; 6; 30; 260). These are the first four terms of the sequence f(n) = nn + n. The programme fails to identify these kind of sequences. But as mentioned above, general methods for solving these sequences can be added. Here are a few more examples where the prototype fails.

1. 1; 2; 2; 3; 3; 3; 4; ...: This is the sequence where the number i is repeated i times.
2. 1; 2; 3; 2; 1; 2; 3;...: This sequence is formed by repeating the sequence 1; 2; 3; 2. The system goes into very deep searching and identifies the sequence incorrectly. The interesting fact to note is that for the sequence 1; 2; 3; 2; 1; 2; 3; 2; 1;... The prototype correctly solves this one and gives the correct answer 2. 9.

RATIONAL SEQUENCES

Rational sequences, ones in which the range of the function f is the set of all rational numbers, are more complicated. Essentially, rational numbers are numbers of the form p = q where p and q are integers and q_6 = 0.

One way to look for the function f given the first few rational numbers is to look at the sequence formed by taking the numerators of the given rationals separately and looking at the denominators separately. If a function f can be identified for the numerator sequence and f can be identified for the denominator sequence, then we can predict the next term of the rational sequence. This idea will take care of simple rational sequences like 1; 1 = 2; 1 = 3; 1 = 4;....

Second idea is generalizing methods for integer sequences

to rational sequences by considering operations on rationals rather than operations on integers.

The current version of the Sequence Expert does not consider rational sequences. But with the kinds of methods that are available for integers, a fairly strong implementation for rational sequences can be obtained by just converting the given rational sequence into a integer sequence and then using the integer-sequence identifier to solve the problem.

For example, a sequence like 1; 1 = 2; 1 = 3; 1 = 4;... can be linearised to give an integer sequence

1; 1; 1; 2; 1; 3; 1; 4; .... This sequence can be easily identified by the integer part of the prototype system.

STRING SEQUENCES

String sequences involve string operators, like concatenation and substring matching. So the basic question here is how to get the next term from the current string by only applying these operators. For example, in the sequence aa; aba; abba; abbba; ... its very clear that the next term if got by inserting an b in the middle of previous string. But not all string sequences can be described by such simple operations.

In many cases the alphabet has some implicit ordering in them. Consider the example, a; b; d; g; .... In this case, the sequence can more easily be understood by transforming it to a integer sequence by replacing a by 1, b by 2 and so on. Sequences like a; ab; abc; abcd ... can be explained by a combination of both the above ideas. Algorithm Identify-String-Sequence(S) 10

1. *Method 1:* Take the last two terms of the string sequence S and nd the edit distance between them. Store the transformations T corresponding to the calculated edit distance. Check to see if the transformations T also describe the previous terms of sequence S. If yes, then the next term is just T applied to the last term of S. If not, then continue with the next method.
2. *Method 2:* Calculate the edit distance between each of the adjacent terms of sequence S. Let D denote

the sequence of the distances (integer sequence) and T be the sequence of transformations.

{Case 1 If D is a constant sequence containing 1, then nd the next transformation and if successful then apply the new transformation to the last term of S. If not successful then try the next method {Case 2 If D is a constant sequence containing 2, then break up T into T and T where T_1 is a sequence of all first transformations and T is a collection of all second transformations.

Find the next transformation for T and T_2. If successful in both then apply both the transformations to the last term in S to get the next term. If not then continue with the next method {Case 3 If D is anything else, then continue with the next method.

3. *Method 3:* Convert each string in the sequence S to an integer. This is done by considering a to represent 1, b_2, c_3, and so on, in base 27. The resulting integer sequence is solved using methods for integer sequences. If the integer methods are successful then the solution integer is converted back to a string. If the integer methods fail, then this method fails. Since there are no more methods to try, the procedure fails for sequence S.

Transformation Sequence

The problem of identifying a string sequence now reduces to nding the next transformation following a given sequence of transformations. For convenience let (insert, ch, n) denote the transformation "insertion of the character ch at position n". So for example, given the sequence (insert; a; 1); (insert; b; 2); (insert; c; 3) the next transformation would be (insert; d; 4) 12.

The technique used to identify the next transformation is to break up the problem into 3 sub-problems. The first one being identifying the next operation, the second is identifying the next character and the third one is identifying the next position.

EXPLANATION FOR STRING SEQUENCES

The explanation generated for string sequences follows the same general idea. Once the rule that generates the next string from the previous string is found, it is printed out based on the templates stored.

For example, consider the sequence S = (az; by; cx). The first method for strings fails here because not the same rule determines the next term in the sequence. Applying method 2, we get the following transformation sequence, T = (replace a by b at position 0; replace z by y at position 1); = (replace b by c at position 0; replace y by x at position 1) and the distance sequence is D = (2; 2), since the edit distance between alternate terms is always 2. Therefore, the next transformation will be found out to be, (using the above mentioned procedure), (replace c by d at position 0; replace x by w at position 1) This gives dw as the next term. The explanation produced for this example looks like this, LIPS> (run).

Input the first few terms of the sequence: az by cx Input sequence is (az by cx)

The way the sequence is built up is

1. Change to b at position 1 and Change to y at position 2.
2. Change to c at position 1 and Change to x at position 2. Therefore, next term can be obtained by
3. Changing to d at position 1 and Changing to w at position 2

Out sequence (az by cx) dw

Identified as a string sequence at level 1

True

The sentence at position 1 in the explanation explains how the second term in the input sequence can be obtained from the rst term. Similarly, 15

STRUCTURE OF MATHEMATICS

A precise notion of 'mathematical structure' other than that given by model theory may prove fruitful in the philosophy of mathematics. It is shown how the language and methods of category theory provide such a notion, having developed out of a structural approach in modern mathematical practice.

As an example, it is then shown how the categorical notion of a topos provides a characterization of 'logical structure', and an alternative to the Pregean approach to logic which is continuous with the modern structural approach in mathematics

The focus of my presentation will be on such structural aspects of mathematics that are known or likely to cause problems or challenges for the process of learning mathematics, and hence for its teaching. I shall interpret the term "the structure of mathematics" in a somewhat broad sense, by taking into account also the nature of mathematics and its characteristics as a discipline and not solely its architectural features as reflected in one or more possible construction(s) of its edifice. In other words, my reflections do not rely on a particular global organisation of mathematics into one coherent structure, à la Bourbaki.

My talk will be centred on three themes. Ultimately they all are related to deep issues in the epistemology of mathematics, which may well be one of the reasons why they give rise to cognitive problems and challenges: The formation, nature, and role of mathematical concepts; the need for, and role of mathematical proof; and symbolism and formalism in mathematics.

The formation, nature and role of mathematical concepts

It is well known from research literature and from teaching practice that the potential gap between "concept definition" and "concept image" (Hershkowitz, Tall, Vinner) in mathematics is a major stumbling block to many students' learning of mathematics. It seems that students form their image of a given concept mainly through the set of specific examples of the concept that they have become familiar with through the teaching they have received. So, a significant source of this gap occurs if the examples shaping the concept image cover only a limited part of the scope implied by the concept definition. In such cases the concept image tends to "win" over the concept definition. A classical example of this is that many students' image of the concept of function does not include functions that are not given by one and only one algebraic expression over the entire domain, e.g. Dirichlet's function, or functions defined by different expressions on different intervals.

It is further well known from the research literature that those mathematical concepts that are formed by encapsulating a process into a mathematical entity give rise to cognitive difficulties with students, e.g. the derivative of a function, created by amalgamating, after the process of differentiating a given (differentiable!) function at all points, the pointwise derivatives into a new function (Tall's procept, Sfard's reification).

In this presentation I should like to point out and discuss a few additional problems and challenges attached to mathematical concepts.

The first is to do with the influence of the (possible) roots in students' experiential world of a mathematical concept. While many mathematical concepts are first introduced and explained in some domain of reality or experience, they soon depart from that domain and obtain residence in a mathematical universe. In other words, the concepts are *abstracted* from an experiential domain. An example of this is fractions. At school students mostly learn about fractions by means of idealised drawings or idealised physical objects such as rectangles or pizzas, which are divided into n equal parts, of which m pieces are taken to form m/n'th of the original unit.

However, in theoretical mathematics a fraction is not primarily an operator on experiential units but a number, and that number can engage in algebraic operations for which it is difficult to find experiential counterparts. Division of the number p/q by the number m/n is defined in algebraic terms (find the number, if there is one, which multiplied by m/n gives p/q), and although not entirely impossible it does become contrived to find decent (correct and relevant) interpretations of this in students' experiential world. The concept of fraction is abstracted from the real world, and, to many students', problems arise when (as is most often the case) not all the mathematical features or operations surrounding such an abstracted concept have counterparts in some experiential domain. Similar phenomena occur with negative numbers, which are often abstracted from experiential domains such as height/depth above/under sea level, temperature, loans etc. Students who insist on/cling to an experiential interpretation of all the mathematical concepts they encounter will, sooner rather than later, run into severe difficulty in coming to grips with the mathematics at issue.

Also the fact that once a mathematical concept has been theoretically defined it is "illegal" to implicate experiential considerations in the context of justification, but not at all in the context of discovery (where such considerations should rather be encouraged), is a major source of confusion with many students.

By their very nature, abstracted concepts do not posses all the properties of the concepts from which they have been abstracted. Over-generalisation in this respect is commonplace amongst students. Examples are legion: Squaring a number gives a bigger number. $(x + y)_2 = x_2 + y_2$. $\log (x/y) = \log x/\log y$. A norm in a normed space is taken to be Euclidean; the metric in a metric space is supposed to stem from a norm; the topology in a topological space is supposed to stem from a metric. In a ring, division is always possible.

Things get worse when we look at concepts that are not abstracted, but *abstract*, typically given as objects in some axiomatically defined structure and subject to the rules that govern their relations with other such objects. Take for instance matrices. Even though all relevant abstract mathematical systems do of course have concrete special cases, it is usually the *system* that is abstracted (albeit it is not always clear from what or how) rather than its individual objects.

Just think of complex numbers (introduced without making use of pairs of reals), a vector, a Boolean algebra, a ®-algebra, a finite automaton, or a Hausdorff space. Also the fact that a given, fixed set of objects can be organised in several different ways (e.g. as algebraic structure or a metric space), irrespectively of their ontological nature, is mind boggling to many students. And worse again when we consider hierarchies of abstract mathematical systems, in which the concepts of the higher levels carry names borrowed from the lower levels even though their specific characteristics are not present at the higher levels: fraction (of real or complex numbers), divisor, straight line (in n-space), open ball, 0-element, or differential) equation.

In the present context I submit that the distinctions between abstracted and abstract, between abstraction and abstractness are significant when it comes to identifying tricky influences of the structure of mathematics on the learning of mathematics.

SYMBOLISM AND FORMALISM

For millennia symbolism and theoretical formalism have formed part of the heart of mathematics and have caused major problems to learners of mathematics. To many lay people symbolism and formalism *are* mathematics. Often mathematics educators focus on students' problems at learning and mastering the specific rules of symbolism and formalism. I should like to venture that the problems go deeper. They are to do with the origin and rationale behind the rules and the systems.

Sometimes it is not so much the operations involved in solving an equation that cause trouble, but the very notion of an equation. What is an equation really, and why is it relevant to try to establish equations, and hence to try to solve them?

Because equations govern the properties and behaviour of objects and systems, a fact which is usually not receiving much attention in the teaching of mathematics. And why can we say that the equation $x_2 + 1 = 0$ has no solution in the real numbers whereas it "suddenly" has two solutions in the complex numbers? Why is it illegal to divide by 0?

A special problem arises when symbolic notation from a concrete domain, e.g. +, •, or 0, 1 in the real numbers, are transferred to other domains, e.g. polynomials, matrices or function spaces? Once again, over-generalisation is an imminent danger

ABSTRACTNESS OF MATHEMATICS

Mathematics is the science of patterns and relationships. As a theoretical discipline, mathematics explores the possible relationships among abstractions without concern for whether those abstractions have counterparts in the real world. The abstractions can be anything from strings of numbers to geometric figures to sets of equations.

In addressing, say, "Does the interval between prime numbers form a pattern?" as a theoretical question, mathematicians are interested only in finding a pattern or proving that there is none, but not in what use such knowledge might have. In deriving, for instance, an expression for the change in the surface area of any regular solid as its volume approaches zero, mathematicians have no interest in any correspondence between geometric solids and physical objects in the real world. A central line of investigation in theoretical mathematics is identifying in each field of study a small set of basic ideas and rules from which all other interesting ideas and rules in that field can be logically deduced. Mathematicians, like other scientists, are particularly pleased when previously unrelated parts of mathematics are found to be derivable from one another, or from some more general theory.

Part of the sense of beauty that many people have perceived in mathematics lies not in finding the greatest elaborateness or complexity but on the contrary, in finding the greatest economy and simplicity of representation and proof. As mathematics has progressed, more and more relationships have been found between parts of it that have been developed separately. For example, between the symbolic representations of algebra and the spatial representations of geometry. These cross-connections enable insights to be developed into the various parts; together, they strengthen belief in the correctness and underlying unity of the whole structure.

Mathematics is also an applied science. Many mathematicians focus their attention on solving problems that originate in the world of experience. They too search for patterns and relationships, and in the process they use techniques that are similar to those used in doing purely theoretical mathematics.

The difference is largely one of intent. In contrast to theoretical mathematicians, applied mathematicians, in the examples given above, might study the interval pattern of prime numbers to develop a new system for coding numerical information, rather than as an abstract problem. Or they might tackle the area/volume problem as a step in producing a model for the study of crystal behaviour.

The results of theoretical and applied mathematics often influence each other. The discoveries of theoretical mathematicians frequently turn out—sometimes decades later—to have unanticipated practical value. Studies on the mathematical properties of random events, for example, led to knowledge that later made it possible to improve the design of experiments in the social and natural sciences.

Conversely, in trying to solve the problem of billing long-distance telephone users fairly, mathematicians made fundamental discoveries about the mathematics of complex networks. Theoretical mathematics, unlike the other sciences, is not constrained by the real world, but in the long run it contributes to a better understanding of that world.

Because of its abstractness, mathematics is universal in a sense that other fields of human thought are not. It finds useful applications in business, industry, music, historical scholarship, politics, sports, medicine, agriculture, engineering, and the social and natural sciences. The relationship between mathematics and the other fields of basic and applied science is especially strong. This is so for several reasons, including the following:

- The alliance between science and mathematics has a long history, dating back many centuries. Science provides mathematics with interesting problems to investigate, and mathematics provides science with powerful tools to use in analyzing data. Often, abstract patterns that have been studied for their own sake by mathematicians have turned out much later to be very useful in science. Science and mathematics are both trying to discover general patterns and relationships, and in this sense they are part of the same endeavor.

- Mathematics is the chief language of science. The symbolic language of mathematics has turned out to be extremely valuable for expressing scientific ideas unambiguously. The statement that $a=F/m$ is not simply a shorthand way of saying that the acceleration of an object depends on the force applied to it and its mass; rather, it is a precise statement of the quantitative relationship among those variables. More important, mathematics provides the grammar of science—the rules for analyzing scientific ideas and data rigorously.
- Mathematics and science have many features in common. These include a belief in understandable order; an interplay of imagination and rigorous logic; ideals of honesty and openness; the critical importance of peer criticism; the value placed on being the first to make a key discovery; being international in scope; and even, with the development of powerful electronic computers, being able to use technology to open up new fields of investigation.
- Mathematics and technology have also developed a fruitful relationship with each other. The mathematics of connections and logical chains, for example, has contributed greatly to the design of computer hardware and programmeming techniques. Mathematics also contributes more generally to engineering, as in describing complex systems whose behaviour can then be simulated by computer. In those simulations, design features and operating conditions can be varied as a means of finding optimum designs. For its part, computer technology has opened up whole new areas in mathematics, even in the very nature of proof, and it also continues to help solve previously daunting problems.

ABSTRACTION

Mathematical thinking often begins with the process of abstraction—that is, noticing a similarity between two or more objects or events. Aspects that they have in common, whether concrete or hypothetical, can be represented by symbols such as numbers, letters, other marks, diagrams, geometrical constructions, or even words.

Whole numbers are abstractions that represent the size of sets of things and events or the order of things within a set. The circle as a concept is an abstraction derived from human faces, flowers, wheels, or spreading ripples; the letter A may be an abstraction for the surface area of objects of any shape, for the acceleration of all moving objects, or for all objects having some specified property; the symbol + represents a process of addition, whether one is adding apples or oranges, hours, or miles per hour.

And abstractions are made not only from concrete objects or processes; they can also be made from other abstractions, such as kinds of numbers (the even numbers, for instance).

Such abstraction enables mathematicians to concentrate on some features of things and relieves them of the need to keep other features continually in mind. As far as mathematics is concerned, it does not matter whether a triangle represents the surface area of a sail or the convergence of two lines of sight on a star; mathematicians can work with either concept in the same way. The resulting economy of effort is very useful—provided that in making an abstraction, care is taken not to ignore features that play a significant role in determining the outcome of the events being studied.

SYMBOLISM OF MATHEMATICS

For our present purposes ... the history of the notation is a detail. The interesting point to notice is the admirable illustration which this numeral system affords of the enormous importance of a good notation. By relieving the brain of all unnecessary work, a good notation sets it free to concentrate on more advanced problems".

It is a profoundly erroneous truism, repeated by all copy-books and by eminent people when they are making speeches, that we should cultivate the habit of thinking of what we are doing.

The precise opposite is the case. Civilization advances by extending the number of important operations which we can perform without thinking about them. Operations of thought are like cavalry charges in a battle—they are strictly limited in number, they require fresh horses, and must only be made at decisive moments.".

"The symbolism of mathematics is in truth the outcome of the general ideas which dominate the science

MATHEMATICS AS SCIENCE OF MEASUREMENT

A. Mathematics and science education, including the metric system of measurement, will be strengthened throughout the system, especially in the early grades.

STRATEGIES

1. Implement the Missouri academic performance standards and frameworks for math and science
2. Develop and implement statewide assessments aligned to the state's content, performance, and skills standards
3. Expand active learning opportunities through the use of technology
4. Make performance assessments available for classroom use
5. Encourage frequent communication between schools and business/industry to assess math and science needs in the changing work force
6. Evaluate and disseminate effective math and science programmes

OBJECTIVE

B. The number of teachers with a substantive background in mathematics and science, including the metric system of measurement, will increase by 50 percent.

Strategies

1. Ensure authentic assessment training for all teachers
2. Increase the availability of math and science professional development activities aligned with the state's knowledge, performance, and skill standards
3. Encourage professional development activities that promote effective, research-based teaching strategies in math and science
4. Institute competency-based teacher certification

MATHEMATICS AND ITS RELATIONSHIP

MATHEMATICS WITH ARTS

The Arts and Mathematics involve student understanding of relationships between time and space, rhythm and line through the experience of these abstract concepts in various arts forms and mathematical ideas. Mathematics provides notions of scale, shape, pattern, proportion and orientation to the visual arts. In the Performing Arts, Mathematics has links with aspects ranging from the frequency of musical notes through to the use of Fibonacci and other sequences in musical compositions. Mathematically related aesthetic considerations, such as the golden ratio, are used across visual, performing and multi-modal arts forms.

Construction in the Arts requires the use and understanding of measurement in the manipulation of space, time and form. Creating patterns in the Arts involves counting, measurement and design in different ways across the various arts forms. The Arts also support the development of critical numeracy skills, by engaging students in the deconstruction of media texts. This can include a consideration of how statistics can be used to analyse hypotheses.

MATHEMATICS WITH CIVICS AND CITIZENSHIP

The concepts developed in the study of Mathematics are applicable to a range of Civic and Citizenship understandings. Mathematical structure and working play essential roles in key aspects of our society as well as key civics concepts. Particular aspects of Civics and Citizenship require mathematical understanding, including concepts of majority rule, absolute majority, one vote one value, representation based on electorates of equal sizes, and the preferential and proportional voting systems.

Mathematical understanding also supports the development of community research and the presentation of findings, for example, the use of data and statistics, and including the analysis and presentation of information in charts and diagrams. The recognition and understanding of this mathematical basis to many social structures and processes is integral to the development of informed and active citizens.

MATHEMATICS WITH COMMUNICATION

Mathematical structure and *Working mathematically* play essential roles in understanding natural and human worlds. In communicating about these worlds, students use a combination of everyday language and mathematical symbols involving numerals, operations, connectives, variables and relations.

Development of the language of Mathematics is crucial to its practical application. Students learn to use the language and concepts of Mathematics both within the discipline itself, and also its applications to modelling and problem solving across the other domains. In this process they employ a range of Communication tools for illustrating relationships and displaying results such as venn diagrams and tree diagrams.

DESIGN, CREATIVITY AND TECHNOLOGY

In Design, Creativity and Technology students apply numbers to everyday situations; they explain and use mental and written algorithms for addition, subtraction, multiplication and division. Students carry out arithmetic computations and choose mathematical models and procedures to apply in the process of designing and making products and systems.

When designing, students use drawing tools, accurately drawing two-dimensional and three-dimensional representations.

They represent depth in their drawings and describe what can and cannot be seen in simple objects and drawings. They use a variety of forms of representation including oblique, isometric and perspective to visually represent objects and use computer drawing packages and computer aided design/computer-aided manufacturing (CAD/CAM) for two- and three-dimensional representations and analysis of design.

In the process of investigating, designing, making and testing products and systems students measure length, perimeter, area, surface area, angle and time for familiar products. They recognise and use different units of measurement for appropriate contexts and use suitable instruments to measure length, angle, volume and time. They select and use suitable procedures to measure, estimate and calculate for instance length, area, volume and angle. In the process they learn to use formulae as appropriate. Students investigate situations and solve problems set in a wide range of practical contexts, for example, the design and construction for packaging involving the use of nets for three dimensional shapes.

MATHEMATICS WITH ENGLISH

The use of logical and analytical thinking in Mathematics, including the use of conjectures and proof, has clear links to the development of structured and coherent argument in speaking and writing. Mathematical structure is strongly related to semantics, syntax and language, and to the use of propositions and quantifiers embedded in principled argument in natural language.

The development of skills for critical analysis of literary, everyday and media texts in English empowers individuals to participate effectively in society. This is complemented by the fundamental role that Mathematics plays in cultural, social and technological advances and in empowering individuals as critical citizens in contemporary society and for the future.

Number, space and measurement, chance and data, are common aspects of people's experience in everyday personal, study and work situations, and are naturally embedded in activities related to the English dimensions of reading, writing, speaking and listening.

MATHEMATICS WITH HEALTH AND PHYSICAL EDUCATION

In Health and Physical Education, Mathematics provides tools and procedures which can be used to model situations and solve problems in areas such as:

- Scoring different sporting events involving time, distance, weight and number as variables
- Combinatorial problems related to developing competition draws and ladders
- Calculating percentage improvement in results from data collected through fitness testing or performance in physical activities
- Collecting, recording, interpreting and presenting health, skill or fitness related data in a range of formats such as graphs and tables predicting trends in key indicators of health status in Australia.

MATHEMATICS WITH HUMANITIES – ECONOMICS

The Economics and Mathematics are related through the use of mathematics to model a broad range of economic, political and social phenomena. Examples include the use of statistical modelling and analysis in a census, sampling populations to predict election outcomes, and modelling and forecasting economic indicators such as the Consumer Price Index (CPI) and business confidence.

The application of mathematical skills plays a key role in financial literacy, in particular the use of ratio, proportion and percentage in related calculations such as percentage increase or decrease in price of a commodity or personal income.

MATHEMATICS WITH GEOGRAPHY

Geography and Mathematics are related through the use of Mathematics to model a broad range of economic, political and social phenomena. Examples include the use of statistical modelling and analysis in a census, sampling populations to predict election outcomes, and modelling and forecasting economic indicators such as the Consumer Price Index (CPI) and business confidence.

The application of mathematical skills plays a key role in financial literacy, in particular the use of ratio, proportion and percentage in related calculations such as percentage increase or decrease in price of a commodity or personal income.

Mathematics provides the basis of measurement, scale and spatial representation used in maps and plans. Geography also uses the concepts of direction, length, angle and bearing, gradient and contour and area.

MATHEMATICS WITH HISTORY

The study of History includes the analysis and interpretation of a range of historical information including population charts and diagrams and other statistical information. The concepts and skills developed in Mathematics support student understanding and interpretation of a range of history sources and their presentation as evidence in demonstrating historical understanding.

MATHEMATICS WITH INFORMATION AND COMMUNICATIONS TECHNOLOGY

In Mathematics, extensive use is made of Information and Communications Technology (ICT), with applications specified at all levels in the standards. From Students make use of increasingly sophisticated calculators to check estimations, perform computations and investigate number, function and algebraic properties.

Computer software includes the use of spreadsheets, dynamic geometry packages, statistical and graphing tools and computer algebra systems. Mathematical investigations on the Internet require effective, efficient and discriminatory use of search engines.

MATHEMATICS WITH INTERPERSONAL DEVELOPMENT

In working mathematically students will engage with

others to formulate and test conjectures, gather, analyse and interpret data and apply mathematics to solve real life problems. These activities are often carried out in teams that require students to collaborate and cooperate, share and discuss, and these behaviours are central in working towards the standards in Interpersonal Development.

MATHEMATICS WITH LANGUAGE OTHER THAN ENGLISH (LOTE)

Common and central to both domains is consideration in language of semantic (meaning of key concepts, ideas, terms) and syntactic (structural relationships in natural and symbolic language) elements and features.

This involves acquiring knowledge of words, symbols, terms and definitions, understanding and application of concepts, and the use of related technical skills. Students develop thinking processes of analysis and synthesis, involving relationships between simple and complex ideas and expressions.

These developments involve the use of Mathematics in everyday activities such as number systems in counting, buying and selling, measuring, designing and building, and estimating and describing chance events using different written and spoken languages in a range of social and cultural contexts.

MATHEMATICS WITH PERSONAL LEARNING

The mathematical processes of inquiry, investigation, problem-solving, modelling and the use of technology give rise to opportunities and challenges for Personal Learning. These mathematical processes provide contexts within which students can acquire self knowledge and dispositions that support learning. Opportunities also occur for students to learn with their peers including seeking and responding appropriately to feedback. Establishing values in which individual differences are respected and appreciated encourages unique and varied approaches to working mathematically.

As students see mathematical connections and are able to apply mathematical concepts, skills and processes in posing and solving problems, they become confident in their personal knowledge of Mathematics. They increasingly manage their own learning and growth through the setting of goals and managing resources. The strategies of planning, monitoring, revising, reflecting and if needs be modifying enable students to develop resilience and become adaptive learners. Students will become progressively empowered through knowledge of mathematics and as numerate citizens they will be able to apply this knowledge critically, in societal and political contexts.

MATHEMATICS WITH SCIENCE

The knowledge and skills students engage with in the various dimensions of Mathematics support students in their studies of all aspects of Science. In Science, students use measurement and number concepts, particularly in data collection, estimation of error, analysis and modes of reporting. The Mathematics domain supports students in developing number handling skills.

In Science, students observe, describe and measure aspects of the world around them, using more sophisticated and accurate measuring tools and instruments as they progress through their schooling. They collect, record, interpret and display data appropriately, looking for patterns, drawing conclusions and making generalisations. Students justify their choice of instruments and the accuracy of their measurements, commenting on the reliability of the procedures, the measurements used, and the conclusions drawn against the hypothesis being tested.

Predictions for further investigations, extrapolations and interpolations may be made from their own experimental results or from reliable second-hand data. The understandings, tools and techniques of Mathematics help students to understand measurement and magnitude; to process and analyse data collected in their own experimental investigations and those of others.

Mathematical conventions used in graphing, conversions of units, calculations and manipulation of formulae, the use of spreadsheets to facilitate computations and generation of graphs, the use of scientific calculator functions, the manipulation of very small and very large numbers, direct and indirect variation and the implication of limitations in instrumental measurement are essential in conducting and reporting on scientific investigations.

Mathematical modelling is used extensively in the natural sciences, physics and in bioinformatics, and by computer scientists.

MATHEMATICS WITH THINKING PROCESSES

The study of Mathematics exemplifies important thinking processes within its own discipline and also provides a context within which these and other thinking processes can be developed and refined.

Mathematical reasoning and thinking underpins all aspects of school mathematics, including problem posing, problem solving, investigation and modelling.

It encompasses the development of algorithms for computation, formulation of problems, making and testing conjectures and the development of abstractions for further investigation. Computation and proof are essential and complementary aspects of Mathematics that enable students to develop thinking skills directed toward explaining, understanding and using mathematical concepts, structures and objects.

Thinking strategies and tools are used extensively in Mathematics. As students progress in their learning they move from using concrete thinking skills to applying higher order processes to their learning. Students are encouraged to take managed risks in developing possible alternate approaches to problems and tasks. Curiosity has an important role to play in stimulating mathematical inquiry, while reflection and metacognition are important components of the problem solving process in which new and often creative approaches are required to find solutions.

MATHEMATICIANS

Mathematics is one of the oldest and most fundamental sciences. Mathematicians use mathematical theory, computational techniques, algorithms, and the latest computer technology to solve economic, scientific, engineering, physics, and business problems. The work of mathematicians falls into two broad classes—theoretical (pure) mathematics and applied mathematics. These classes, however, are not sharply defined and often overlap.

Theoretical mathematicians advance mathematical knowledge by developing new principles and recognizing previously unknown relationships between existing principles of mathematics. Although these workers seek to increase basic knowledge without necessarily considering its practical use, such pure and abstract knowledge has been instrumental in producing or furthering many scientific and engineering achievements. Many theoretical mathematicians are employed as university faculty, dividing their time between teaching and conducting research.

Applied mathematicians, on the other hand, use theories and techniques, such as mathematical modeling and computational methods, to formulate and solve practical problems in business, government, engineering, and the physical, life, and social sciences. For example, they may analyse the most efficient way to schedule airline routes between cities, the effects and safety of new drugs, the aerodynamic characteristics of an experimental automobile, or the cost-effectiveness of alternative manufacturing processes.

Applied mathematicians working in industrial research and development may develop or enhance mathematical methods when solving a difficult problem. Some mathematicians, called cryptanalysts, analyse and decipher encryption systems—codes—designed to transmit military, political, financial, or law enforcement-related information.

Applied mathematicians start with a practical problem, envision its separate elements, and then reduce the elements to mathematical variables. They often use computers to analyse relationships among the variables and solve complex problems by developing models with alternative solutions. Individuals with titles other than mathematician do much of the work in applied mathematics.

In fact, because mathematics is the foundation on which so many other academic disciplines are built, the number of workers using mathematical techniques is much greater than the number formally called mathematicians. For example, engineers, computer scientists, physicists, and economists are among those who use mathematics extensively.

The contributions in the subject of mathematics of some famous mathematicians are furnished below.

ARCHIMEDES

Archimedes is remembered as the greatest mathematician of the ancient era. He contributed significantly in geometry regarding the areas of plane figures and the areas as well as volumes of curved surfaces.

His works expected integral calculus almost 2000 years before it was invented by Sir Isaac Newton and Gottfried Wilhelm von Leibniz. He also proved that the volume of a sphere is equal to two-thirds the volume of a circumscribed cylinder.

He regarded this as his most vital accomplishment. So, he desired that a cylinder circumscribing a sphere ought to be inscribed on his tomb. He found an approximate value of pi by circumscribing and inscribing a circle with regular polygons of 96 sides. His works have original ideas, impressive demonstrations and excellent computational techniques. Some of these which have survived are:

- On the sphere and cylinder
- Measurement of a circle
- On conoids and spheroids
- On spirals
- On plane equilibriums
- The sand reckoner
- Quadrature of the parabola
- On floating bodies
- Stomachion

EUCLID

Euclid is the most famous mathematician of all time. "Euclid's Elements" is divided into 13 books. The initial six are related to plane geometry seven, eight and nine are pertaining to number theory number ten is regarding Eudoxus's theory of irrational numbers eleven to thirteen comprise of solid geometry the last part throws light on the properties of five regular polyhedrons and an evidence that there can be maximum five of these. These Elements have an impressive clarity regarding the selection and order of the theorems and problems. There are minimum assumptions, less extraneous material and an excellent logic in the propositions. The Elements was first published in 1482. The other works of Euclid which survive are:

- Optics
- Phaenomena
- On divisions of figures
- Data

The works of Euclid that have not survived are:

- Elements of music
- Book of
- Fallacies
- Conics
- Porisms
- Surface loci

SIR ISAAC NEWTON

Newton created the basis for elementary differential and integral calculus during the plague years. This occurred several years prior to its independent discovery by the German mathematician Gottfried Wilhelm von Leibniz. He called it as the method of fluxions. He proposed that the integration of a function is the opposite procedure of its differentiation. Using differentiation as a basic operation, he developed simple analytical methods concerning issues like finding areas, lengths of curves, areas, maxima and minima. Newton is credited for development of a potent problem solving and analysis tool in pure mathematics and physics.

PYTHAGORAS

He was a Greek mathematician. His belief was that all relations could be expressed as number relations i.e. all things are numbers. He deduced this conclusion due to observations in mathematics, music and astronomy. The Pythagorean theorem is thought to be first proved by the Pythagoreans. However, it is thought that this was known in Babylonia, where Pythagoras traveled in his young days. The Pythagoreans also observed that vibrating strings created harmonious tones if the ratios of the length of the strings are whole numbers. These ratios could be extended to other devices also. The important discovery was that the diagonal of a square was not an integral multiple of its side. This led to the proof of existence of irrational numbers.

BLAISE PASCAL

The French mathematician had been involved in imaginative and subtle work in geometry and other branches of mathematics. In 1645, Pascal invented the first calculating machine and sold it. His work in hydrostatics led to the invention of the syringe and hydraulic press. In 1647, he published an essay on conic sections using the methods of Gerard Desargues and deserted the field of mathematics. However, later he developed an interest in probability due to his involvement in gambling.

CARL FRIEDRICH GAUSS

Gauss was a German mathematician. While he attended Caroline college from 1792 to 1795, he formulated the least-squared method and a surmise on the distribution of prime numbers amongst all numbers. In 1795, he discovered the basic theorem of quadratic residues relating to the concept of congruence in number theory. In 1796, he proved the possibility of constructing a 17-sided regular polygon with the help of a ruler and compass only. In 1799, his dissertation revealed the first evidence of the fundamental theorem of algebra. In 1801, his treatise – Disquisitiones arithmeticae set a basis for future research and enabled Gauss to have a major recognition amongst mathematicians. His became very popular when he correctly predicted where the asteroid Ceres would reappear by calculating the orbit by an improved theory.

ARYABHATTA

"Aryabhatiya" is the name of Aryabhatta's work. There are an introductory 13 verses followed by 108 verses, all of them divided into 4 chapters. Aryabhatta found out the approximate value of pi and writes about it in the second part of his works (Ganitapada 10). It is possible that he found out that pi is irrational. In Ganitapada 6, he mentions the formula to calculate the value of a triangle. He developed the "Kuttaka" method to solve first order Diophantine equations.

This is termed as the "Aryabhatta algorithm". The number place-value system was obviously present in his work. Later, this system was noticed in the 3rd century Bakhshali manuscript. Georges Ifrah, the French mathematician, states that the number "zero" was implicit in this system.

RAMANUJAM

Srinivasa Ramanujan Iyengar contributed to number theory, mathematical analysis, infinite series and continued fractions. He was a great Indian mathematical genius of the 20th century. He compiled about 3900 results that were original and highly unconventional. The Ramanujan prime and the Ramanujan theta function have lead to a tremendous further research. A few major discoveries entered the mathematical mainstream a bit slowly. After his death, his formulae were found useful in string theory and crystallography. The Ramanujan Journal is an international publication that publishes his works concerning those areas that have been influenced by them. Some other famous mathematicians are:

- Stefan Banach
- Georg Cantor
- Joseph Fourier
- John von Neumann
- Brook Taylor

Unit II

Aims and Objectives of Teaching Mathematics

NEED OF TEACHING MATHEMATICS

Teaching is a career that guides the thoughts of the next generation, training them to think clearly where others would only founder. It calls for a combination of skills demanded by few other professions - and brings rewards like no other, too. It is a career respected by the whole community - and it also pays pretty well.

WORK IT OUT

If mathematics teaching isn't the career you were thinking of, perhaps it should be. Chances are the idea of teaching paying well comes as a particular surprise: even a newly qualified graduate teacher earns over 14,000 a year - which compares very well with the typical graduate salary of just 12,500 - and some schools will pay more still to get the best and the brightest. With experience, pay rises to over 33,000, and head teachers can earn in excess of 55,000.

And at a time when many professions are feeling the drastic effects of "downsizing" of staffing levels, the demand for mathematics teaching shows no signs of collapsing. To meet the projected demand for mathematics teachers over the next few years, the Training and Development Agency for Schools (TDA) estimates that it will need about a third of all mathematics graduates to go into teaching over the coming years: around 2,000 a year.

ADD SOMETHING TO THE WORLD

"It is important for us to attract newly-graduated mathematicians into teaching", says Anthea Millett, Chief Executive of the TTA. *"There is a real problem in the declining numbers of people who are being trained in mathematics, which in turn could lead us into a shortfall in the numbers of mathematics teachers for the future. We're looking to break this vicious cycle."*

The daily experience of most mathematics teachers is very positive. Knowing that a good performance in core subjects like mathematics is now vital to their future, pupils are keen to do well - and they look to their teachers to give them both the knowledge and motivation they need.

Teachers themselves are given a degree of responsibility and autonomy unimaginable in many professions - and at an earlier stage in their careers.

Within broad limits, you can achieve your teaching goals however you think best suits your pupils. And if your pupils do well, there is no vast hierarchy of management to steal the credit from you.

PRIME IMPORTANCE

The importance of teaching the next generation the skills they will need in the 21st century is recognised far beyond schools. An NOP Consumer Market Research survey was recently commissioned to gauge the relative standing of different professions in society, from the armed forces to the media. It revealed that a majority of people - 59 per cent - rate teachers as being of value to the community, a figure second only to doctors. In contrast, journalists and accountants came in at just 3 per cent.

That same NOP survey also revealed that more than 1 in 5 people have thought about going into teaching. If you are a mathematics graduate, there has never been a better time to turn that thought into action.

Many of us wondered about the advantages of Mathematics during our childhood days. Many of us were not able to comprehend the benefits of mathematics beyond the daily usage of calculating simple numbers. Let us see in detail what are some of the benefits of learning mathematics and marveling at this arduous subject at early age. The importance of mathematics is two-fold, it is important in the advancement of science and two, it is important in our understanding of the workings of the universe. And in here and now it is important to individuals for personal development, both mentally and in the workplace.

Mathematics equips pupils with a uniquely powerful set of tools to understand and change the world. These tools include logical reasoning, problem-solving skills, and the ability to think in abstract ways. Mathematics is important in everyday life, many forms of employment, science and technology, medicine, the economy, the environment and development, and in public decision-making.

One should also be aware of the wide importance of Mathematics, and the way in which it is advancing at a spectacular rate.

Mathematics is about pattern and structure; it is about logical analysis, deduction, calculation within these patterns and structures. When patterns are found, often in widely different areas of science and technology, the mathematics of these patterns can be used to explain and control natural happenings and situations. Mathematics has a pervasive influence on our everyday lives, and contributes to the wealth of the individual.

The study of mathematics can satisfy a wide range of interests and abilities. It develops the imagination. It trains in clear and logical thought.

It is a challenge, with varieties of difficult ideas and unsolved problems, because it deals with the questions arising from complicated structures. Yet it also has a continuing drive to simplification, to finding the right concepts and methods to make difficult things easy, to explaining why a situation must be as it is.

In so doing, it develops a range of language and insights, which may then be applied to make a crucial contribution to our understanding and appreciation of the world, and our ability to find and make our way in it.

AIMS IN TEACHING MATHEMATICS

TO DEVELOP A GOOD UNDERSTANDING OF NUMBERS AND THE NUMBER SYSTEM

- Maximising their counting ability.
- Achieving a sound grasp of the properties of numbers and number sequences including negative numbers.
- Achieving a good understanding of place value and ordering, including reading and writing numbers.
- Understanding the principles and practice of estimating and rounding.
- Achieving a sound grasp of the concepts of fractions, decimals and percentages, and their equivalence. Developing these concepts to gain understanding of ratio and proportion.

To Develop the Ability to Undertake Calculations with Confidence, Accuracy and

IMPROVING SPEED

- Achieving a good understanding of number operations and relationships.
- Achieving rapid mental recall of number facts.
- Maximising the ability to undertake mental calculation, including strategies for deriving new facts from known facts.
- Maximising the ability to undertake calculation using pencil and paper methods.
- Maximising the ability to undertake calculation using a calculator. Developing the ability to check that the results of calculations are reasonable.

TO DEVELOP A GOOD ABILITY TO SOLVE PROBLEMS

- Developing the ability to make decisions e.g. deciding which operation and method of calculation to use (mental, mental with jottings, pencil and paper, calculator etc.)

- Being able to reason about numbers or shapes and make general statements about them.
- Improving the ability to solve problems involving numbers in context (e.g. everyday uses such as money, measures etc.)

TO DEVELOP A GOOD KNOWLEDGE AND UNDERSTANDING OF MEASURES, SHAPE AND SPACE

- Achieving a sound knowledge of measures, including the ability to choose units and read scales logically and accurately.
- Achieving a sound knowledge of the properties of 2-D and 3-D shapes, and a good understanding of position, direction and movement.

To Develop a Good Ability to Handle Data with Confidence, Accuracy and

IMPROVING SPEED

Improving the ability to collect, present and interpret numerical data with understanding. Our aims in Maths broadly reflect those set out in the National Numeracy Strategy.

Ginn's Abacus numeracy textbooks are used to provide a progressive framework for teaching from Years 3 to 6, although many others resources will be used to supplement learning as deemed appropriate by the class teachers. The following topics are taught in each term, with concepts and strategies being developed each time.

- Place Value (hundreds, tens, unit digits)
- Addition strategies
- Subtraction strategies
- Multiplication strategies
- Division strategies
- Money (shopping and change)
- Fractions
- Time

Throughout the year the children will complete open-ended investigations that are related to the topic being taught. These topics are taught in the following terms:

PRACTICAL AND SOCIAL TEACHING MATHEMATICS

Excellent mathematics teachers make a major difference to the learning outcomes of the students they teach. What are the professional skills and knowledge that really matter?

Teaching Secondary School Mathematics is a research based introduction to the professional knowledge, attributes and practices needed to teach mathematics well at secondary level.

The authors explain the challenges that secondary mathematics teachers face today, and how they can build on the experiences students bring from primary school and from outside the classroom to ensure students develop concepts and skills in mathematical thinking and a positive attitude to mathematics.

They outline the secondary mathematical curriculum and methods of assessment, and examine the pedagogical strategies teachers can use to engage student interest in mathematical concepts. They emphasise the importance of working with mathematical reasoning and problem solving, real world applications, and mathematical communication skills. The core mathematical topics covered at secondary level are reviewed, and the authors also explore the issues teachers need to consider with students of diverse backgrounds.

'I highly recommend this book to practising mathematics teachers as well as pre-service teachers. The combination of research and practical teaching ideas ensures current and worthwhile advice for teaching secondary or middle school students.'

INSTRUCTIONAL OBJECTIVES

Instructional objectives are specific, measurable, short-term, observable student behaviors.

Objectives are the foundation upon which you can build lessons and assessments that you can prove meet your overall course or lesson goals.

Think of objectives as tools you use to make sure you reach your goals. They are the arrows you shoot towards your target (goal).

The purpose of objectives is not to restrict spontaneity or constrain the vision of education in the discipline; but to ensure that learning is focused clearly enough that both students and teacher know what is going on, and so learning can be objectively measured. Different archers have different styles, so do different teachers. Thus, you can shoot your arrows (objectives) many ways. The important thing is that they reach your target (goals) and score that bullseye!

Instructional objectives (also known as *behavioral objectives* or *learning objectives*) are basically statements which clearly describe an anticipated learning outcome. When objectives were first coming into their own in education, they almost always began with the phrase: "Upon completion of this lesson, the student should be able to...." This phrase focused on the outcome of learning rather than on the learning process. In fact, one of the criteria for a well-written objective is that it describe the outcome of learning, that is, what the learners can do after learning has occurred that they might not have been able to do before the teaching and learning process began.

A well-written objective should meet the following criteria:

- Describe a learning outcome.
- Be student oriented.
- Be observable (or describe an observable product).

A well-written objective should describe a learning outcome (e.g., to correctly spell the spelling words on page seventeen). It should not describe a learning activity (e.g., to practice the words on page seventeen by writing each one ten times). Learning activities are important in planning and guiding instruction but they are not to be confused with instructional objectives.

A student-oriented objective focuses on the learner, not on the teacher. It describes what the learner will be expected to be able to do. It should not describe a teacher activity (e.g., to go over the words on page seventeen with the students, explaining their meaning and telling them how the words are pronounced). It may be helpful to both the teacher and the student to know what the teacher is going to do but teacher activities are also not to be confused with instructional objectives.

If an instructional objective is not observable (or does not describe an observable product), it leads to unclear expectations and it will be difficult to determine whether or not it had been reached. The key to writing observable objectives is to use verbs that are observable and lead to a well defined product of the action implied by that verb.

Verbs such as "to know," "to understand," "to enjoy," "to appreciate," "to realise," and "to value" are vague and not observable. Verbs such as "to identify," "to list," "to select," "to compute," "to predict," and "to analyse" are explicit and describe observable actions or actions that lead to observable products.

There are many skills that cannot be directly observed. The thinking processes of a student as she tries to solve a math problem cannot be easily observed. However, one can look at the answers she comes up with and determine if they are correct. It is also possible to look at the steps a student takes to arrive at an answer if they are written down (thus displaying his thinking process). There are many end products that also can be observed (e.g., an oil painting, a prose paragraph, a 3-dimensional map, or an outline.)

CHARACTERISTICS OF A USEFUL OBJECTIVE

To be useful for instruction, an objective must not only be well written but it also must meet the following criteria:

- Be sequentially appropriate
- Be attainable within a reasonable amount of time
- Be developmentally appropriate.

For an objective to be sequentially appropriate it must occur in an appropriate place in the instructional sequence. All prerequisite objectives must already have been attained. Nothing thwarts the learning process more than having learners trying to accomplish an objective before they have learned the necessary prerequisites. This is why continuous assessment of student progress is so important.

A useful objective is attainable within a reasonable time. If an instructional objective takes students an inordinately long time to accomplish, it is either sequentially inappropriate or it is too broad, relying on the accomplishment of several outcomes or skills rather than a single outcome or skill. An objective should set expectations for a single learning outcome and not a cluster of them.

Developmentally appropriate objectives set expectations for students that are well within their level of intellectual, social, language, or moral development. Teachers, parents, and others who are working with preschool or elementary school children should be especially aware of the developmental stages of the children they are working with. No author or researcher has more clearly defined the stages of intellectual development than Jean Piaget.

Familiarity with his work as well as with the work of other child development specialists (e.g., Lev Vygotsky's language development, Lawrence Kohlberg's moral development and Erik Erikson's social development) should produce better instructional objectives.

TYPES OF OBJECTIVES

Instructional Objectives for Learner

- Table of contents objectives (these are the things we're going to teach you).
- Performance Objectives (this is what you'll do..).
- Motivation (why you should pay attention).
- Focusing Objectives (what you should pay attention to).

Instructional Objectives for Developers

- Instr. Des Objectives (what we want learners to learn, behaviors for them to do).
- Evaluation Objective (these are the things we're going to measure).

- Situation (these are the list of situations).
- Organizational Objectives (the benefits that will come to the organization).

Psychomotor

Physical skills (e.g., "The student will be able to ride a two-wheel bicycle without assistance and without pause as demonstrated in gym class."); actions which demonstrate the fine motor skills such as use of precision instruments or tools, or actions which evidence gross motor skills such as the use of the body in dance or athletic performance.

Cognitive

Understandings, awarenesses, insights (e.g., "Given a description of a planet, the student will be able to identify that planet, as demonstrated verbally or in writing." or "The student will be able to evaluate the different theories of the origin of the solar system as demonstrated by his/her ability to compare and discuss verbally or in writing the strengths and weaknesses of each theory.").

This includes knowledge or information recall, comprehension or conceptual understanding, the ability to apply knowledge, the ability to analyse a situation, the ability to synthesize information from a given situation, and the ability to evaluate a given situation.

Affective

Attitudes, appreciations, relationships (e.g., "Given the opportunity to work in a team with several people of different races, the student will demonstrate an positive increase in attitude towards non-discrimination of race, as measured by a checklist utilized/completed by non-team members.").

EXAMPLES

Audience - Green
Behaviour - Red
Condition - Blue
Degree - Pink

Psychomotor: "Given a standard balance beam raised to a standard height, the student (attired in standard balance beam usage attire) will be able to walk the entire length of the balance beam (from one end to the other) steadily, without falling off, and within a six second time span."

Cognitive (Comprehension Level): "Given examples and non-examples of constructivist activities in a college classroom, the student will be able to accurately identify the constructivist examples and explain why each example is or isn't a constructivist activity in 20 words or less."

Cognitive (Application Level): "Given a sentence written in the past or present tense, the student will be able to re-write the sentence in future tense with no errors in tense or tense contradiction (i.e., I will see her yesterday.)."

Cognitive (Problem solving/synthesis level): "Given two cartoon characters of the student's choice, the student will be able to list five major personality traits of each of the two characters, combine these traits (either by melding traits together, multiplying together complimentary traits, or negating opposing traits) into a composite character, and develop a short (no more than 20 frames) storyboard for a cartoon that illustrates three to five of the major personality traits of the composite character."

Affective: "Given the opportunity to work in a team with several people of different races, the student will demonstrate an positive increase in attitude towards non-discrimination of race, as measured by a checklist utilized/completed by non-team members."

If you're paying attention here, you'll notice two things: As you move up the "cognitive ladder," it become increasingly difficult to *precisely* specify the degree.

Affective objectives are the hardest objectives for most people to write and assess. They deal almost exclusively with internal feelings and conditions that can only be artifically observed externally.

The verbs you use to describe the overt, measurable activity can be tricky to write. Fortunately,

GENERAL INSTRUCTIONAL OBJECTIVE

An intended outcome of instruction that has been stated in appropriate general terms to encompass a domain of student performance. It must be further defined by a set of specific learning outcomes.

Formulate general objectives of instruction that describe types of behaviour students should exhibit in order to demonstrate that they have learned. Under each general objective, list up to five specific learning outcomes (what you should be able to perform).

Examples of General Objectives and Specific Outcomes:

OBJECTIVE

By the end of the course, learners should know the basic operations of Mac System 7.5. (and never use an IBM any more)

SPECIFIC OUTCOMES

Learners should be able to:

- Install new software.
- Copy and erase files.
- Use Chooser to select a file server and a printer.
- Use Control Panel for setup.
- Add aliases into Apple menu and Startup folder.

General instructional goals and objectives provide the foundation for both instruction and assessment of student learning (Linn and Miller, 2005). When instructional objectives are viewed as learning outcomes and are defined in performance terms, numerous types of intended outcomes might be included (Linn and Miller, 2005). In addition to the more obvious knowledge outcomes, these in the areas of understanding, application, thinking skills, performance skills, attitudes, interests, and appreciation should also be included (Linn and Miller, 2005).

General instructional goals and objectives provide direction for the instructional process, convey instructional intent to students, and provide a basis for assessing student learning (Linn and Miller, 2005). The final step in the instructional process is to determine the extent to which students have achieved the learning objectives. Students are expected to demonstrate certain knowledge, understanding, applications, integration of ideas and concepts, and skills as a result of instruction (Linn and Miller, 2005).

This is accomplished by using quizzes, tests, research reports, research projects, oral presentations, class and homework assignments, and other types of assessments that are specially designed to measure the intended learning outcomes.

SPECIFIC LEARNING OUTCOMES

Learning outcomes (LOs) describe what a student is expected to know, understand or be able to demonstrate at the end of a course in order to obtain a passing grade. They express a desired state and are often described in terms of knowledge, skills and attitudes. Learning outcomes can be set for both individual courses and entire degree programmemes.

Learning outcomes describe the measurable skills, abilities, knowledge, or values that students should be able to do or demonstrate as a result of a completing a programme of study, a course, or lesson.

Learning outcomes are student-centered rather than teacher-centered, in that they describe what the students will do, not what the instructor will teach. Learning outcomes are not standalone statements. They must all relate to each other and to the title of the unit and avoid repetition.

Learning outcomes are statements that describe significant and essential learning that learners have achieved, and can reliably demonstrate at the end of a course or programme. In other words, learning outcomes identify what the learner will know and be able to do by the end of a course or programme.

Spady, (1994), an educational researcher who spearheaded the development of outcomes based education, suggests that the ability *demonstrate* learning is the key point. This demonstration of learning involves a performance of some kind in order to show *significant* learning, or learning that matters.

He claims that significant content is essential, but that

content alone is insufficient as an outcome. Rather, knowledge of content must be manifested through a demonstration process of some kind. An outcome statement that incorporates this knowledge within a performance demonstration might include:

- The learner will have demonstrated the ability to make engine repairs on a variety of automobiles.
- In the above statement, the ability to make engine repairs implies that the person has the requisite knowledge to do so.
- Performance statements include higher level thinking skills as well as psychomotor skills.

Consider the following learning outcome statement:

- The learner will have demonstrated the ability to analyse engines and make decisions regarding required repairs for a variety of automobiles.
- Spady, also addresses the context or performance setting in which the performance demonstration occurs. He suggests a range of performance contexts from that of demonstrations of classroom learning to those which involve living successfully in the larger society. Thus, his highest level outcomes refer to generic skills such as the preparation of learners to be problem solvers, planners, creators, learners and thinkers, communicators etc., regardless of subject areas studied.
- Learning outcomes refer to observable and measurable:
  - Knowledge
  - Skills
  - Attitudes

Articulating learning outcomes for students is part of good teaching. If you tell students what you expected them to do, and give them practice in doing it, then there is a good chance that they will be able to do it on a test or major assignment. That is to say, they will have learned what you wanted them to know. If you do not tell them what they will be expected to do, then they are left guessing what you want. If they guess wrong, they will resent you for being tricky, obscure, or punishing.

LEARNING OUTCOMES NEED TO BE SMART

Specific: The learning outcome should be well defined and clear. It states exactly what will be accomplished.

Measurable: The learning outcome should provide a benchmark or target so that the institution can determine when the target has been reached, by how much it has been exceeded or by how much it has fallen short.

Agreed Upon: Important stakeholders must be in general agreement with the institutions mission, goals and learning outcomes. Stakeholders may include university, school administration, faculty, students, alumni, and/or community members.

Realistic: Learning outcomes should be reasonable given the available resources. Learning outcomes should neither be easy nor impossible to attain, but somewhere in between.

Time-Framed: A learning outcome should include a specific date by which it will be completed. It is important to allow enough time to successfully implement the steps needed to achieve the objective, but not so much as to elicit procrastination.

Learning cannot be forced; it is a process that each learner goes through independently. When you use learning outcomes, you shift the responsibility more towards the learner and move towards more student-oriented instruction. When students know exactly what is expected of them, they can choose the studying methods they consider the most efficient. Therefore, if a student is expected to learn, the teacher must be able to define specifically what needs to be learnt.

LEARNING OUTCOMES HAVE DISTINCT ADVANTAGES

If expectations are stated accurately, students are more likely to be able to control their learning. By defining the learning outcomes, instructors can see what they actually expect from students.

Learning outcomes help focus the assessment on the right criteria. Learning outcomes help discover the most appropriate assessment methods. Learning outcomes of a degree programmeme explain to outsiders what a graduate knows.

HOW TO WRITE LEARNING OUTCOMES

Learning outcomes should define the most important points that the student is expected to learn be attainable and possible to assess be explicit and simple

There is no rule as to the number of learning outcomes per course, but the usual recommendation is four to eight. Basic courses often have several learning outcomes, whereas advanced ones may have only few.

When you start to define learning outcomes, you should list the issues each student must know, remember or be able to do in order to obtain a passing grade. Learning outcomes thus describe the threshold level students need to reach to pass the course.

A recommended starting point is an analysis of the core content of the course. The core content is something all students in the course should assimilate, and necessary in the assimilation of new information. This represents the threshold achievements for a passing grade, which serves as a basis for the learning outcomes.

Accurate learning outcomes always include a verb describing what the student should be able to do at the end of the course. Moreover, they should explain the threshold level of these competences. For instance, if you list "writing a programmeme" as a learning outcome, this would also include programmemes that do no function. However, if you restrict the LO to functioning programmemes, you set a clear limit. Nevertheless, often such specifications are not needed, as the LO itself contains limiting criteria. For instance, if you list "solving a differential equation with the Runge-Kutta method" as an LO, you imply that the solution to the equation must be correct.

Since the learning outcomes must be fulfilled in order to pass the course, there must be a way to test them.

Consequently, you should avoid verbs such as understand, know, comprehend, can etc. which describe activity that cannot be perceived with the naked eye.

For instance, if the outcome states that a student has to understand certain principles, there is no way of verifying that it has actually happened. If, instead, the student is required to explain these principles, this would demonstrate whether they have understood them. The sentence should thus convey how students are to demonstrate their skills. One dynamic verb is sufficient for one learning outcome; if there are more, the sentence may become open to interpretation. If need be, the outcome can be expanded on with another sentence.

Learning outcomes for a degree programmeme can be introduced e.g. as follows: "A graduate from the degree programmeme is expected to know:". And those of a course: "At the end of the course a student is expected to know:". After this, you can list the individual learning outcomes. Here are a few examples of different learning outcomes:

TYPES OF OBJECTIVES/LEARNING OUTCOMES

With the general acceptance of objectives as a key component of the systems approach to course and curriculum design, it has become fashionable to think in terms of broad types of objectives. Here, another American, Benjamin Bloom, has been extremely influential in clarifying and organizing educational thought regarding the classification of objectives, his original work being carried out during the 1950's.

Bloom and his co-workers contended that objectives are attainable in three distinct areas, or domains, to which they assigned suitably impressive jargon names: the cognitive domain, affective domain and psychomotor domain. At the risk of over-simplification, these can be thought of as being respectively concerned with knowledge-related objectives, attitude-related objectives and motor skills-related objectives. Let us now examine them in more detail.

THE COGNITIVE DOMAIN

This contains objectives which are related to the

acquisition and application of knowledge and understanding, and probably includes the great majority of educational and training objectives. An example of such an objective might be:

"The student should be able to calculate all the dimensions of a triangle given the lengths of two sides and the size of the angle between them".

Bloom and his co-workers also divided the cognitive domain into six distinct levels, each level building on those below and representing a progressively higher level of cognitive activity. Their hierarchy of the cognitive domain.

Level 6: Evaluation: Making judgements/critical comparisons on the basis of agreed criteria.

Level 5: Synthesis: Bringing elements together to form a new, coherent whole.

Level 4: Analysis: Breaking a system down into its constituent elements.

Level 3: Application: Applying procedures/systems/rules in specific situations.

Level 2: Comprehension: Understanding and interpreting information.

Level 1: Knowledge: Recalling information

THE AFFECTIVE DOMAIN

This contains objectives that are concerned with attitudes and feelings which are brought about as a result of some educational or training process. An example of such an objective might be:

"The trainee lecturer should exercise empathy when counselling students".

The affective domain was also divided into a number of distinct, hierarchical levels, as shown in Figure. This work was carried out by Bloom and his co-worker Krathwohl.

Level 5: Characterization: integrating one's beliefs, ideas and attitudes into a total, all-embracing philosophy.

Level 4: Organization: Making adjustments or decisions from among several alternatives.

Level 3: Valuing: Committing oneself to taking up an attitudinal position.

Level 2: Responding: Showing active interest in something.

Level 1: Receiving: Developing an awareness of something.

THE PSYCHOMOTOR DOMAIN

This contains objectives that deal with the development of manipulative or physical skills - things like measuring, setting up and using equipment, using tools, drawing graphs, and so on. An example of such an objective might be:

"The student should be able to assemble and use the distillation apparatus provided".

A number of hierarchical classifications of the psychomotor domain were subsequently produced, probably the best known being the one by Kibler shown in Figure.

Level 4: Speech Behaviors: Sound production and projection; sound/gesture coordination.

Level 3: Non-Verbal Communication: Facial expressions, gestures, bodily movements.

Level 2: Finely-Coordinated Movements: Movements of hand and fingers, hand and eye, eye and foot, etc.

Level 1: Gross Body Movements: Movements of arms, shoulders, trunk, feet and legs.

Although the work of Bloom and his successors has had a tremendous influence on educational thinking, the above tripartite classification of objectives/learning outcomes has since been modified in a number of important respects. First, it has been recognised that most of the levels of the cognitive domain overlap to a considerable extent, and that the only real gap is that between Level 2 (Comprehension) and Level 3 (Application).

For this reason, it is now customary to talk simply of lower cognitive objectives (encompassing Levels 1 and 2 of Bloom's hierarchy) and higher-cognitive objectives (encompassing Levels 3-6 of Bloom's hierarchy). Second, it has been recognised that Bloom and his co-workers completely ignored one of the most important of all groups of objectives - those covering the various 'life skills' such as decision-making, problem-solving, creative thinking, communication and interpersonal skills.

Some of these fall naturally into the class of 'higher-cognitive objectives', while others can be thought of a constituting a completely new 'domain' - the interpersonal domain. Third, it has been recognised that many objectives and learning outcomes defy rigid classification of the type advocated by Bloom and his successors, since they have overlapping aspects that fall into more than one category.

For the above reasons, a much simpler, less rigid scheme for classifying educational objectives and learning outcomes has achieved widespread acceptance in recent years, and is commended to all teachers and lecturers.

This incorporates all you really need to know about such classification, and should prove of immense value in helping you to choose appropriate instructional methods, plan your teaching, design supportive materials, and plan your student assessment. It recognises the following five broad types of objectives and learning outcomes:

Lower Cognitive

Comprising the first two levels (knowledge and comprehension) of Bloom's cognitive domain, and containing all objectives and learning outcomes related to the acquisition of knowledge and basic understanding.

Higher Cognitive

Comprising the top four levels (application, analysis, synthesis and evaluation) of Bloom's cognitive domain, and including all objectives and earning outcomes related to interpretation of information, decision making, problem solving and planning.

Affective

Comprising all five levels of the affective domain, ie including all objectives and learning outcomes related to feelings, attitudes and values.

Psychomotor

Comprising all four levels of the psychomotor domain, ie

including all objectives and learning outcomes related to motor skills, manual dexterity, hand-eye coordination, practical abilities, and so on.

Interpersonal

Covering all the various 'life skills' that were not catered for by Bloom's original tripartite classification, including all objectives and learning outcomes related to communication (written and oral), listening, working as part of a team, interacting with other people, acting as a leader, and so on.

Unit III

Teaching Skills of Mathematics

MICROTEACHING

Microteaching is so called since it is analogous to putting the teacher under a microscope so to say while he is teaching so that all faults in teaching methodology are brought into perspective for the observers to give a constructive feedback. It eliminates some of the complexities of learning to teach in the classroom situation such as the pressure of length of the lecture, the scope and content of the matter to be conveyed, the need to teach for a relatively long duration of time (usually an hour) and the need to face large numbers of students, some of whom are hostile temperamentally.

Microteaching also provides skilled supervision with an opportunity to get a constructive feedback. To go back to the analogy of the swimmer, while classroom teaching is like learning to swim at the deeper end of the pool, microteaching is an opportunity to practice at the shallower and less risky side.

Microteaching was developed in the early and mid 1960's by Dwight Allen and his colleagues at the Stanford Teacher Education Programme. The Stanford model emphasized a teach, review and reflect, re-teach approach, using actual school students as authentic audiences. The model has been adapted for college and university teaching where it has been used most often for graduate teaching assistants. It often offers a concentrated, focused form of peer feedback and discussion. A very similar model called Instructional Skills Workshop (ISW) was developed during the early 1970s by British

Columbia's Education Ministry as a training support programme for all college and institute faculty in British Columbia and has now spread throughout Canada, the US and internationally. While there are significant differences between the two models, they both share some commonalities and were designed to enhance teaching and promote open collegial discussion about teaching performance.

A micro lesson is an opportunity to present a sample "snapshot" of what/how you teach and to get some feedback from colleagues about how it was received. It is a chance to try teaching strategies that you may not use regularly. This is a good, safe time to experiment with something new to you or to get feedback on a technique you've been trying but are not sure about its effectiveness.

The Microteaching cycle starts with planning. In order to reduce the complexities involved in teaching, the student teacher is asked to plan a "microlesson" i.e a short lesson for 5-10 minutes which he will teach in front of a "microclass" i.e a group consisting 3-4 students, a supervisor and peers if necessary. There is scope for projection of model teaching skills if required to help the teacher prepare for his session. The student teacher is asked to teach concentrating one or few of the teaching skills enumerated earlier.

His teaching is evaluated by the students, peers and the supervisor using cheekists to help them. Video recording can be done if facilities permit. At the- end of the 5 or 10 minutes session as planned, the teacher is given a feedback on the deficiencies noticed in his teaching methodology. Feedback can be aided by playing back the video recording.

Using the feedback to help himself, the teacher is asked to replan his lesson keeping the comments in view and reteach immediately the same lesson to another group. Such repeated cycles of teaching, feedback and reteaching help the teacher to improve his teaching skills one at a time. Several such sequences can be planned at the departmental level. Colleagues and postgraduate students can act as peer evaluators for this purpose. It is important, however, that the cycle is used purely for helping the teacher and not as a tool for making a value judgement of his teaching capacity by his superiors.

ADVANTAGES OF MICROTEACHING

Microteaching has several advantages. It focuses on sharpening and developing specific teaching skills and eliminating errors. It enables understanding of behaviours important in classroom teaching. It increases the confidence of the learner teacher.

It is a vehicle of continuous training applicable at all stages not only to teachers at the beginning of their career but also for more senior teachers. It enables projection of model instructional skills. It provides expert supervision and a constructive feedback and above all if provides for repeated practice without adverse consequences to the teacher or his students.

Life is not a bed of roses; and we usually confront as many problems in our daily life. Problem is not a problem itself however we convert it to a difficult one by dealing with trivial issues or sometimes ignoring the significant ones. Our attitude to such problems compels us to face more complicated issues in even small problems.

In our daily life, the busy schedule tends us to invite more problems and we get caught in situation by one way or another. If these problems are not attended properly; these tend to tease you on every step. They say if you are not a part of solution than you are a part of problem; however the significance lies in the solution of the problem, no matter what procedure one adopts to acquire the solution.In every day life, we are confronted with many problems. Some of them continue to persist if left unsolved.

Basically, I am a school teacher, teaching Mathematics at Primary level. Teachers and students are two important cogs of the machinery of education. Both of them are some how related to one another. Teachers teach the students and the students learn from the teachers. It is our common observation that when new session commence each year there is a stream of newly admitted students in the school. From primary to secondary, there is mixed queue of students having diversified level of intelligence.

I spent about four to five hours with the children, confronting with their problems with behaviour and studies. In my experience, I learnt that most of the students rate Mathematics as a difficult subject. Many parents also complaint about their wards unable to comprehend some exercises in Mathematics. Not all the students are gifted with the same skills to understand and easy pick up of complicated problems. As a teacher, I am responsible to provide these students the easy way to understand these difficult exercises. To overcome, any problem, one must analyse the nature of the problem and decide further action plan to deal with it.

Analyzing the nature of the problem is to reach the core of it so that the root cause may be prevented in the future. When the new session starts in August, we are provided with new students, having different intelligence level. Among them, some are sharp and some are dull. These students suffer the most because it is their hesitant nature that keeps them away from the teacher and they try to avoid asking specially the novice students, who are still unsettled in the class. Active and brilliant students are always participating in the class work however the problem lies with these dull students. What we teachers are expected, is to provide all our students with quality education, irrespective of their Intelligence level.

PURPOSE OF MICRO TEACHING

The purpose of microteaching is to give you confidence, support, and feedback by letting you try out with a small group of colleagues a short sample of the kind of teaching you are currently doing or which you are preparing yourself for. The microteaching will be organized as follows:

1. You need to prepare a short teaching episode (between 10 and 15 minutes) drawn from the kind of teaching you are involved in or want to develop. It can be an extract from a session you have actually taught, something you are going to be teaching, or just something you want to try out.

2. We normally organize the microteaching in small groups of 5-7, each with a facilitator. Members of the group take it in turn to give their teaching episode, with the other group members in the role of 'student' or 'observer'.
3. The microteaching will take place in a 'classroom' setting but you will be able to re-arrange the room, as appropriate to the kind of teaching methods involved.
4. AV equipment will be available – including OHP, whiteboard, flip chart, PC + projector.
5. If appropriate, you can prepare a handout (e.g. a task or problem sheet, case study, or vignette). If you provide the handout on Monday 11th June or email it in advance, Julie Hanks, the Course Co-coordinator, will make photocopies of your handout ready for your microteaching session. Otherwise, you will need to make sufficient copies yourself and bring them to the session.
6. Those involved give one another constructive feedback on their teaching. The person who has 'performed' should be the first to comment, giving their own self-evaluative views and, if they wish, identifying particular areas for others to comment on.
7. A digital video recording of the microteaching will be made. You will have the opportunity for a one-to-one review of your microteaching video with a course tutor. The recording is regarded as the property of the person whose teaching is recorded. A copy will be provided for each participant as soon as possible after the event. (The original recordings are wiped unless you give consent for them to be kept for training purposes.)

PREPARATION OF MICRO TEACHING

- To prepare a short lesson for a small group of learner.
- Your lesson can be excerpted from the beginning, middle or end of one course lesson and you will be

able to explain this in setting up your lesson and as part of your application or instruction form.

- You have several decisions to make concerning the preparation of your micro lessons:
  - *Topic:* Choose a teaching topic that you are comfortable with in order to focus on a particular teaching method or element. Or, preparing material that you especially would like to make sure your students understand by the end of your next class.
  - *Lesson objectives:* Think about and be able to articulate what you want your students to learn from your lesson (e.g., facts, concepts, skills, and/or values) and how your teaching methodology might work to fulfill your objectives.

What you want feedback on. You can specify to the group what you would like them to focus on. For example, you may wish to have overall, general feedback or perhaps you might wish for the group to simply attend to a specific issue, such as how you use questions or reinforcement with students. Not only plan out how to treat the subject matter, but also give some thought to how you are going to present yourself, manage the class, and involve the students.

Striving to create as natural a classroom setting as possible. While one person takes his or her turn as teacher, everyone else plays the roles of students. It is the job of these pretend pupils to ask and answer questions realistically. It is the job of the pretend teacher to involve his or her "class" actively in this way.

- A timer is used to keep to the strictly enforced time limit.
- Don't be offended if you are cut off; it will be necessary to keep to the time limit so that everyone might participate fully.

OBSERVATION

- When you are in the role of students, you should combine the role of student and observer.

- Do not feel like you must role play specific student behaviors, but do feel free to ask questions and comment as a learner in the classroom environment.
- Try to focus on what is happening during the micro lesson.
- The best way to give feedback is to identify a small number of things the person can improve, so think about what is best to focus on for each micro-teacher.

SKILL EMPHASIS

Emphasis on Skills is a training and development firm that designs and delivers genuinely tailor-made in-house programmemes for you.

The grid below shows what training we offer and for whom. For each skill area you will find specific information about what we can help you with and example courses.

Our emphasis is on SELF-AWARENESS by helping you to realise the potential that lies within you, and also your performance and the way you do things. Our software programmes shows organized simple ways to do these same things differently and avoid discomfort and distress.

Our products are simple processes and tests that have been converted into software to enable universal and versatile application.

They can be used by any individual or organization to enhance their potential, productivity, values, and over all "feel good factor".

The software will help you think well, reduce stress, and feel better and hence can maximize the enjoyment within your current avocation and lifestyle.

It adds zest to your life, and is reliable.

It is a challenger.

It stands by you in times of need.

QUESTIONING

Questioning is a basic tool for rebellion. It breaks open the stagnant hardened shells of the present, and opens up the options that might be explored.

Questioning reveals the profound uncertainty that is imbedded deep in all reality beyond the facades of confidence and sureness. It takes this uncertainty towards growth and new possibilities.

Questioning can change your entire life. It can uncover hidden powers and stifled dreams inside of you ... things you may have denied for many years.

Questioning can change institutions and entire cultures. It can empower people to create strategies for change.

Asking a Question that leads to a strategy for action is a powerful contribution to resolving any problem.

Asking Questions that open up more options can lead to many unexpected solutions.

Asking Questions that help adversaries shift from their stuck positions on an issue can lead to acts of healing and reconciliation.

Asking Questions that are unaskable in our culture at the moment can lead to the transformation of our culture and its institutions.

Asking Questions and listening for the strategies and ideas embedded in people's own answers can be the greatest service a social change worker can give to a particular issue.

TYPES OF QUESTIONING

Open and Closed Questions

A closed question usually receives a single word or very short, factual answer. For example, "Are you thirsty?" The answer is "Yes" or "No"; "Where do you live?" The answer is generally the name of your town or your address.

Open questions elicit longer answers. They usually begin with what, why, how. An open question asks the respondent for his or her knowledge, opinion or feelings. "Tell me" and "describe" can also be used in the same way as open questions. Here are some examples:

What happened at the meeting?

Why did he react that way?

How was the party?

Tell me what happened next.
Describe the circumstances in more detail.

Open Questions Are Good For

Developing an open conversation: "What did you get up to on vacation?"

Finding our more detail: "What else do we need to do to make this a success?"

Finding out the other person's opinion or issues: "What do you think about those changes?"

Closed Questions Are Good For

Testing your understanding, or the other person's: "So, if I get this qualification, I will get a raise?"

Concluding a discussion or making a decision: "Now we know the facts, are we all agreed this is the right course of action?"

Frame setting: "Are you happy with the service from your bank?"

A misplaced closed question, on the other hand, can kill the conversation and lead to awkward silences, so are best avoided when a conversation is in full flow.

Funnel Questions

This technique involves starting with general questions, and then homing in on a point in each answer, and asking more and more detail at each level. It's often used by detectives taking a statement from a witness:

"How many people were involved in the fight?"

"About ten."

"Were they kids or adults?"

"Mostly kids."

"What sort of ages were they?"

"About fourteen or fifteen."

"Were any of them wearing anything distinctive?"

"Yes, several of them had red baseball caps on."

"Can you remember if there was a logo on any of the caps?"

"Now you come to mention it, yes, I remember seeing a big letter N."

Using this technique, the detective has helped the witness re-live the scene and gradually focus on a useful detail. Perhaps he'll be able to identify young men wearing a hat like this from CCTV footage. It is unlikely he would have got this information if he's simply asked an open question such as "Are there any details you can give me about what you saw?"

Tip: When using funnel questioning, start with closed questions. As you progress through the tunnel, start using more open questions.

Funnel Questions Are Good For

Finding out more detail about a specific point: "Tell me more about Option 2." Gaining the interest or increasing the confidence of the person you're speaking with: "Have you used the IT Helpdesk?", "Did they solve your problem?", "What was the attitude of the person who took your call?"

Probing Questions

Asking probing questions is another strategy for finding out more detail. Sometimes it's as simple as asking your respondent for an example, to help you understand a statement they have made. At other times, you need additional information for clarification, "When do you need this report by, and do you want to see a draft before I give you my final version?", or to investigate whether there is proof for what has been said, "How do you know that the new database can't be used by the sales force?"

An effective way of probing is to use the 5 Whys method, which can help you quickly get to the root of a problem.

Tip: Use questions that include the word "exactly" to probe further: "What exactly do you mean by fast-track?", "Who, exactly, wanted this report?"

Probing Questions are Good For

- Gaining clarification to ensure you have the whole story and that you understand it thoroughly.

- Drawing information out of people who are trying to avoid telling you something.

Leading Questions

Leading questions try to lead the respondent to your way of thinking. They can do this in several ways:

With an assumption: "How late do you think that the project will deliver?". This assumes that the project will certainly not be completed on time.

By adding a personal appeal to agree at the end: "Lori's very efficient, don't you think?" or "Option 2 is better, isn't it?"

Phrasing the question so that the "easiest" response is "yes" (our natural tendency to prefer to say "yes" than "no" plays an important part in the phrasing of referendum questions): "Shall we all approve Option 2?" is more likely to get a positive response than "Do you want to approve option 2 or not?". A good way of doing this is to make it personal. For example, "Would you like me to go ahead with Option 2?" rather than "Shall I choose Option 2?". Giving people a choice between two options, both of which you would be happy with, rather than the choice of one option or not doing anything at all. Strictly speaking, the choice of "neither" is still available when you ask "Which would you prefer of A or B", but most people will be caught up in deciding between your two preferences. Note that leading questions tend to be closed.

Leading Questions are Good For

Getting the answer you want but leaving the other person feeling that they have had a choice.

Closing a sale: "If that answers all of your questions, shall we agree a price?"

Tip: Use leading questions with care. If you use them in a self-serving way or one that harms the interests of the other person, then they can, quite rightly, be seen as manipulative and dishonest.

Rhetorical Questions

Rhetorical questions aren't really questions at all, in that they don't expect an answer. They're really just statements phrased in question form: "Isn't John's design work so creative?"

People use rhetorical questions because they are engaging for the listener - as they are drawn into agreeing ("Yes it is and I like working with such a creative colleague") - rather than feeling that they are being "told" something like "John is a very creative designer". (To which they may answer "So What?")

Tip: Rhetorical questions are even more powerful if you use a string of them. "Isn't that a great display? Don't you love the way the text picks up the colors in the photographs? Doesn't it use space really well? Wouldn't you love to have a display like that for our products?"

Rhetorical Questions are Good For

Engaging the listener

Using Questioning Techniques

You have probably used all of these questioning techniques before in your everyday life, at work and at home. But by consciously applying the appropriate kind of questioning, you can gain the information, response or outcome that you want even more effectively.

Questions are a powerful way of:

Learning: Ask open and closed questions, and use probing questioning.

Relationship building: People generally respond positively if you ask about what they do or enquire about their opinions. If you do this in an affirmative way "Tell me what you like best about working here", you will help to build and maintain an open dialogue.

Managing and coaching: Here, rhetorical and leading questions are useful too. They can help get people to reflect and to commit to courses of action that you've suggested: "Wouldn't it be great to gain some further qualifications?"

Avoiding misunderstandings: Use probing questions to seek clarification, particularly when the consequences are significant. And to make sure you avoid jumping to conclusions, the The Ladder of Inference tool can help too.

Diffusing a heated situation: You can calm an angry customer or colleague by using funnel questions to get them to go into more detail about their grievance. This will not only distract them from their emotions, but will often help you to identify a small practical thing that you can do, which is often enough to make them feel that they have "won" something, and no longer need to be angry.

Persuading people: No one likes to be lectured, but asking a series of open questions will help others to embrace the reasons behind your point of view. "What do you think about bringing the sales force in for half a day to have their laptops upgraded?"

EFFECTIVE USE OF QUESTIONING

Questioning can.....

- arouse curiosity
- stimulate interest in the topic
- clarify concepts
- emphasize key points
- enhance problem-solving ability
- encourage students to think at higher cognitive levels
- motivate student to search for new information
- ascertain students' knowledge level to aid in modifying instruction

Bloom's Taxonomy

The types of questions and the manner in which questions are asked have a direct impact on the effectiveness of the questioning.

TECHNIQUES OF EFFECTIVE QUESTIONING

Establish an Appropriate Environment

Only certain questions should be posed in front of the patient; bedside questions should focus principally on knowledge and recall and to a lesser extent on comprehension.

Bloom's Taxonomy of Thinking Skills	
Knowledge	Students are required to recall the information learned and repeat it to the teacher. *Example:* What are the major causes of fistula?
Comprehension	Students must explain topics, review items, and discuss issues; this includes translation, interpretation, extrapolation, and focuses on the meaning and intent of the material. *Example:* What study would you order to confirm the diagnosis of myocardial infarction in a patient with a left bundle branch block?
Application	Students must use an abstraction (principle, theory, etc.) brought from other experiences. It requires that students apply previously learned knowledge and skills to new situations and necessitates the use of abstractions in specific situations. *Example:* A 35-year-old woman presents to your office with a 1-month history of polyarthritis, rash, pleuritic pain, and low grade fever. What is the most likely diagnosis?
Analysis	Students must break down material into its component parts and then use a systematic process to reach a logical conclusion. *Example:* How would you distinguish between polymyositis and viral myositis in a 42-year-old man with weakness and a rash?
Synthesis	Students must hypothesize, predict, and use the available information to arrive at a generalization---putting together elements or parts from many sources to constitute a new pattern or structure. *Example:* If the blood culture were negative of the patient with echocardiographic valvular vegetations, how would you proceed with the antibiotic treatment?
Evaluation	Students must use specific criteria to assess situations or to justify previous responses. *Example:* Explain your rationale for using combination drug therapy instead of mono therapy to treat a patient with pulmonary tuberculosis.

Create a Climate Conducive to Learning

A happy facial expression, nod, or verbal acknowledgement of a correct response encourages other students to participate in the discussion. Pose questions in a non-threatening way and receive answers in a supportive fashion. A harsh tone, especially when used to interrupt a response from the student, can be devastating for both the student and his or her peers.

Prepare the Students For the Questioning Session and discussion

Explain to students the format, expectations, and how this knowledge will help them.

Use Both Pre-planned and Emerging Questions

Pre-planned questions are those incorporated into the educational plan prospectively that are asked during the teaching session to introduce new concepts, focus the discussion on certain items, steer the discussion in specific directions, or identify student knowledge level on the topic. Emerging questions derive from the discussion itself and the specific answers given to previous questions. Think quickly and act decisively to phrase these questions accurately and pose them at appropriate times in the discussion.

Use an Appropriate Variety and Mix of Questions

One good strategy is to start with convergent questions and then continue with divergent questions, perhaps asking questions in hierarchical sequence and building from the recall of facts to higher levels of thinking and problem-solving. If a question requiring a higher level thinking skill stymies the student, go down to a question requiring a lower-level thinking skills and then work up the hierarchy.

Avoid Trick Questions and Those That Require Only a yes or no Response

Trick questions should be avoided, as they frustrate students and tend to encourage frivolous responses. YES or NO questions encourage students to respond without fully understanding or thinking through the issue. When used, such questions should be followed by other questions to determine the thinking process of the student.

Phrase the Questions Carefully, Concisely and Clearly

Improper phrasing and the use of multiple questions related to the same topic may result in unintentional cueing and inability to accurately assess student understanding.

Address Questions to the Group, Versus the Individual

Pose the question to the entire group and wait before identifying a student to respond. The wait time encourages all students to think about the response, as they do not know who is going to be called upon to answer the question. Select students at random to answer questions, as it tends to keep everyone attentive and involved.

SELECT BOTH VOLUNTEERS AND NON-VOLUNTEERS TO ANSWER QUESTIONS

Adapt Questions to the Needs of the Learners

Assess the students' needs and tailor questions to maximize the number of correct answers while moving toward more and more difficult questions. Remember, no two groups of students will be alike or at the same level.

Use Sufficient Wait Time

The teacher can significantly enhance the analytic and problem-solving skills of students by allowing sufficient wait times before responding, both after posing a question and after the answer is given. This allows everyone to think about not only the question but also the response provided by the student. Three to five seconds in most cases; longer in some, maybe up to 10 seconds for higher-order questions.

Respond to Answers Given by Students

Listen carefully to the answers given by students; do not interrupt students while they are responding to questions unless they are straying far off course, are totally unfocused, or are being disruptive. Acknowledge correct answers and provide positive reinforcement.

Do not use sarcasm, reprimands, accusations, and

personal attacks. Repeat answers only when the other students have not heard the answers; other repeats waste time. Keep questioning until the learning objectives for the session have been achieved; this may be the best opportunity to teach a particular concept. Handle incomplete answers by reinforcing what is correct and then asking probing questions.

Types of probing questions:	
Extension	Require students to elaborate on the response given to an earlier question. Such questions indicate to the learner that the original response was in the right direction but was not adequate.
Clarification	Useful when the student's response is unclear or incomplete.
Justification	Require the learner to provide rationale for the previously-given response. Useful in providing insights into thinking and reasoning processes of students and revealing errors in these processes.
Prompting	Useful when students do not respond to the original question
Redirection	Used to elicit a variety of opinions during problem-solving sessions or discussions.

Use Questions to Identify Learning Objectives for Follow-up Slf-study

Pose questions towards the end of the teaching session to identify specific areas for additional learning opportunities that students can pursue on their own time.

USING BLACKBOARD

When you evaluate the performance of a protocol, you need information on internal state changes of your protocol, maybe even from protocols that you use. You could monitor these changes using e.g. vector files from within you protocol and remove these monitors once you are done. Another way is to use a blackboard. The state changes are published on it, and the monitors subscribe to these values. This allows other researchers to tap your protocol for performance evaluation, while imposing nearly no runtime penalty when the information is not needed.

May be even more importantly, the blackboard allows you to exchange information between layers, without passing pointers to the modules around. Some items might not only be interesting for the layer they are created/changed in. The physical layer for example can sense whether a channel is busy or not. If the MAC protocol is based on carrier sense it needs the information the physical layer has. The *Blackboard* is a module where the corresponding information can be published and then is accessible for any module interested in it.

The *Basic Module* provides everything necessary to interact with the blackboard. It is derived from *Modifiable* - a pure virtual base class that allows the blackboard to inform your module of changes - and contains a pointer named *bb* to the blackboard module.

The majority of the teaching on this course will be delivered using software called Blackboard. Blackboard is one of many Virtual Learning Environments used to teach over the internet. It can be used to present study information online either to complement traditional face-to-face classes, or as a main method of teaching. This document will introduce you to Blackboard and how to use it during the course.

Section One demonstrates how to log into Blackboard, and describes the Blackboard student homepage. Section Two introduces the Delve Deeper distance learning pages.

In order to use Blackboard, you will need a Newcastle University login and password.

These will be posted out to you before the beginning of your course. There are several formatting conventions used in this document. Please take note of the formatting styles:

- Buttons and drop-down lists will be indicated in Bold.
- Locations on the screen are indicated in *italic*

REINFORCEMENT

The principle of reinforcement is a psychological concept

based on the idea that the consequences of an action will influence future behaviour. Rewarding behaviour is considered reinforcement, because it teaches the subject that the behaviour is desired, and encourages the subject to repeat it. Punishing a behaviour, on the other hand, teaches the subject that the behaviour is not desired, and should not be repeated.

There are actually two types of reinforcement: positive reinforcement and negative reinforcement. Positive reinforcement refers to introducing a new stimulus to the subject's environment in order to reward desired behaviour. For example, a child might be given a balloon after behaving well at the dentist, or a rat might learn to press a bar for a treat. Positive reinforcement associates a pleasant outcome with the desired outcome. Negative reinforcement, on the other hand, involves removing an unpleasant stimulus from the environment. For example, a mouse entering a cage with an electrified floor would quickly learn to press a button if the current was stopped every time the button was pressed.

Negative reinforcement is used in escape and avoidance conditioning. In escape conditioning, the subject learns to quickly remove him or herself from a situation where the negative stimulus exists, much as people evacuate a building with a screaming fire alarm. Avoidance conditioning involves learning to avoid the potentially unpleasant situation altogether, and the most classic example of avoidance conditioning is eating when you expect to be hungry, to avoid the unpleasant sensation of hunger.

Likewise, punishment is divided into positive and negative aspects. In a positive punishment situatión, something unpleasant is introduced the the environment, such as a spanking for a misbehaving child. Negative punishment removes a pleasant thing from the environment, much as a parent might take ice cream away from a screaming child.

MACRO TEACHING

Macros are programmes that generate programmes: Mention macros to most programmemers, perhaps even you, and the first image that comes to mind is string substitution - you use a macro to glue together a few parameters in a new way, maybe with a bit of compile-time decision making thrown in. And because of the typical (in languages other than Lisp) disparity between the macro language and the programmeming language, the difficulty of writing a macro increases much faster than its complexity.

Lisp macros are Lisp programmes that generate other Lisp programmes. The generated Lisp code has a fully-parenthesized notation, as does the macro that generates the code. In the simplest case, a macro substitutes forms within a template, clearly establishing a visual correspondence between the generating code and the generated code.

Complex macros can use the full power of the Lisp language to generate code according to the macro parameters; often a template form is wrapped in code that constructs appropriate subforms, but even this approach is just a typical use pattern and not a requirement (or restriction) of the Lisp macro facility.

In the following sections, we'll examine the mechanism by which the Lisp system translates code generated by a macro, then we'll see several increasingly sophisticated examples of macros.

LESSON PLAN

A lesson plan is developed by the teacher to guide the instruction. Planning the instruction is much more difficult than delivering the instruction. Planning is when you look at the curriculum standards and develop lesson content that match those standards. Luckily, textbooks that are adopted for your subject areas are typically are written with this in mind.

All details should be written down to assist the smooth delivery of the content. The extent of the detail will vary depending on the number of years of experience that the teacher has and the number of times he/she has taught the lesson. Obviously a teacher with several or many years of experience may have plans that are much less detailed than beginning teachers. There will be requirements mandated by the school system that employs you regarding your responsibilities.

Below you will find a basic lesson plan model, typical components and explanations as well as "directions" for writing your plan using the template that is provided here for download. While all lesson plan models are not identical (different states may use slightly different models), the major components are found in all models.

Writing Lesson Plans is a preliminary and essential stage that helps increase the success-rate of anything you are teaching. A well-planned lesson or unit is much less likely to flop! While districts, school boards, administrators and principals may have differing opinions of the importance of Lesson Plans, the vast majority of teachers are required to use them to varyin degrees. Here are some helpful resources to guide you through the process.

DEVELOPING GOOD LESSON PLAN

The first thing to consider, obviously, is what you want to teach. This should be developed based upon your state (or school) standards. You also need to be aware of what grade level you are developing the lesson plan for (and keep that in mind of course), and also record a time estimate for your lesson plan to help in time budgeting.

Once you have your topic, you can begin determining how you want to teach the topic. If you didn't use the state standards to help in developing your topic, refer to them now to see what specific standards your lesson plan can fulfill. Having your lesson plan correctly aligned with state standards helps to prove its worthiness and necessity.

It also helps in assuring that your students are being taught what your state requires. If you are able to correlate your lesson plan with standards, record links to those standards in your lesson plan. If writing this lesson plan for a website (The Lesson Plans Page) be sure to include a title that properly reflects your topic.

To make sure your lesson plan will teach exactly what you

want it to; you need to develop clear and specific objectives. Please note that objectives should not be activities that will be used in the lesson plan. They should instead be the learning outcomes of those activities. As an example, if you wanted to teach your class how to add 2 + 3, your objective may be that "the students will know how to add 2 + 3" or more specifically "the students will demonstrate how to add 2 + 3."

Objectives should also be directly measurable (we'll get to this in assessment/evaluation). In other words, make sure you will be able to tell whether these objectives were met or not. You can certainly have more than one objective for a lesson plan.

To make objectives more meaningful, you may want to include both broad and narrow objectives. The broad objectives would be more like goals and include the overall goal of the lesson plan, i.e. to gain familiarity with adding two numbers together. The specific objectives would be more like the one listed above, i.e. "the students will demonstrate how to add the numbers 2 and 3 together."

You would probably find out exactly what materials you are going to use later, but they should be shown early in your lesson plan. This way if someone else were going to use your lesson plan, they would know in advance what materials are required. Be specific here to make sure the teacher will have everything they need. For the addition lesson, you should make sure you have 10 or so unifix cubes per student, paper, and pencils.

You may also want to write an Anticipatory Set, which would be a way to lead into the lesson plan and develop the students' interest in learning what is about to be taught. A good example deals with a lesson on fractions. The teacher could start by asking the students how they would divide up a pizza to make sure each of their 5 friends got an equal amount of pizza, and tell them that they can do this if they know how to work with fractions.

Now you need to write the step-by-step procedures that will be performed to reach the objectives. These don't have to involve every little thing the teacher will say and do, but they should list the relevant actions the teacher needs to perform. For the adding 2 + 3 lesson, you may have procedures such as these:

A. The teacher will give each child 2 unifix cubes.
B. The teacher will ask the students to write down how many unifix cubes they have on paper (2).
C. The students should then write a + sign below the number 2, like this: 2+.
D. The teacher will then pass out 3 more unifix cubes to each student.
E. The students will be asked to write down how many unifix cubes they were just given. They should write this number below the number 2 that they just wrote, so that it looks like this: 2 + 3.
F. Students should now draw a line under their 3.
G. Now the students should count how many unifix cubes they have together and write this number just below the 3, like this:

$$2 + 3 = 5$$

H. Ask students how many unifix cubes they had to start, how many they were given to add to that, and how many they had total after the teacher gave them the 3 unifix cubes.

- After the procedures have been completed, you may want to provide time for independent practice. For the example of above, students could be given time to add different numbers of unifix cubes together that a partner would provide them with.
- Just before moving on to the assessment phase you should have some sort of closure for the lesson plan. A good idea for this is to return to your anticipatory set, i.e. ask students how they would divide up that pizza now that they know how to work with fractions (refer to the example in step 4).
- Now you want to write your assessment / evaluation. Many lesson plans don't necessarily need an assessment, but most should have some sort of

evaluation of whether or not the objectives were reached. The key in developing your assessment is to make sure that the assessment specifically measures whether the objectives were reached or not. Thus, there should be a direct correlation between the objectives and the assessments. Assuming the objective were to be able to add two single digit numbers together, an example would be to have students approach the teacher and add two single digit numbers (that the teacher provides via unifix cubes) on paper using unifix cubes as a guide.

- Adaptations should also be made for students with learning disabilities and extensions for others. Examples would be adding 1 unifix cube to 1 unifix cube for students with learning disabilities and adding 9 unifix cubes to 13 unifix cubes for gifted students. This is best done with specific adaptations for specific students, to take into account their individual differences.
- It's also a good idea to include a "Connections" section, which shows how the lesson plan could be integrated with other subjects. An example would be to have students paint 2 apples, then 3 more apples below them, etc. to integrate Art into the lesson plan. A better integration would involve creating 2 or 3 different types of textures on those apples, assuming texture was being studied in art class. Putting a lot of work into this can develop complete thematic units that would integrate related topics into many different subjects. This repetition of topics in different subjects can be extremely helpful in ensuring retention of the material.

UNIT PLAN

A unit plan is developed by the teacher and serves as a long-range plan. It contains multiple lessons that are related. Below you will find the Suggested Unit Plan Format (Tennessee Framework for Evaluation and Professional

Growth) components followed by explanations of each. While all unit plans are not identical (different states may use different formats), the major components will remain the same.

A unit is an organized group of lesson plans with a beginning, various activities, and a culmination. Your task is to arrange the unit into organized and sequential blocks of content and learning activities. The unit will consist of a number of daily lessons designed to achieve the broader goals of the unit. A unit may be subject based, interdisciplinary, or thematic.

The unit can last as long as a semester or as short as a week. For the purpose of planning, consider three weeks to be the appropriate length of time for your unit. Just as with lesson plan formats, there is no single best format for a teaching unit that works best for every time of unit. While a unit will have a general outline and plan for implementation, the daily lesson plans demonstrate in detail how the unit is carried out in the classroom. Often, lesson plans are created as you move through the unit, rather than ahead of time, since there are often changes from the original plan.

A Language Learning Unit Plan is a subdivision of your language learning programme made up of a series of daily lesson plans. The Units may be determined in various ways, depending on the overall approach to language learning being followed.

HERBARTIAN STEPS

Herbart. Known as the father of scientific pedagogy based on psychology . . . . thought that the mind acted as a unit, and that it had the power of what he called apperception—the capacity to assimilate new ideas through ideas already acquired . . . . developed teaching methods that he believed assisted the mind in making use of the power of apperception. His methods "elevated the importance of the teacher and made the pupil a listener, whose mind was to be molded according to a preconceived plan of studies and by formal steps of method." By the middle of the 19th century, the Herbartian steps of teaching had become common practice—indeed, slogans—in almost every North American normal school. The methods used in drawing lessons were determined by these steps.

Herbart was the first scientist to distinguish instructional process from subject matter. According to Herbart, interest develops when already strong and vivid ideas are hospitable towards new ones, thus past associations motivate apperception of current ones. Herbartianism, in predicting that learning follows from building up sequences of ideas important to the individual, gave teachers a semblance of a theory of motivation.

He also stressed the study of the psychological processes of learning as a means of devising educational programmes based on the aptitudes, abilities, and interests of students. The success of Herbart's methods led to their adoption in the teacher-training systems of numerous countries.

Based on his work, Herbart's followers designed a five-step teaching method:

1. Prepare the pupils to be ready for the new lesson.
2. Present the new lesson.
3. Associate the new lesson with ideas studied earlier.
4. Use examples to illustrate the lesson's major points.
5. Test pupils to ensure they had learned the new lesson.

THE HERBARTIAN STEPS AS CRITERIA

Preparation

In this case, 'preparation' does not refer to what the teacher did before the lesson, i.e. how s/he prepared for it. Rather it refers to the manner in which s/he prepares the mindsets of students for the new knowledge, concepts and skills that are to be introduced. There are many ways in which this can be done, the more common being:

- Stating what the topic or /theme is and/or stating what the expected outcomes for the lesson are.
- Recalling what was learned in the previous lesson and indicating how this will be added to and applied.

- Asking questions based on what students already know or can do, these leading to a key question, or task, whose solution/completion becomes the focus of the lesson. In some cases, a single question (without leading questions) will suffice.
- Sharing an anecdote (a short narrative, usually of something the teacher has experienced) that arouses interest around the theme/topic of the lesson to follow. This could alternately be a news report, a legend/fable, or a scenario that presents a problem whose solution becomes the focus of the lesson.
- Doing an activity of some kind (e.g. song, improvisation, eurhythmic activity, game, listening to a recording, watching a video). Ideally, the activity should relate to one or more of the intended outcomes for the lesson, but this is not always necessary. Music classes often begin with an activity (e.g. echo clapping, sight singing) aimed at long term goals (e.g. improving kinesthesia, rhythmic memory, vocal quality, etc.). Even though it may not relate directly to the specific outcomes for the lesson, the activity at least 'breaks the ice' and helps to bring about an appropriate mindset.
- Attending to work assigned in the previous lesson.
- Doing warm-up exercises relevant to activity that will follow.

Herbart's main interest in philosophy however, is the problem of Education—its object, its method, its possibilities. Education is in fact both the starting point and the goal of all his philosophical inquiries. The end of education is, he holds, determined by ethics. It is the formation of noble, cultivated, moral character. Morality is goodness of will. Moral conduct cannot be embraced, as Kant imagined, under one principle. It is best included under the five practical ideas. Ideal character is to be attained by "many-sided interest". The full development of the individual, the realization of all his capabilities should be then the constant aim of the process of education.

The main foundations on which Herbart's whole theory of education rests are his doctrines of apperception and interest. Apperception, with Herbart means the act or process of assimilating, appropriating and identifying an object, impression or idea. All progress in knowledge after the first percipient act is a process of apperception, and the character of each new perception is determined by those which have gone before. The first sensation or impression affords no knowledge, but results in a presentation which persists in existence gradually sinking down below the surface of consciousness.

This original presentation existing in the sub-conscious state of our mental life will be partially wakened and called up into conscious activity by the next impression. Thus aroused it modifies the reception of the latter and partially fuses with it. Again this pair of presentations or this compound state similarly sinking down into subconscious life still remains ready to appropriate the next impression assimilating it in like fashion.

But the method of the reception and the character of the appropriation is constantly varying with the increasing collection of presentations or ideas already in the mind. The facility and completeness with which each fresh idea is assimilated is determined by what has gone before. Herein, according to the Herbartian school, lies the importance of directing the process of apperception by judicious selection of the materials which are to constitute the experience of the child.

As the mind, in this view is simply built up entirely out of the ideas which it has received, the kinds of ideas presented to it and the order in which they come are of the utmost moment in the work of education. Ideas or objects are assimilable or apperceivable when partially familiar; a totally foreign idea has no friends already lodged in the mind to welcome it.

In the pleasure of the process of apperception lies the great fact of interest. Interest depends on what is already in the mind. It is the factor of most vital importance in education—

and in moral life, as a whole. Interest and knowledge react on each other. Interest stimulates voluntary attention and sustains involuntary. It thus ties at the root of the mental activity of observation.

It determines what we shall see and also what we shall desire and will. With Herbart interest is not simply a means: it is an end in itself. "Many-sided interest" frees from narrow prejudices and counteracts evil possessions, but it is also an ideal worthy of all admiration in se. Ignorance is really the main factor in vice. All action springs out of "the circle of thought"; hence the decisive influence of the matter or content of instruction in the work of character building.

"Make your instruction educative," is the great Herbartian maxim. Connected with the insistence on the psychological agencies of apperception and interest is the Herbartian principle of correlation and the five formal steps of instruction. The former should, according to the school, govern the drawing up of the curriculum. Organize the course of studies so that the matter of the different branches simultaneously treated, e.g. the literature, history and geography, may be connected with one another; and as far as possible let the subsidiary subjects be arranged in concentric circles around the chief study.

The five formal steps prescribe the order and method of procedure in an ideal lesson. Prepare the mind for the reception of the new matter by repetition of questions which freshen the pupil's recollection of ideas related to the subject of the coming lesson. Next present the matter clearly, developing it in an orderly method. Then, or pari passu by comparison or illustration associate the new ideas or facts with those already familiar. After this generalize the results and finally apply the knowledge gained in some form of practical exercise. These latter doctrines and other deductions from Herbart's principles—some of them very disputable—have been elaborated in very pedantic fashion by certain of the later Herbartians.

Besides instruction, practical education includes two other factors,—government and discipline. Though character, according to Herbart, is formed in very large measure by the instruction, i.e. by the ideas apperceived and absorbed by the mind, yet he allows something to these other agencies.

Government is mainly repressive, checking disorder and providing the conditions for instruction. Training and discipline are of greater importance.

They look to the future building up of the will and forming lasting habits. But as discipline is effected not merely by the form but also by the matter of the school exercises, we come back once more to instruction as the essential factor.

CRITICISM ABOUT HERBART STEPS

Undoubtedly there is much that is stimulating and valuable in Herbart's works on Education. His insistence on certain psychological laws established by experience; his frequent invocation of rational principles in opposition to mere empiricism in education; his accentuating the value of interest; his earnest advocacy of an ethical aim; his demand for wide culture; his faith in the potency of education, and his enthusiasm for the vocation of the teacher are all deserving of warm commendation But there are other features in his theory to which serious objections are made.

Firstly, his account of the soul, as being capable originally only of simple reactions to impressions and as being then virtually swallowed up by, or dissolved into the stream of subsequent presentations or ideas, is metaphysically erroneous, and in educational practice exceedingly dangerous if carried to its logical conclusions.

For it implies an entirely mechanical view of the mind, as rigidly determinist as that of the English Associationists, with which indeed, notwithstanding Herbart's spiritualism, it has sundry points of similarity. It leaves no place for free-will, nor, if logically pressed, for individual responsibility. The soul seems to be conceived merely as the arena for chance experiences coming from without. Our whole mental life is solely the resultant of the collision or coalescence of the presentations flowing in upon us.

Every volition is the inexorable product of the circle of

thought. Yet Herbart himself, as well as the best educationists of today, insist much on the duty of respecting and developing the individuality of the pupil; but where the individuality is seated, or in what it consists, is not easy to understand in the Herbartian system. Here especially lies the strength of the rival doctrine of the Fröbelian School, which so earnestly inculcates the importance of self-activity.

Again, the ethical aim of Herbartianism is after all the Ego. It is not God—not an end outside of self, not even humanity—but self-culture. Further, knowledge and intellectual culture, however varied or refined, are not virtue. Herbart has here fallen into the old Socratic error.

Knowledge is desirable and its attainment may be a duty; but virtue is essentially a quality of the will, not of the intellect. Its essence lies in self-control, and self-denial, often in "action in the line of greatest resistance" as Professor James well calls it. Asceticism, so obnoxious to the Herbartian, is therefore not unintelligent. Many-sided interest, too, though ethically helpful is not virtue. Intellectual ignorance and narrow-mindedness may and often are combined with a high quality of moral fibre, whilst men of abundantly many-sided interest as e.g., Francis Bacon or Goethe, may fall sadly short of being ethical models.

Furthermore, although, as Catholic doctrine insists, the positive moral and religious teaching of the young and the ethical quality of the ideas on which their intellects are fed exert a real influence on the will and moral disposition of the child, yet the value of mere instruction in comparison with that of discipline is exaggerated by the Herbartian school. It is not the mere cognition of the facts of history and literature, or in general the content of the instruction in these subjects, that makes for morality, but the exercise of our faculties, our moral judgment, imagination, sympathy, aversions etc. upon these facts. Moral sensibility is developed by action in harmony with the intimations and suggestions of conscience, rather than by the acquisition of moral information.

Again, whilst interest is to be fostered and advantage taken of every psychological law which facilitates learning, we must not forget the educational worth of effort and the conquest of difficulties, nor the disciplinary value of stiff formal studies such as mathematics. Strenuousness of character will not be cultivated by a "soft" pedagogy which would eliminate all obstacles from the student's path—though this latter attempt is not the outcome of the true Herbartian spirit.

The evil also of an unenlightened formalism has exhibited itself in a somewhat slavish adhesion to details of the Herbartian method by certain members of the school. Nevertheless it remains true that Herbart has given a substantial contribution of permanent value to educational theory and educational method.

FORMAT OF TYPICAL LESSON

A TYPICAL LESSON MIGHT LOOK LIKE THE FOLLOWING

- *Tune Up:* Guitars need regular tuning. The more they are played, the more the strings slip out of tune.
- *Knowledge Review:* Review of notes, strings, chords, technique, and other recently covered material. To a beginner, I might say, "Show me all the notes you know, and tell me their names." To a more advance student, I might say, "Show me the I, IV, and V chords in the key of D" (if that material was recently covered.)
- *Skill and Drill:* Drills focus on fine motor skills for either the right hand or the left hand, sometimes both.
- *Performance Goal Check:* Each week, students try to acheive short term goals and complete assignments. Goals can be related to repertoire (songs), theory, fretboard, technique, etc. After warm up, the student is asked to show mastery of the goal.
- *Check Off:* If the student shows mastery of the new goal, I ask the student to feel good about the accomplishment. We add a level of refinement to the goal (e.g. expressiveness, quality, nuance, soloing,

strumming, etc) or move on to new material. If there are problems, we move to....

- *Problem Correction:* If the student has diffuculty reaching the goal, we address them during the lesson. Is it a problem related to skill, ability, knowledge, understanding, etc.... OR is it that they just....
- *Didn't Practice:* If the student didn't practice during the week, it is really a downer, and the lesson time becomes practice time. Little or no new material, skills, or techniques will or can be introduced; I promise. Click here for a few thoughts on how to practice on your own at home.
- *New Goal:* We set a new short term goal for the week—a new song, new chords, new technique, new concept, etc. We practice the new goal several times to be sure it is understood before the student leaves.

LESSONS OFTEN INCLUDE THE FOLLOWING AS WELL

- *Student Questions:* Students often ask questions about guitar strings, kinds of guitars, reading music notation, special guitar techniques like note bending. These questions are usually prompted by experiences or problems encountered during the previous week.
- Discussion of a Music Theory concept like scales, modes, different kinds of chords, keys, modulation, turn-arounds, etc.
- *Discussion of Guitar Techniques:* using a pick, playing fingerstyle, note bending, sliding, slurring, hammer-on's, pull-offs, arpeggios, special rhythms like samba or blues shuffle, etc.

LESSONS DON'T INCLUDE

Guitar Maintenance: Guitars need technical TLC from time to time. Neck adjustments, action adjustments, new strings, etc. etc. I shy away from these types of things for several reasons. First and foremost, I don't want to damage your guitar while attempting to fix it. Secondly, most repair work or adjustments require patience and time, more time than a typical lesson offers. See my links page for my favourite guitar repair shops.

TEACHING AIDS

A teaching aid is something a classroom teacher uses in her class to help students improve reading and other skills, reinforce a skill, or to make learning fun. Teaching aids can be used in any of the core classes. There are several types of teaching aids to be utilized in your classroom.

CHART

A chart is something that shows a group of facts in the form of a diagram, table, or a graph. Teachers can use small alphabet charts on student desks to aid in learning the alphabet. Charts can be large enough to mount on a wall. Wall charts can be used for whole group lessons; the teacher can write an outline or word definitions on the wall chart.

FLASH CARDS

A flash card is part of a set of cards that has numbers, letters, pictures or words on it. They are commonly used for drilling students on facts. Flash cards may also be used to enhance student memory. Try playing a memory game with the facts on the cards. This is a great and fun way to help students memorize.

Most teachers use flash-cards in their English lessons when they have to introduce new vocabulary. Using flash-cards our students will be able to understand the new vocabulary without any kind of translation. Anyway, we have to take into account that there are lexical fields that cannot be illustrated through flash cards (abstract words such as feelings, for example). In this article, I'm going to suggest some activities with flash-cards that can be applied to any kind of vocabulary and almost any age and level.

To start with, we will always choose comprehension activities. This means that the students are not required to say the new words, just to understand them.

After this stage, it is good to introduce activities which require repetitive production.

Then they will be ready to develop tasks in which they have to speak without models.

Finally we will have to introduce interaction activities, which involve contextualized use of the language.

Saying hello (only in infant education): Very young children enjoy saying hello to the animals, the people and even the objects. We can put the flash cards in different places of the classroom and greet them alternatively.

When the students have mastered the main vocabulary, we can make errors like saying 'Hello kangaroo, how are you?' when we are speaking to the monkey. Children will be delighted to say 'Nooo! that is the monkey!!

The chain: We put all the flash-cards in different places. We choose one student and we say one word, for example 'donkey'. The student has to find the corresponding flash-card. It doesn't matter if they don't know the vocabulary yet. They can try luck. If one student fails, we choose another one, and so on until someone finds the donkey. Then we say another word, for example 'monkey', and we go on until the student fails. Then we choose another student and we start the chain again 'donkey, monkey,...'. The idea of the chain is that when one student finds out the meaning of a word, the others will try to remember it. You will see that in twenty minutes all your students will have mastered all the vocabulary.

Point to: The teacher says 'point to the donkey, point to the kangaroo, ...' and the students have to perform the actions. When you see that the students are getting tired of this boring activity, you can transform it into a memory game: say 'point to... the monkey, the elephant, the snake and the hippo' and they have to make it in the right order. If you speak very quickly they will find it funny.

Where is it?: We turn all the cards upside down (on the floor or on a table). Then we choose one student and we ask 'where is the donkey?' and the students uncovers one card. If s/he gets right, we ask again 'where is the elephant?', and so on until s/he fails. Then we turn all the cards upside down, we choose another student and we start the chain again (' Where is the donkey?, where is the elephant?, where is the kangaroo?...').

be quick! We put all the flash-cards in different places of the classroom. (Another good idea is to ask some students to hold them up). Then we ask two students to stand up. Then we say one word, for example 'giraffe' and both students will try to take it in first place. We go on with the other words. At the end, the student that has taken more flash-cards is the winner.

FLIP CHARTS

Flip charts are useful for teaching large groups at one time. A flip chart is a large group of papers that are attached at the top so that the papers can be flipped over one at a time to show a new page of paper. Flip charts are often placed on an easel, which allows the teacher to easily move it. A teacher can use a flip chart when she is showing different parts of a lesson, stages in the process of something, steps of something, or the progress of a story as it unfolds. Flip charts are very versatile and can be used for all classes.

MAPS

Maps are something teachers can use for various projects or lessons. A map is something to use when a teacher is describing where a city, state, country, or continent is located. Teachers can show students different types of terrain, the population of a specific state or country, or the amount of precipitation in various areas. Maps are great for social studies and science and give students a great understanding of spatial relations.

CALENDAR

A calendar is a chart that shows dates in each month of the year. Teachers can use calendars for teaching days of the month and the months to her class. Using a calendar that is in a different language is also a unique way to teach days of the month in that particular foreign language.

NEWSPAPERS

Many teachers may not know that a newspaper is a great teaching aid. Newspapers can be used for any of the core classes. Teachers can use them to teach about people, places and things in language arts. Newspapers can be used for math activities, such as clipping coupons and doing basic math. A teacher can use a newspaper for finding parts of speech, teaching about life skills, or to keep kids current on news events.

GRAPHS

Graphs are a wonderful teacher's aid and can be used for any subject. Teachers can make their own graphs and use them to compare population growth in social studies, numbers or ratios of objects in math class, or even use them for charting student growth. Teachers can make their own graphs using computer programmes or can choose to go the old-fashioned way and use graph paper.

SURVEYS

These are another great teaching aid. Teachers can make their own survey to pass out to the class. On that survey, the teacher may ask the students to answer yes, no, multiple choice, or short answer questions regarding a recent teaching unit, the overall performance of the teacher or the school in general. Surveys are a great way for a teacher to get feedback and use that feedback to improve teaching skills or change future lessons for more success.

MOTIVATION

One of the most important factors that lead one to their goals is the drive. This drive is known as motivation. It is a zest and determination with a kind of excitement that leads one to persevere to reach greater heights, in no matter what avenue of their life; be it – personal or professional. The drive may come from an internal or external source. The individual determines this.

The factors that motivate an individual keep changing as

one climbs the ladder of age and maturity. And also, achievement of one goal sets the ball rolling for another one to be achieved. Thus, to be motivated is a constant need. There are times when one faces a period of de-motivation and everything seems bleak. It is then that they need to find what would motivate them back into action.

For every individual there is a variable driving force. In fact, it is not just a single factor, but a combination of factors that lead people to achieve their goals. The fact is that with routine monotony steps in and then everything seems like stagnant waters. It feels like there is nothing new.

Breaking this cycle of monotony has helped many bounce back with enthusiasm. This is why human resource managers create a training calendar, which will take away employees from the routine they are stuck to, as well as enhance their skills in various areas.

Others pursue hobbies during the weekend, thus giving them something to look forward to, as each week comes to a close. There are people who redefine their goals and ambitions from time to time in order to fill them with newer levels of enthusiasm to achieve greater feats. One needs to take stalk every now and then and find the motivator required to carry them through.

SEVEN RULES OF MOTIVATION

Set a major goal, but follow a path: The path has mini goals that go in many directions. When you learn to succeed at mini goals, you will be motivated to challenge grand goals.

Finish what you start: A half finished project is of no use to anyone. Quitting is a habit. Develop the habit of finishing self-motivated projects.

Socialize with others of similar interest: Mutual support is motivating. We will develop the attitudes of our five best friends. If they are losers, we will be a loser. If they are winners, we will be a winner. To be a cowboy we must associate with cowboys.

Learn how to learn: Dependency on others for knowledge supports the habit of procrastination. Man has the ability to learn without instructors. In fact, when we learn the art of self-education we will find, if not create, opportunity to find success beyond our wildest dreams.

Harmonize natural talent with interest that motivates: Natural talent creates motivation, motivation creates persistence and persistence gets the job done.

Increase knowledge of subjects that inspires: The more we know about a subject, the more we want to learn about it. A self-propelled upward spiral develops.

Take risk: Failure and bouncing back are elements of motivation. Failure is a learning tool. No one has ever succeeded at anything worthwhile without a string of failures.

PRESENTATION

Presentation is a stimulus delivery and experimental control software system for neuroscience. Presentation runs on Windows and uses standard PC hardware. Presentation was designed for behavioral and physiological experiments that collect fMRI, ERP, MEG, reaction time, and electrophysiological (e.g. single neuron) data. At the same time, Presentation is very flexible and has many features that make it applicable to a diverse range of applications. Presentation is designed to provide the best possible timing accuracy and timing verification on standard hardware. Presentation is also completely programmemable

PRESENTATION MODE

As a Moderator, you can change the view of the Whiteboard or an Application Sharing window so it fills the entire CCC Confer window. This is called Presentation Mode. When you use Presentation Mode, everyone in the session automatically will have the same full-window view – until either they "opt out" of Presentation Mode or you end Presentation Mode and return the content to a normal view.

When Presentation Mode is engaged, the menu bar, status bar and all of the interaction features (such as Chat, Audio and the Participants window) are hidden from view. Those wishing to interact with others in the session (by sending Chat messages, using Audio, raising their hands, etc.) can still do so, but they must first opt out of Presentation Mode. You cannot use the Graphing Calculator, Multimedia, Quiz, Web Tour and File Transfer during resentation Mode.

If you have them open when Presentation Mode begins, they will be closed, and you won't be able to open them until Presentation Mode ends. If open, the Video, Notes, Timer and Closed-Captioning windows will remain open when you start Presentation Mode. You also can open them after Presentation Mode has been engaged.

Use Presentation Mode when you want to reduce distractions and focus everyone's attention on what is being presented; project your CCC Confer session onto a large screen to a group assembled in a conference room or classroom (since the group is logged in as one session attendee, interaction features are not as important as maximizing the content being presented); demonstrate software applications, where it is important to have a "full-screen" view of the application in order to easily see all the menus and options; and record CCC Confer sessions for instructive purposes, where the interaction features cannot be used (as there is no live participation in the session) and you want to keep the viewer's focus directed toward the content.

APPLICATIONS

An application is a specific survey operation that the instrument and survey train or assembly is required to perform. Lets look at a few examples:

Directional Surveying provides data that defines the position of the borehole in 3 dimensional space. This provides answers to questions such as "Exactly where did this rock (core or chip) sample come from?" or "Is the hole going to hit the destination target?".

Say, for example, that the hole was being drilled steeply downward to depths of 1000m (3300 feet) using NQ* equipment in a temperate climate. The NQ designation immediately conveys the size of the drilling equipment and the fact that we can lower and retrieve the instrument by the same system that is used to transport the core-barrel assembly inside the drill rods.

If the instrument used is a magnetic azimuth type, then the survey train has to pass through the drill bit to place the instrument beyond the influence of the magnetic drill rods. In this application the drill rods would have to be raised from the bottom of the hole to allow the survey assembly to pass through.

If the instrument chosen used nonmagnetic could be done inside the drill rods. In this case the directional reference would be set at the surface and transferred by the instrument to the survey site.In this particular application we have a wide choice of instruments because the size of the hole in the bit is fairly large (47.5 mm or 1.87 inches), the hole is steep downwards (greater than 40° from horizontal) and the temperature will not be extremely hot nor cold.

The protective casing or container for the instruments may vary in size (both in diameter and length), most instruments have limits on the inclination angles and temperatures they can operate within, and all have depth limits that depend on the strength of the protective casing or the length of cable for systems that can be viewed on the surface for example.

The survey train has to be at least partly specific to NQ because the train has to attach to NQ lowering gear and pass through the NQ rods or the NQ drill bit (depending on the instrument type) without causing significant survey errors. Errors can arise from the instrument not being perfectly aligned with the drill hole, or, for example, some of the components of the train may be sufficiently magnetic to influence a magnetic azimuth sensor.

RECAPITULATION AND ASSIGNMENT

RECAPITULATION

Recapitulation is a core technique used to heal emotional charges. On a deeper level, it is used to reclaim energy and return it to self. Recapitulation was first introduced into mass consciousness by Carlos Castaneda in his book, The Eagles

Gift, published in 1982. However, its roots go deeper. In his book, *The Toltec Path of Recapitulation: Healing Your Past to Free Your Soul,* Victor Sanchez speaks about learning procedures from the Wirrarika people (native to Mexico), who he calls the 'surviving Toltecs', similar to the process of recapitulation. I studied with Mother Sarita, don Miguel Ruiz's mother who was in her 80's at the time, who spoke about recapitulation like processes with don Miguel's grandfather.

One purpose of recapitulation is to eliminate emotional charges. Emotional charges cause one to misperceive the world around them and make it impossible to perceive the Nagual with clarity. For example, if a young girl is relentlessly teased about her curly hair by her father, she may become emotionally charged.

Later, when she is a adult, whenever someone compliments her, particularly her hair, she becomes angry. She may not know why compliments cause her to get angry as she doesn't remember how her father used to tease her as a young child. What is worse is that she misperceives another person's good intent, i.e. giving her a compliment, as teasing her about her looks. This misperception causes upset both in her life and other people in it.

The average person is full of emotional charges, many that they are not aware of as they were suppressed as painful memories during childhood. This causes the average person to misperceive the world and the people in it. Systematic recapitulation decharges emotions and frees one up to perceive the world clearly. Recapitulation releases negative emotions that are trapped in one's subconscious freeing up their life. Many people have a habitually negative emotional state, or are moody for reasons they do not know why. More times than not, the reason lies in the suppressed emotional charges that lie in their subconscious.

On a deeper level, recapitulation is used to reclaim one's energy. Everywhere one has lived they leave an energetic piece of themselves. In every person you interact with you live energetic cords or filaments that, unless reclaimed back to self drain you of your vital energy. This is particularly true of sexual encounters. Through the consistent use of recapitulation you restore the vital energy necessary to progress on a spiritual path. Most do not realise how much energy is required to break free of the Dream of the Planet. You need every ounce of energy you have. This is why Toltecs place so much importance on the Recapitulation.

ASSIGNMENT

An assignment is the legal transfer of a right or property from one party to another. For state business, this is the transfer of a vendor's right to payment. The party transferring their right to payment is called the *assignor*. The party receiving the right to payment is called the *assignee.*

For example, ABC Construction Company enters into a contract to perform a job for a state agency and hires a subcontractor, XYZ Asphalt, to complete a portion of the work. The construction company may *assign* payments for that portion of the job to the subcontractor. ABC Construction Company becomes the *assignor* of the payment, and XYZ Asphalt becomes the *assignee.*

Unit IV

Psychological Theories and Factors influencing of Mathematics, Individual Difference

PSYCHOLOGICAL OF LEARNING MATHEMATICS

Teaching and learning mathematics have many myths associated with them. Two of them are: mostly men can learn and enjoy mathematics, and math is a combination of rote computational activities and the logic of word problems – nothing more, nothing less.

As is the case, understanding and using mathematics involves many more strategic operations than implied by memory and logic. Instead, math involves the application of a rather specific sequence of operations. Some are logical, others linguistic, and a few are social. In addition, many prove to be rather difficult for teachers and students to understand, teach and learn. However, recent research in cognitive psychology and the use of technology offer additional pedagogical assistance that may help to overcome this diversity of operations.

Multiple Perspectives on Mathematics Teaching and Learning offers a collection of chapters that take a new look at mathematics education. Leading authors, such as Deborah Ball, Paul Cobb, Jim Greeno, Stephen Lerman, and Michael Apple, draw from a range of perspectives in their analyses of mathematics teaching and learning. They address such practical problems as: the design of teaching and research that acknowledges the social nature of learning, maximizing the impact of teacher education programmes, increasing the learning opportunities of students working in groups, and ameliorating the impact of male domination in mixed classrooms.

These practical insights are combined with important advances in theory.

Several of the authors address the nature of learning and teaching, including the ways in which theories and practices of mathematics education recognize learning as simultaneously social and individual. The issues addressed include teaching practices, equity, language, assessment, group work and the broader political context of mathematics reform. The contributors variously employ sociological, anthropological, psychological, sociocultural, political, and mathematical perspectives to produce powerful analyses of mathematics teaching and learning.

So far our efforts have been directed towards trying to understand some of the factors which affect the learning and understanding of mathematics, on the assumption that we, or the student concerned, want to do so. But now, let us in all seroiusness ask the question: Why should anyone want to learn mathematics? It is indeed arguable that this question should have come right at the start of the inquiry, since without some kind of motivation there should be no reason to expect anyone to make the neccessary effort. However, if you have bought this book you probably have some kind of motivation. So let us now look at what this might be - or these, since several motivations may combine in a single activity.

"Motivated" is a description we apply to behaviour which is directed to-wards the satisfaction of some need. If we say that a certain piece of behaviour seems motiveless to us, we mean that we do not know, and cannot even guess, what need is satisfied by means of it. So questions about motives are usually, in disguise, questions about needs.

But there are some people for whom mathematics is a pleasurable and worthwhile activity in itself, regardless of any other goals which it may also serve. These are the people whom I regard as true mathematicians; and if this view is accepted, then some seven-, ten-, and twleve-year-olds merit the description as much as, or more than, many sixth-form and adult students. Why people to should enjoy learning and practising mathematics for its own sake, however, far from obvious we keep to our original hypotheseis that any motivated behvior satisfies some need.

Let us approach the problem indirectly, by the way of other examples. Look at a child, out for a walk with parents, balancing along a low wall in preference to walking along a pavement. Or look at a dinghy sailor, sitting precariously out over the water in prefernce to the greater certainty and convenience of an outboard motor. Or look at a mountaineer, laboriously and hazardously climbing a mountain, which he could ascend quickly and safely by a funicular railway. Wall-walking, sailing, mountaineering are not basic needs; but neither do they appear to be used as a means to other go.

The complicacy of teaching mathematics in classroom is due not only to teachers personality and belief system, but also to social aspects of teachers mathematical communication. Internal psychological aspects are discussed in an earlier paper where mathematical models for mathematical communication are introduced.

A good source for finding important factors taking part in the social aspects of teaching mathematics can be borrowed from sociology of science. The amount of similarity between the scientific community and the process of mathematical education of students in classroom depends on how natural the process of learning is implemented by teacher.

The psychology of mathematics teachers, with particular working criteria's in views of necessary attention in their social aspects of learning are described.. We try to give mathematical models for teaching mathematics and try to understand the behaviour of teachers using these models.

Different Models for a Mathematics Classroom

Field study has indicated that the meaning of doing, teaching and learning mathematics varies in different classes.

This variation is partially due to the perspectives of teachers towards mathematics and towards the role of teacher in education and these perspectives are affected by the their mathematical knowledge and their professional abilities as a teacher.

Both of these could be strengthened by teachers? education programmes, but promotion of the level of abstractness of teacher?s knowledge and his/her professional abilities takes time and is not easily achieved. Therefore, not every teacher could teach every style.

We have to introduce different models for a mathematics classroom, so that different teachers with different levels of sophistication in teaching could find a model appropriate for their professional capacities.

Mathematics Teacher as a Source of Information

Knowledge in such a classroom is nothing but row information and teaching and learning are nothing but transformation and communication of information. Teacher either orally explains the information to the class or writes the information on board or shows students demonstrations on computer or on data show.

Some other information are made available to students by handing them books and papers. Student?s access to information is not always in full detail. Most of the time teacher chooses the key information and makes it known to his/her pupils.

Teacher also gives some explanations on the meaning and the relations between the packages of information. This role of such a teacher could be easily played by computers. Information technology could provide students with more detailed, accurate, advanced, and accessible information.

The role of student in such a class is taking notes and trying to memorize them. Repetition helps students to keep information in mind for a longer period of time.

Decisions that a teacher should make in such a classroom are very formal and can be modeled to be performed by a computer. Teacher decides about the language and tools which each piece of information shall be demonstrated to the class, and also the exercises which help students internalize the information. Teacher has to choose the key information and decide about appropriate references to introduce students for further study. Teacher has to decide about how to assess a piece of information too. We shall introduce models for different personalities of teachers in making such decisions.

Mathematics Teacher as a Physician

In such a classroom, teacher is trying to give special treatments to the minds of his/her students. For this kind of teacher, knowledge is only used as a means of communication in order to get information on how students think. A teacher tries to replace an unorganized mind by an ordered healthy mind.

This is why he/she demonstrates some examples of truthful deductions and accurate reasoning to the class. The main occupation of the teacher in this classroom, is discovering the mental weaknesses of students and trying to bring them to a normal position in which all of their different abilities demonstrate a coherent progress during the process of mathematical education.

Only a very well-trained experienced teacher can play this role in the classroom. There is some chance that some day a detailed classification of learner?s behaviour plus a well developed theory of information engineering could partially replace the role of these teachers in the educational system.

In this classroom, students try to awaken the abilities of their mind, by learning and imitating examples of deductions and reasoning presented in class. They try to cooperate with their teacher in discovering their mental weaknesses.

Teacher has to have a classification of human mathematical mind so that he/she can decide each student belongs to which class and then comparing student?s abilities with the particular class he/she has chosen, decide about weaknesses and strength of the student. Classification of weaknesses is an abstract procedure, because abnormal situations are exceptions; but teacher has to put similar ones in the same class, so that he/she be able to study them by their symptoms. Making such decisions is very abstract and complicated.

Mathematics Teacher as a Coach

In this classroom, teacher is trying to discover his/her students? personal talents and train them in direction of perfection of these talents. The particular characteristics of the mathematical knowledge being discussed in class has an important role in this training. Teacher makes determining decisions in choosing the material to be discussed in class. Different examples demonstrated in class are aimed to train different groups of students of different talents.

Teacher shall be able to teach students the particular practices and exercises which help them in perfection of their talents. Teacher supports and protects his/her students in the storm of their mental contradictions. He/she has to provide an appropriate atmosphere in classroom for treatment of students? mental contradictions.

The role of student in this classroom is doing mathematics. Student personally gets actively involved in enrichment of his/her knowledge up to a level in which he/she be able to overcome mental contradictions leaning on his/her own personal abilities. Students also cooperate with teacher in the process of discovery of their talents.

Teacher has to introduce a classification of mathematical talents and decide about the manners in which these talents show off so that he/she can decide about talents of students and exercises which can lead students to perfection of their talents. Teacher has to decide about different levels of student access to each of these talents.

Mathematics Teacher as a Role Model

In this classroom various forms of mathematical knowledge are discussed. Teacher tries to openly demonstrate the process of thinking to the class. Students could learn how to solve problems, only if they can openly watch their teacher wrestle with hard problems. Teacher must be able to think loudly so that students could imitate his/her skills of problem solving. Teacher could serve as a good role model, only if students can watch his/her thoughts inside out. In this classroom, teacher shall do mathematics which is not familiar with, in front of the students. Teacher tries to make students involved in his/her process of problem solving. If this role could be successfully played in classroom, students have been given the best possible education for group thinking. A teacher for this class should be very experienced and knowledgeable in mathematics.

The role of students in such a classroom is doing mathematics while keeping the teacher in mind as a role model. Students are able to construct their mathematical abilities personally and guide the direction of progress in their mental skills.

Most of the decisions that such a teacher should make are personal decisions which he/she makes in problem solving and the class is supposed to imitate him in making personal decisions.

Mathematics Teacher as a Life Companion

In this classroom, teacher tries to apply mathematics to students? everyday life situations. To this teacher, knowledge is what is practically useful. Teacher tries to introduce mathematics as a human endeavor. The aim of teacher is to translate problems of everyday life situations to the abstract language of mathematics and solve them using mathematical machinery and then translate the solution back to the language of everyday life. This ability should be internalized in students so that they use their mathematical skills outside school.

In such a class, the human history of evolution of mathematical concepts is under focus. Also, the process of discovery in problem solving should be recorded carefully by students. Strategies of problem solving and skills of decision making in course of discovery are taught carefully in this classroom.

Students engage in groups in solving everyday life problems using mathematics. Learning is a group activity but each student has a particular interest and perspective in doing mathematics. Every student helps his/her colleagues during the learning process and takes advantage of the helps offered by other colleagues.

Teacher has to decide about different skills that students should learn and about different levels of sophistication in these skills. Teacher has to decide about the skills which each of the students could learn better by having a classification of students? learning strategies.

Mathematics Teacher as a Scientist

In this classroom, teacher unveils the mathematical order of the universe we live in. For this teacher, mathematical knowledge is based on ideas borrowed from nature. Teacher makes sure his/her students learn to observe nature, discover mathematical ideas from it and use them in development of mathematics.

History of science is under focus. Students should learn how mathematical ideas taken from nature have affected human civilization. Proposing reasonable conjectures base on scientific methodology is an important skill which students should learn. The aim of teacher is not only familiarizing students with applications of mathematics to other branches of science, but also teaching them skills of discovering new applications of mathematics to other areas of science. These applications do influence the practice of scientists in other areas.

Students in such a classroom search in groups for mathematical ideas in nature. They recognize mathematics as the language of nature and try to get a better understanding of nature through this language. Student also tries to apply mathematics to other branches of science.

Teacher has to decide about how he/she can motivate students to become interested in nature and its order. Teacher has to decide about the branches of science that a student is fascinated by, so that he/she could insert mathematical ideas to teach the student how to apply mathematics in basic different branches of science.

Mathematics Teacher as a Philosopher

In this classroom, mathematics is an abstract knowledge independent of nature which is governed by the mathematical essence of the world of creation. Mathematical ideas could be borrowed not only from nature, but also from beyond. Teacher tries to discover the mathematical order with the aim of demonstrating his/her students unity in the essence of creation. Teacher tries to find similar ideas in different parts of mathematics and use them to unveil the unity beyond these ideas.

In such a class, the abstract science of mathematics is formulated independent of nature. Mathematics has many abstract layers and teacher tries to connects these layers by unifying different mathematical theories in each layer. This is a new perspective to learning mathematics in which each student does mathematics in a particular layer of abstractness.

Student tries to structure the abstract mathematical nature of his/her mind and is interested in knowing the essence beyond the mathematical ideas. Relating different branches of mathematics and performing computations and comparing them in different branches are tools which students use to extend the abstract structure of their mind.

Learning and doing mathematics is no longer possible in groups because of the high level of abstractness of this kind of mathematical activity. Student is learning mathematics for reasons beyond mathematics. So, again the particular mathematical content of mathematics does not play any important role in such a classroom.

In such a classroom, teacher has to decide about the particular level of abstractness each student could handle. Teacher also has to make sure if unification of a few different examples and creation of a more abstract generalization has actually occurred for a particular student. Teacher has to have a personal knowledge of different layers of abstractness and be able to decide each particular mathematical content belongs to which of these abstract layers. Teacher chooses a particular mathematical content which he/she is most familiar with its abstract layers.

Personality of Teachers in Decision Making

Many different decisions has to be made by teachers and the examples we have already mentioned is by no means a complete list. Nor is the different models we introduced for a mathematics classroom.

Therefore, we shall find a way in which mathematical modeling of the personality of teachers in decision making be independent of the particular decisions that they have to make. Otherwise classification of their behaviour in class would be a complicated task. To do this, we shall focus on the social aspects of learning. This will help us to understand the personality of the teacher independent of the particular meaning of learning in different classes.

THE SOCIAL ASPECTS OF LEARNING

Learning mathematics and problem solving in classroom has a completely different nature from individual attempts in doing mathematics.

When working in groups, not only decision making in different stages of problem solving is influenced by group discussions, but also diversity of perspectives towards the solution of the problem smoothens the process of individual learning. Human forms of communication makes the process of learning and its content to be considered in more human perspectives. For example, mathematical arguments instead of being considered as abstract human independent truth, seem like an address which is directing our mind to a particular place.

Different addresses could lead to the same conclusions and at the end, the new places discovered are of main importance, not the particular nature of the addresses leading to that place. In better words, different minds could be satisfied with arguments of different natures. Students eventually develop different personalities in accepting arguments and the teacher will not be able to force them to think the same about the truth of a mathematical proposition. Teacher can only focus on skills of students in applying the mathematics they learn to different aspects of their life.

THE MANAGEMENT OF GROUP LEARNING

Management of learning in a classroom is very similar to management of development of science in a scientific society. Different social aspects of science [4], could be regarded as different aspects of group learning in classroom, and the teacher has to make decisions about each of these aspects for the good of his/her students? learning. Teacher?s decision making is affected by many external factors. Here we mention a few of them:

The mathematical subject which is to be discussed could have numerical, geometric, algebraic or analytic nature. This could cause different decisions of teacher in his/her particular approach in teaching the subject matter.

Students motivation in learning mathematics could be of many different levels of abstractness. Students with different motivations could not be treated the same and this affects the process of teachers decision making.

Different learning strategies of students, and their particular mental process of thinking calls for different educational treatments and different styles of teaching mathematics. Efficient decision making of teachers could cause a more fruitful education for each of student's minds.

GAGNES TYPE OF LEARNING

INTRODUCTION

As an instructional psychologist, Gagné was primarily interested in determining what knowledge and skills are required for a person to effectively perform a given job.

Gagne suggested that there are five categories of learning. Such categories can be formed because each leads to a different class of human performance and each requires a different set of instructional conditions for effective learning (Gagné. 1974). The categories are:

1. *Intellectual skills:* These skills are the capabilities that make the human individual competent. They enable him to respond to conceptualizations of his environment.

2. *Cognitive strategies:* These skills are the ones that govern the individual capability to learn, think and remember.
3. *Verbal information:* Stored in our memory to recall when needed, such as names of months, days of week, letters, numeral e.t.a.
4. *Motor skills:* The capability to learn: to ride a bike, drive a car, write, draw a straight line.
5. *Attitudes:* All of us possess attitudes of many sorts towards different things, persons and situations. These attitudes may affect our position toward those things.

These categories of learned capabilities are distinctive categories that also require different arrangements of conditions in order for the learning of each to occur.

Within these various types of learning there must be nine general instructional events:

1. *Gaining attention:* To ensure reception of coming instruction we give the learner a stimulus
2. *Tell the learners the learning objective:* Tell the learner what they will be able to do because of the instruction
3. *Stimulating recall of prior learning:* Ask for recall of existing relevant knowledge.
4. *Presenting the stimulus:* Display the content.
5. Providing learning guidance.
6. *Eliciting performance:* Ask the learner to respond, demonstrating learning
7. *Providing feedback:* Give informative feedback on the learner's performance.
8. *Assessing performance:* Require more learner performance, and give feedback, to reinforce learning.
9. Enhancing retention and transfer to other contexts. Provide varied practice to generalize the capability

Designing instruction would involve *analyzing requirements, selecting media* and *designing the instructional events.* Skills should be learned one at a time and lower level objectives must be mastered before higher-level objectives can be met. Objectives must be stipulated in concrete behavioral terms.

Like Skinner he emphasizes use of positive reinforcement in a repetitive manner. When designing instruction, the analysis phase must identify and describe the prerequisite lower level skills and knowledge required for an instructional objective. Each new skill learned should build on previously acquired skills.

Gagné distinguished eight different classes of intellectual skills in which human beings learn.

These intellectual skills can be categorized on a dimension of complexity. The more complex kinds of intellectual processing are based upon these simpler varieties (Gagné., Briggs., 1974).

1. *Signal Learning:* The individual learns to make a general, diffuse response to a signal. Such was the classical conditioned response of Pavlov.
2. *Stimulus-Response Learning:* The learner acquires a precise response to a discriminated stimulus.
3. *Chaining:* A chain of two or more stimulus-response connections is acquired.
4. *Verbal Association:* The learning of chains that are verbal.
5. *Discrimination Learning:* The individual learns to make different identifying responses to many different stimuli that may resemble each other in physical appearance.
6. *Concept Learning:* The learner acquires a capability of making a common response to a class of stimuli.
7. *Rule Learning:* A rule is a chain of two or more concepts.
8. *Problem Solving:* A kind of learning that requires the internal events usually called thinking (Gagné., Briggs., 1992).

Gagne's work has contributed greatly the field of instructional technology especially regarding the design of instruction. According to Gagné the following steps should be clearly thought out when designing instruction.

1. Identify the types of learning outcomes.

2. Each outcome may have prerequisite knowledge or skills that must be identified.
3. Identify the internal conditions or processes the learner must have to achieve the outcomes.
4. Identify the external conditions or instruction needed to achieve the outcomes.
5. Specify the learning context.
6. Record the characteristics of the learners.
7. Select the media for instruction.
8. Plan to motive the learners.
9. The instruction is tested with learners in the form of formative evaluation.
10. After the instruction has been used, summative evaluation is used the judge the effectiveness of the instruction.

Evaluation of courses, programmes and instructional programmes usually has the following questions in mind:

- Have the objectives of instruction been met.
- Is the new programme better than the previous one.
- What additional effects does the new programme produce.(Gagné., Briggs., 1992).

Formative evaluation is undertaken while the new unit is being developed. The purpose is to supply data on feasibility and efficiency to develop and improve the course.

Summarise evaluation is concerned with the effectiveness of the course or programme regarding the student's performance. Based on the students performance measures are taken of the kind of student capabilities the programme is intended to establish.

Although objectively analyzing the condition for learning Gagné says: "Since the purpose of instruction is learning, the central focus for rational derivation of instructional techniques is the *human learner*. Development of rationally sound instructional procedures must take into account learner characteristics such as initiate capacities, experimental maturity, and current knowledge states. Such factors become parameters of the design of any particular programme of instruction".

GAGNE'S LEARNING OUTCOMES

Verbal Information

Stating previous knowledge: facts, concepts, principles, procedures

- Draw attention to distinctive features in print or speech.
- Present information so that it can be made into chunks.
- Provide a meaningful context for effective encoding of information.
- Provide cues for effective recall and generalization of information.

Intellectual Skills

Discriminations-Distinguishing objects, features, symbols

Concrete concepts-Identifying classes of concrete objects, features or events

Defined Concepts-*Classifying New Examples of Events or Ideas by Their Definition*

Rules-Applying a single relationship to solve a class of problems.

Higher Order Rules-*Applying a New Combination Rules to Solve a Complex Problem*

- Call attention to distinctive features.
- Stay within the limits of working memory.
- Stimulate the recall of previously learned component skills.
- Present verbal cues to the ordering or combination of component skills.
- Schedule occasions for practice and spaced review.
- Use a variety of contexts to promote transfer.

Cognitive Strategies

Using personal ways to guide learning, thinking, acting and feeling.

- Describe or demonstrate the strategy.
- Provide a variety of occasions for practice using the strategy.
- Provide informative feedback as to the creativity or originality of the strategy or outcome.

Attitudes

Choosing personal actions based on internal states of understanding and feeling

- Establish an expectancy of success associated with the desired attitude.
- Assure student identification with an admired human model.
- Arrange for communication or demonstration of choosing personal action.
- Give feedback for successful performance; or allow observation of feedback in the human model.

Motor Skills

Executing performances involving the use of muscles:

- Present verbal or other guidance to cue the excutive subroutine.
- Arrange repeated practice.
- Furnish Immediate feedback as to the accuracy of performance.
- Encourage the use of mental practice.

LEARNING TYPES AND LEARNING STYLES

Personality and Learning

The study of personality as it emerges from the works of many psychologists (G. Lindzey ed., 1970; B. Semenoff ed., 1970; L. J. Bischof, 1970) is primarily based on the highlighting of differences (e.g. types: Jung 1928, Spranger 1928; traits: Allport 1937, 1962; character structures: Horney 1937).

In sharp contrast to this depiction of human personality variety, a series of opposing theories have been elaborated in the area of learning studies (Bower G. H. & Hilgard E.R., 1981) that seem all aimed at giving a unique fully comprehensive explanation of human learning valid for every type of person in every type of situation.

In its extreme formulations, learning appears to be either the product of something induced from the outside (conditioned learning in its various range of positions, i.e. classical: Pavlov; reinforced: Hull; operant: Skinner) or something originated from the inside of a human being (insightful learning: Kohler; Koffka; Wertheimer; Lewin).

As remarked by O'Connell (1973) referring to conditioned learning (but the sphere could be extended) "S-R learning theorists are often criticised for their narrow and limited view of learning and their inability to take into consideration the specificity of each individual."

Because of this neglect of the individual, one of the most widely used textbook on learning theory (Bower and Hilgard) in his 1975 edition does not contain any mention of individual learning strategies, included only starting from the 1981.

Learning Styles

Nevertheless, already in 1956 in USA, Bruner, Goodnow and Austin in their classical "A study of thinking", had introduced the concept of strategy referring to the mental processing behaviour of individuals engaged in problem solving.

Through the administration of tests to a group of subjects, they discovered that individuals use different strategies ("successive scanning" or "conservative focusing" as defined by H. Gardner, 1987) to reach the solution of the same problem.

In England, one of the first to stress a relationship between differences in personality and varieties in thinking/learning approaches, has been dr. L. Hudson. In his study on the psychology of the English schoolboy (L. Hudson, 1966) he pointed out the existence of two learning personalities (the "converger" and the "diverger") that manifest themselves in two different learning styles.

The findings of Dr. Hudson and other psychologists (Witkin, Kagan) on differences in learning approaches, were reviewed in a unit prepared by A. Cashdan and V. Lee for the Open University "Educational Studies Course" under the title "Learning styles and strategies" (1971).

The expression "learning style" (and the one affine "cognitive style" employed in another Open University Unit, "Personality and Learning", block 5, 1976) seems not to have been in use before the '70s.

So, it seems that only starting from that period, the variety of learning approaches in relation to differences in personality has been recognized by a large part of the scientific community of educationalists and psychologists.

This appears to be the result of a progressive shift in the same scientific community from a behaviourist to a cognitivist approach to learning.

As remarked by Tessmer and Jonassen (1988) 'since the late '50s a gradual revolution in educational psychology has occurred"; "the mechanistic behaviourist model of human learning, with its view of learning as a simple, reflexive and quantifiable activity, was replaced by an active and organicistic model. In this view, learners have organized knowledge bases and actively participate in the construction of their reality."

LEARNING TYPES

Besides "learning styles", another concept has emerged, that of "learning types" (Gagné, 1965).

For learning types, Gagné refers to the content of learning and the intellectual skills involved in mastering it. He differentiates eight types of learning (from signal learning to problem solving) arranged in a hierarchical order, being the lower level prerequisite to proceeding to higher levels. Gagné stresses the fact that each type of learning is associated with characteristic strategies of instruction (A. J. Romiszowski, 1981).

Taking all this into consideration, what seems to have emerged in recent times is the acknowledgement of the existence of different life situations seen, from an educational point of view, as different types of learning to whom different styles of learning are connected, in accordance to the specific personality of the learner. In all this construct, variety seems the stressed feature for learning to take place.

The School System

Starting specifically from the second half of the XXth century, a very large amount of learning time, in most countries of the world, has been given to particular institutions called 'schools', in order to be administered and dispensed. From what has previously emerged, one should expect variety (of learning styles, of learning types) to be the dominant feature of a school.

But, having the school system assimilated many aspects of the mechanical industrial world (A. Toffler, 1970), his main traditional characteristics were, in origin, and still are, in large part:

- Massification of learning processes
- Standardization of learning contents
- Fragmentation of learning topics.

This system has undergone many changes in recent times, with a few radical experiments (e.g. Summer hill) and some new approaches (student centered, independent learning), variously accepted or more often rejected (R. Meighan, 1980). But the main traditional structure still survives throughout the various school levels with his unsatisfactory aspects, as pointed out by many social and educational analysts (Gross, 1972; Goodman, 1973; Postman and Weingartner, 1971; Reimer, 1971; Illich, 1971, 1974; Buckman, 1973; Lister, 1974).

The Rationale Against the School System

Stated in a concise way, based on what has emerged up to now, the critical argument relies on the following reasoning:

- Given the existence of different life situations and personalities that manifest themselves as learning experiences (learning types) and learning strategies (learning styles).
- This means that there is a need for individualization/ personalization of learning processes (whatever this means in actual terms) if a (more) effective learning

(defined in terms of skills acquisition that manifest themselves in performances and results) is to be achieved.

- But, being the present mass school system, around the world, generally organized according to a massification/standardization/fragmentation pattern, it derives that no (sufficient) place can be reserved to learning types and learning styles.
- From this, it follows that a less effective learning process takes place and this means that human resources are wasted, in a certain measure.

This wastage of human resources could be considered a problem.

The Rationale For the School System

From a different perspective, this reasoning could be rejected point by point. It could be argued:

- That the mass schooling system has given access to education to a huge number of people (massification as democratization).
- That the only way to perform this educational gigantic task has been to standardize the provision of educational services (standardization as organization).
- That, in order to standardize them, it has been necessary to decompose knowledge into bits and to administer it in such a manageable way (fragmentation as simplification).
- That the mass school system provides, at the same time, the homogenization and the specialization that society requires.
- That there is no wastage of resources being the lack of effective learning the result of lack in personal learning abilities.

According to this position, the statement that the mass school system wastes human resources, is not only rejected but turned upside down. The school appears to make the best possible use of resources given the restraints imposed by economic and technological factors and by the natural learning capabilities of the individual.

The Problem Stated

This position seems to hold insofar as:

- Certain values are supported.
- A certain technology is present.

If a different set of value are expressed and new technological devices (that foster those values) appear, the same situation seen as not problematic, could be viewed as leading to the emergence of a problem.

This means that for a situation to be identified as a problem there should be:

- A specific set of values that point to it.
- A specific set of problem solving devices that solve it.

From this it follows that a problem concerning the waste of human resources in the present system of mass school learning, could be deemed to exist only if:

- A certain set of values is postulated that, based on the variety of types and styles of human learning as recognized by the scientific community, stresses the exigency for this variety to emerge.
- A certain set of technological tools is available to translate those values into reality, at least potentially, not being the existence of technological devices, condition 'per se' sufficient for their use.

The first points involves aspects (values) that cannot be dealt in terms of true/false, so no evidence can be given in support of it (i.e. in support of the preferability for this variety to emerge). The second point involves facts whose occurrence can be practically assessed (i.e. posing and answering the question if a certain set of technological devices exist that can support a variety of learning styles, assist a variety of learning types and promote a recomposition in the process of learning topics).

A Possible Solution

As it will examined in the following chapter (Chapter 2:

Information and information technology) a series of tools have emerged or have become economically available that could alter the way learning experiences (within or without a school system) are approached, processed, mastered. These tools could facilitate:

Individualized learning: Each individual is activated in the learning process interacting with a learning tool.

Personalized learning: The interaction follows certain paths and is conducted at a pace chosen by the learner.

Integrated learning: The path is open to the crossing of boundaries and to the interconnection of topics kept insofar distinct.

This means that the previous school's pattern of massification/standardization/fragmentation could be replaced by a new pattern based on individualization/personalization/integration of learning experiences.

A Reformulation of the Argument

Assumed the existence of these learning tools (to be reviewed and assessed in general terms) and postulated the option towards the preferability for a variety of integrated learning experiences (styles, types) to emerge as being conducive to a more effective learning, the argument can be re-formulated in the following way, leading to the highlighting of what can be now defined, the problem:

- The present mass school system (broadly defined) causes.
- A certain wastage of human resources because less than effective learning processes take place because-learning styles, learning types and integrated learning are neglected.
- Being massification/standardization/fragmentation the dominant feature because this is what a certain set of uphold values recommend and a certain set of employed tools allow.

A possible contribution to the solution of this unsatisfactory state felt as a problem (the waste of human resources) could lie in:

- The transformation of schools in the form of resources centres where.
- Learners could use learning tools that facilitate individualization/personalization/integration of learning experiences because.
- Learning styles, learning types and integrated learning are taken into consideration, and this should mean that.
- A more effective (to be defined) learning process could take place, that means that.
- The waste of human resources could be reduced and this means that.
- The problem could, in a certain measure, be solved (i.e. the situation could be improved).

IDEA OF PIAGET AND BRUNER

Jean Piaget

Piaget considers the most critical factor in a child's cognitive development to be interaction with peers. Interaction lends opportunities for the child to have cognitive conflict, which results in arguing or debating with peers. This type of interaction requires children to *decenter*, or consider another person's point of view. Piaget observes that children are most challenged in their thinking when they are with peers, because they all are on an equal footing and are more free to confront ideas than when interacting with adults.

However, when children are too similar in their thinking, there may be little to debate about, resulting in fewer developmental gains (Stone, 1995; McClellan, 1994). The multiage setting maximizes a child's opportunity for cognitive conflict because it brings together children at a variety of developmental levels. For further information, refer to Thinking About Piaget in Relationship to the Mixed-Age Classroom (McClellan, 1993).

A rather more serious figure in the field of developmental psychology is the Swiss philosopher and psychologist, Jean Piaget. Piaget was originally interested in the philosophical question of epistemology - how do we know what we know? - and decided that metaphysical argument needed to be grounded in a scientific understanding of how children's knowledge of the world develops. He began by studying his own children.

Piaget starts from the premise that human beings, like all other biological organisms, are active in their relationships with the world. Knowledge of the world is connected to actions in the world - thus he says:

To know an object or a happening is to make use of it by assimilation into an action schema.

Human beings know the world in selective ways - if a stimulus cannot be incorporated into an action schema, it will remain outside the domain of knowledge.

The construction of knowledge by the child, then, is an active process. At the beginning, the action is purely physical - then, through a process of internalisation, the actions become mental. Ideas are not given in the perceptive features of the brain, or encoded in language - that is, ideas are neither thoroughly mentalistic nor cultural - but are arrived at through the child's physical interaction with the world.

Piaget is centrally concerned with the development of such categories as space, time, number, causality and so on - the Kantian categories of knowledge. He sees this as going through four stages.

Sensorimotor Stage

Up to 7/9 months, the child concentrates on her own body, and then enters a second sub period in which space and objects within space are recognized under the rubric of 'practical intelligence'. At the end of the period, the child has learnt to distinguish between objects and subjects, and has grasped the idea of a causal relationship.

Initial exploration of the world through perception is followed up by active exploration, using hands and arms. The child learns to 'make interesting events last' - a rattle, at first set off accidentally, becomes the object of intentional activity. Through this, the child comes to value repetition as a strategy within the world. At the end of the stage, the child is also capable of symbolic representation - mental activity is now possible.

Period of Representational Thought

The advent of representation leads to a knowledge explosion. One example is the rapid growth of language - but in Piaget's scheme of knowledge, language is not all-important - it is seen as a socially derived conventional system, and subsidiary to thought.

During this period, children are said to achieve 'semilogics' - that is, their thinking appears to get stuck half-way. For example, the child confuses 'longer than' with 'goes further than' - this Piaget derives from his results on experiments in the conservation of matter.

A child is asked to ascertain whether, when liquid is poured from one container into another, there is more of it, the same amount, or less. Up until the end of this period, the child is likely to say that if the liquid is poured from a short fat container into a long thin one, then there is more of it. On the other hand, if the liquid is poured from a long thin container into a short fat one, she will say that there is less of it. Similarly, a piece of plasticine is conceived of as changing in mass as it changes in form.

Concrete Operations

At this stage, the child acquires rules that allow them to make deductive inferences. They also emerge from their initial egoism - in this, Piaget appears to agree with Freud - and recognize the other's point of view. Thus, the child at this stage will be able to appreciate that a view seen from one angle will not look the same when seen from another angle.

Deductive inferences allow the child to conserve weight, volume, length and so on. These inferences are reversible - that is, the idea that what has been taken away can be put back, and what has been added can be subtracted.

Formal Operations

At this stage, the child becomes capable of applying

operations to operations - second order constructions. It is now that the child is capable of reasoning through an operation rather than solving the problem by trial and error. - that is, the child is capable of constructing hypotheses and then of testing them. Essentially, it is only at this stage that the individual becomes capable of fully scientific thought.

Piaget's work gave a basis for almost all subsequent investigation of developmental processes, and one cannot overestimate its importance. Nevertheless, there are a number of criticisms that can be made of it. in the light of subsequent research. Thus, Michael Rutter makes the following comments:

1. The idea of the child as an active agent in learning is still accepted today.

Children do explore their environments, do prefer novel stimuli to familiar ones, and do take an experimental attitude towards the world. Animal studies also back this up - animals that are allowed to explore an environment actively learn far more about it than do those who perceive it passively. Indeed, rhesus monkeys reared under conditions in which little movement is possible appear to be less intelligent than their genetic peers who are reared in environments in which they can move about and play:

2. The idea that development is achieved through a series of discrete stages, at each of which overall cognition functions according to a specific structure is misleading.

In fact, it has been found that children are quite capable at being at stage four on certain tasks, while remaining at stage three on others.

3. Many of Piaget's findings on questions such as conservation appear to be as much artefacts of his experimental method as they are measures of the real abilities of children.

It has been found that, if the question is put otherwise, and if there is a clear explanation of what the experimenter expects of the child, the tasks can often be carried out quite successfully by children who, according to the stage theory, should not be able to do so.

As a corollary, we can present experiments in such a way that adults fail them. Success is often a question of context - Brazilian street-vendors are capable of doing maths in their everyday transactions that they cannot do when the same problems are presented in schoolbook style.

4. Special training can lead to the development of particular skills.

Children who are very good at chess develop advanced memory skills, and Australian aborigine children who have spent their lives navigating the vast spaces of the desert have superior spatial reasoning.

Piaget ignores both individual and cultural differences, assuming that there is a unique path to development that is followed by all human beings.

Webster R. Callaway performs an intensive investigation into the language Piaget developed in his year of writing. He determines that Piaget was assigning inconsistent meanings to the terms he used. For example, Callaway writes: "While reading Biology and Knowledge (1971a) and Psychology and Epistemology. (1971b), I began to suspect that Piaget was methodically using the word 'biology' with two drastically different meanings. Sometimes there appeared to be a switch of meaning in the same paragraph, or even the same sentence, but there was never a forewarning or overt clue of any kind that the meaning was being changed.

The changes were frequent, unexpected and usually involved 'tricky' or cryptic language." (Callaway, p. 1).The language problem Callaway identifies is only one aspect of Piaget's work that has fallen under criticism. David Elliott urges the perspective that Piaget was "one of the greatest minds of the nineteen-forties." And if one considers Piaget's theories of assimilation and accommodation, it is clear other, more recent perspectives shape the way we think about cognitive development.

Robert J. Sternberg, an opponent of Howard Gardner, as I discuss below, outlines several important methodological and theoretical challenges to Piaget's theory of intellectual development. Sternberg draws upon Brown and Desforges as well as Siegel and Brainerd in their psychological critiques and papers proposing alternatives to Piagetian theory.

The first problem is that of replicability. Sternberg writes, "interexperimenter variance owing to flexibility of Piaget's clinical method is a major problem in replication attempts." (Sternberg 1990). In other words, there are serious problems with his methodology. David Elliot echoes this when he observes that Piaget used only his own children to form the basis of his research.

The other areas of concern are:

- *Interpretation:* Are apparent failures really failures and successes really successes?
- *Interpretation:* What does "failure" or "success" on a given task mean in terms of evaluating a child's intelligence?
- Usefulness of the theory.

Jerome Bruner

Jerome Bruner was born in New York in 1915. At the age of 2 he underwent operations to correct vision impaired due to cataracts. His father died when Jerome was 12, after which the family moved frequently and Jerome had an education interrupted by frequent changes of school. Despite this, Bruner's grades were good enough to enter Duke University in Durham, NC where he obtained a B.A. in 1937 followed by a Ph.D. from Harvard in 1941.

Bruner was Professor of Psychology at Harvard (1952-1972) and Watts Professor at Oxford (1972-1980), and has spent time at the New York University School of Law and the New School for Social Research in New York City.

For the past 45 years Bruner has been a leader in the establishment of cognitive psychology as an alternative to the behaviourist theories that dominated psychology in the first half of the 20th century.

Bruner's cognitive approach to his work in childhood learning and perception has made him a key figure in educational reform in the United States and Britain.

Bruner served on the President's Science Advisory

Committee during the Kennedy and Johnson presidencies and has received many awards and honours, including the International Balzan Prize (for his "lifelong contribution to the understanding of the human mind"), the CIBA Gold Medal for Distinguished Research and the Distinguished Scientific Award of the American Psychological Association.

Bruner is currently Research Professor of Psychology and Senior Research Fellow in Law at New York University. Over the past 40 years he has published many books, including *The Process of Education* (1960), *Acts of Meaning* (1991) and *The Culture of Education* (1996).

Bruner's Work on Cognition and Constructivism

Jean Piaget and Jerome Bruner demonstrated how thought processes could be subdivided into three distinct modes of reasoning. While Piaget related each mode to a specific period of childhood development, Bruner saw each mode as dominant during each developmental phase, but present and accessible throughout. Bruner's model of human development as a combination of enactive skills (manipulating objects, spatial awareness), iconic skills (visual recognition, the ability to compare and contrast) and symbolic skills (abstract reasoning) has influenced psychological and educational thought over the past 50 years.

Bruner's work came at a time when psychological thought was dominated by behaviourism, which was popular because a measurable response could be observed to a defined stimulus. This satisfied the need for scientific rigour, but explained learning without accounting for mental processes that were assumed to be not measurable. Bruner was able to apply a similar scientific rigour to unobservable mental processes.

Bruner was instrumental in the move from behaviourism to cognitivism in 1950s and 1960s mainstream psychology. An important work in the early days of the cognitive movement was *A Study in Thinking* which Bruner published in 1956 with Jacqueline Goodnow and George Austin, and where they defined cognitive processes as "the means whereby organisms achieve, retain and transform information." Bruner suggested that people remember things "with a view towards meaning and signification, not toward the end of somehow 'preserving' the facts themselves." This view of knowledge – and memory – as a constructed entity is consistent with constructivism, with which Bruner is also closely associated.

A constant theme in Bruner's work is that education is a process of discovery. As a structural theorist, Bruner believes that information or knowledge is most effectively gained by personal discovery, and then classified enactively, iconically or symbolically. Bruner advocated that if students were allowed to pursue concepts on their own they would gain a better understanding. Within the education system, a teacher would then engage students in active dialogue and guide them when necessary so that students would progressively build their own knowledge base, rather than be 'taught'. New information would be classified and understood based on knowledge already gained.

Implications and Applications of Bruner's Theories

Bruner's theory of how children construct knowledge involves three basic modes of instruction.

In their very early years, young children rely extensively upon enactive modes to learn. As a child learns to roll over, sit up or walk, they are learning to do so through their own actions. While this mode is present in people of all ages it is more dominant when a person is young. An example of this dominance is the way a young person can often learn to play a musical instrument more quickly than an older person.

Iconic representation normally becomes dominant during the next stage of childhood years. Children learn to understand what pictures and diagrams are and how to do arithmetic using numbers and without counting objects.

Later – usually around adolescence - the symbolic mode of learning becomes most dominant. Students can understand and work with concepts that are abstract.

According to Bruner, developmental growth involves mastering each of the increasingly more complex modes -

enactive to iconic to symbolic. Mastering this incorporates becoming more skilled in translating between each mode. An example of this sort of translation could be a discussion (symbolic mode) of what students had learned from an experiment (iconic mode).

An implication of Bruner's developmental theories is that children should be provided with study materials, activities, and tools that are matched to and capitalise on their developing cognitive capabilities. For example, a teacher wanting to help children learn about dinosaurs could use all three modes. Students could be asked to construct models of dinosaurs (enactive); they might watch a film about, or involving, dinosaurs (iconic); or they could consult reference texts and then discuss their findings (symbolic).

The influence of Bruner's work extends beyond psychology and education. Bruner's work influenced Xerox PARC researchers in their efforts to create graphical user interfaces (GUIs) that addressed enactive, iconic and symbolic ways users understand and manipulate the world around them. Bruner was a key member in founding and teaching the Colloquium on the Theory of Legal Practice which involves the study of how law is practised and how its practice can be understood through the use of tools developed within anthropology, psychology, linguistics and literary theory.

Bruner observes that the process of constructing knowledge of the world is not done in isolation but rather within a social context. The child is a social being and, through social life, acquires a framework for interpreting experiences (Bruner & Haste, 1987). Bruner (1966) also notes that "there is no unique sequence for all learners, and the optimum in any particular case will depend upon a variety of factors, including past learning, stage of development, nature of the material, and individual differences". Effective curriculum then, must provide many opportunities and choices for children (Anderson & Pavan, 1993). Within the multiage setting, opportunities exist for children to make choices about their learning experiences. In addition, the variety of teaching methods used in the multiage classroom provides opportunities for children to construct knowledge in a multitude of ways.

Jerome Bruner was a guest lecturer in our music education curriculum development class at New York University in November of 2001. His energetic presence and enthusiasm for intellectual discourse pervaded the atmosphere of the room that night. I remember asking him about a quote from his "Essays for the Left Hand" which started, "how can I know who I am until I feel what I do?" He pointed to the necessity for teachers to inspire their student's to "achieving their highest level of excellence."

His theory of cognitive growth in the 1960's looked to environmental and experiential factors and suggested that intellectual ability developed in stages through step-by-step changes in how the mind is used. "Bruner is surely right to insist that the child acquires ways of performing particular kinds of communicational acts. However, it is crucial that communicational acts must not be treated as if they were separable—or as if they could be studied independently—from their conceptualization within a particular cultural form of life."

This view emphasizes the difference between the constructivist thinking Bruner developed, and a more behaviorist approach as represented by E.D. Hirsch. Hirsch urges the notion that certain facts are necessary for an individual to know in order to be "culturally literate." The thinking Bruner develops along constructivist lines is different; Bruner views the process of discovery as essential to learning. He values this above the need to memorize facts.

It is important to include a word here about psychology in relation to music education. Top scholars ranging to beginning practitioners look to the work of cognitive psychologists –like Bruner, Piaget, and Gardner- to form theories of learning and teaching as well as to illuminate the path toward effective curriculums. But this action must be exercised with caution when these very psychologists are non-musicians. Jerome Bruner, by his own admission, is a non-musician, and as such, does not possess the experience or understanding most music educators possess having been educated in a school of music, conservatory, or perhaps a school of education with a music department.

Bruner emphasizes the structure of a discipline and gave great emphasis to mathematics and science as the major disciplines for teaching structure. Thorndike influenced Bruner, but there were differences between them. One is that Thorndike found that no one subject was more important than another for meaningful learning.

PSYCHOLOGICAL ASPECT OF MATHEMATICS

Recently, attempts to create a unified theory of learning have been made by psychologists, and one may try to approach practical problems via such a unified theory. We have adopted three principles from this theory:

- Progress in small steps.
- Active response.
- Immediate confirmation and reinforcement.

We have studied the implementation of these principles in the classical teaching situation, that is, in the regular classroom as it has existed for many years and have found that this can be done through the question-and-answer method. The mere fact that the entire lesson proceeds by way of questions and answers is not sufficient to ensure the three principles. Questions and answers alone do not yet constitute the question-and-answer *method*.To implement the three principles, the following additional rules must be adhered to:

- The first principle requires that the questions split up the material into elements of knowledge (clauses) which lead in combination to a complete solution of our problem. We have no satisfactory definition of 'element of knowledge' and must resort to a description: it is an item of knowledge that cannot be further subdivided (examples have been given in the text).
- The second principle requires that every question be asked *before*the respondent is chosen. By this and other means the number of students answering each

question, whether silently or by show of hands, must be maximized. Moreover, those that do not respond may need special attention.

- The third principle requires that the answer received be incorporated in the next question, or even confirmed by a word such as 'correct' before such incorporation.

Psychology covers a very broad range of topics, but at its simplest level it is the systematic study of the behaviour of individuals. It considers emotions, personality, and the way individuals interact, and it considers the neurophysiological, sensory and perceptual aspects of behaviour.

Psychology is a growing and ever-changing subject - that's what makes it so fascinating.

Questions psychologists may ask include:

- How do people perceive, learn, think, develop, behave and relate to each other?
- How does the structure of the brain affect our behaviour?
- What makes people different from each other?
- How does being in groups affect people's behaviours; how do social groups affect what we do?
- How do factors like culture, gender, poverty and mental illness affect the way we think and behave?

And on a wider level, psychology helps us to make sense of the human impact on the world in which we live. Political turmoil, conflict, corruption, drug abuse, crime, sexual abuse and poverty are fundamentally related to human behaviour. Psychology students see their subject as a way to understand and perhaps change or prevent the behaviours that cause those problems.

THE PSYCHOLOGY PROGRAMMEME

Psychology can be defined as the scientific study of behaviour and mental processes. However, this definition does not reveal the diversity of content that characterises psychology. Psychology can be considered to be both a natural science and a social science. As a natural science, psychology focuses on perception, cognition, learning, and the biological bases of behaviour. As a social science, psychology focuses on development, personality, social processes, and abnormal behaviour.

The natural science and social science aspects of psychology are linked together by a common core of research methods, which includes experimental design, data analysis, and psychometrics. Another important aspect of psychology is its applicability to the world outside the laboratory, to assist in the solution of individual and social problems.

The range of psychology papers offered at Massey reflects the diversity of psychology. Undergraduate papers cover the natural science aspect of psychology, the social science aspect of psychology, research methods used in psychology, and applications of psychology.

The table below shows how the various papers offered at Massey fit into the different categories. An introduction to both the natural science and the social science aspects of psychology is provided by the two 100-level papers. The 200-level papers offer further study of both aspects, and research methods are introduced. At 300-level, all aspects of psychology are covered in a wide range of papers, and applied areas of psychology are included.

Majoring requirements in psychology are structured so that students include papers from the natural science category, the social science category, and the research methods category within the major. There is also flexibility within the majoring requirements, so that students can pursue their particular interests within psychology.

INTEREST IN PSYCHOLOGY

To study psychology is to understand behaviour, both what people actually do and the mental processes underlying their actions. The psychologist's challenging job not only involves studying individuals and groups but also requires the researcher to take into account the environmental, physiological, and cultural factors that influence human behaviour. Students of psychology employ a variety of clinical and scientific methods to discover how and why the human mind behaves as it does.

Psychology is a field that includes many vibrant areas of intellectual interest. Clinical psychology studies normal personality as well as mental disorders and their treatment. Social psychology investigates significant social issues, and community psychology explores how community organizations develop to meet the changing needs of our society.

Health psychology studies how to prevent and treat illness using biological, psychological, and social perspectives. Physiological psychology examines the biological bases of behaviour, especially those involving the nervous system. Experimental psychology focuses on the basic processes of sensation, perception, learning, memory, thinking, language, emotion, and motivation.

Psychologists have always been interested in interest, and so modern research on interest can be found in nearly every area of the field: Researchers studying emotions, cognition, development, education, aesthetics, personality, motivation, and vocations have developed intriguing ideas about what interest is and how it works. Exploring the Psychology of Interest presents an integrated picture of how interest has been studied in all the wide-ranging areas of psychology. Using modern theories of cognition and emotion as an integrative framework, Paul Silvia examines the nature of interest, what makes things interesting, the role of interest in personality, and the development of peoples idiosyncratic interests, hobbies, and avocations. His examination reveals deep similarities between seemingly different fields of psychology and illustrates the profound importance of interest, curiosity, and intrinsic motivation for understanding why people do what they do. The most comprehensive work of its kind, Exploring the Psychology of Interest will be a valuable resource for student and professional researchers in cognitive, social, and developmental psychology.

Human-computer interaction and computer simulation of psychological processes bring students into the advanced area of artificial intelligence. Developmental psychology looks at patterns of all psychological processes, including meta-cognition and insight, as they occur and change over the life span.

The psychology curriculum acquaints students with a wide range of psychological theories and methods that form the basis for contemporary psychology. The department also strives to develop the student's competency in conducting and evaluating empirical research in the classroom and in faculty research labs. Many opportunities exist for students to gain internship experience and see the practical applications of psychological principles.

Students begin their studies with three foundation courses: Introduction to Psychology, Statistics, and Psychology Methodology. Seven other courses are selected, in conference with the student's faculty adviser, based on department guidelines and student interest. Course sizes range from nine students (at the upper level) to 39 students (at the introductory level).

Requirements for the major ensure that students get a broad exposure to the subfields of psychology. Students interested in clinical or counseling psychology benefit from relevant practicum experiences as well as from courses in personality, abnormal psychology, social psychology, and psychology of women. Students interested in basic research in psychology gear their coursework toward experimental, developmental, social, health, community, human-computer interaction, and physiological psychology.

Psychology describes and attempts to explain consciousness, behaviour and social interaction. Empirical psychology is primarily devoted to describing human experience and behaviour as it actually occurs. In the past 20 years or so psychology has begun to examine the relationship between consciousness and the brain or nervous system. It is still not clear in what ways these interact: does consciousness determine brain states or do brain states determine consciousness - or are both going on in various ways? Perhaps to understand this you need to know the definition of "consciousness" and "brain state" - or is consciousness some sort of complicated 'illusion' which bears no direct relationship to neural processes?

An understanding of brain function is increasingly being included in psychological theory and practice, particularly in areas such as artificial intelligence, neuropsychology, and cognitive neuroscience. The department has an active practicum programme, and most psychology majors pursue a practicum experience in an area of interest. The programme provides supervised experience and training in psychological activities in a variety of local institutions and businesses. The practicum programme is offered to junior and senior psychology majors as an important supplement to their academic and research development.

Perhaps the greatest strength of Lewis and Clark's psychology department is the opportunity for students to do research in the major areas of psychology. Research conducted at Lewis and Clark is at the professional level. The department has a strong commitment to involving students in faculty research projects and providing guidance for students who wish to work on independent projects.

Students, in collaboration with faculty, may develop their own research and frequently present their papers at national psychology conferences. Students are also frequently credited as coauthors on articles in leading psychology journals. Psychology students may also tie in their overseas study experiences with their interest in psychology.

Based on an evaluation of academic performance and the quality of a research proposal prepared in cooperation with a faculty member, a select group of senior students is invited to participate in the psychology honors programme. Students work closely with a thesis committee to undertake and defend their honors theses to the department. Exceptional senior projects are awarded honors on graduation.

Fields of Research Psychology

Research psychology encompasses the study of behaviour for use in academic settings, and contains numerous areas. It contains the areas of abnormal psychology, biological psychology, cognitive psychology, comparative psychology, developmental psychology, personality psychology, social psychology and others. Research psychology is contrasted with applied psychology.

Abnormal Psychology

Abnormal psychology is the study of abnormal behaviour in order to describe, predict, explain, and change abnormal patterns of functioning. Abnormal psychology studies the nature of psychopathology and its causes, and this knowledge is applied in clinical psychology to treating patients with psychological disorders.

Cognitive Psychology

The nature of thought is another core interest in psychology. Cognitive psychology studies cognition, the mental processes underlying behaviour. It uses information processing as a framework for understanding the mind. Perception, learning, problem solving, memory, attention, language and emotion are all well researched areas. Cognitive psychology is associated with a school of thought known as cognitivism, whose adherents argue for an information processing model of mental function, informed by positivism and experimental psychology.

Cognitive science is very closely related to cognitive psychology, but differs in some of the research methods used, and has a slightly greater emphasis on explaining mental phenomena in terms of both behaviour and neural processing.Both areas use computational models to simulate phenomena of interest. Because mental events cannot directly be observed, computational models provide a tool for studying the functional organization of the mind.

Such models give cognitive psychologists a way to study the "software" of mental processes independent of the "hardware" it runs on, be it the brain or a computer.

Developmental Psychology

Mainly focusing on the development of the human mind

through the life span, developmental psychology seeks to understand how people come to perceive, understand, and act within the world and how these processes change as they age. This may focus on intellectual, cognitive, neural, social, or moral development.

Researchers who study children use a number of unique research methods to make observations in natural settings or to engage them in experimental tasks. Such tasks often resemble specially designed games and activities that are both enjoyable for the child and scientifically useful, and researchers have even devised clever methods to study the mental processes of small infants.

In addition to studying children, developmental psychologists also study aging and processes throughout the life span, especially at other times of rapid change. Urie Bronfenbrenner's theory of development in context is influential in this field, as are those mentioned in "Educational psychology" immediately below, as well as many others. Developmental psychologists draw on the full range of

ATTENTION AND CONCENTRATION

Concentration, attention, to focus, is difficult think many. Most can not concentrate. To be able to concentrate, focus one's attention, concentration, even merely paying basic attention to focus on ordinary things is regarded as the greatest power. Concentration and attention, concentrating and focusing, have been described as the power which if one possessed would make all other known power insignificant to one. Focusing attention, concentration, is what intelligence is, is about. Here is how to acquire focus -concentration, attention.

Concentration and attention, first, know that one can easily, quickly acquire. What are attention, concentration, focus? There are three simple definitions relevant to attention and focus, concentration - intelligence.

Intelligence is knowing how to avoid distractions and concentrate on issues -it is concentration, focusing attention; concentrating, knowing how to concentrate and focus attention

-success in life situations by effective concentration, effective focus of attention.

Attention is part of focus, concentration, a component of intelligence. Attention, focus of attention, only lasts a few seconds *(tests suggested up to 90 but 30 seconds is regarded as maximum for focusing attention).* Attention is the act or process of focusing on one or more particulars in the content of one's consciousness to give special clearance to essentials by restricting one's sensory input from the environment's unwanted aspects. Attention is never entire; it digresses, but can be re-focused at will.

Concentration and attention are subject to will. When one is trying to concentrate, paying attention, waves of electricity called 'alpha rhythm' are given by one's brain at a frequency of 8-12 Hz.; but attempts by bio-feedback on an electroencephalograph (EEG) or a 'mind-mirror' to usefully experiment with focusing attention to concentrate failed without direct input from the brain tissue, and because in 10% of subjects no waves were recordable -in concentration, while trying to focus attention, sensory input in attentive states can be sealed off at sense-organ level. Practice helps improve attention.

Concentration is exclusively to focus on, to give one's attention to, the task at hand by habitually bringing one's digressed attention back to quicker focus that attention, and to focus that attention more accurately. Concentration, concentrating, is being able also to re-focus attention if and when one is much distracted, or immediately after any rest or other one or more breaks, on the same task or other tasks (as opposed to 'concrete thinking' -which is not attention or concentration but obsession with a specific fact or task and inability to switch focus of attention, concentration, to any other). The strength of the ability to concentrate, focus of attention for concentration, is *by mental conditioning.*

Concentration, attention, focus, involve thought. Thought outwardly directs itself creatively when uncontrolled, and with 5 a minute break ideally the ability to focus and refocus attention, concentration, lasts at best 20-40 minutes. But focus and re-focus, attention and concentration, are aided by a network of nerve fibres within the brain stem, and because this ('reticular-activating system' -RAS) despatches signals to other parts of the brain, the brain is capable of being stimulated for attention also by conscious attitude -i.e., focus of attention, concentration, increases by confident familiarity with, excited interest in, the task at hand -it becomes easier and quicker to focus and re-focus attention on the subject of your concentration.

Diet and Exercises to improve focus of attention, and re-focus of attention, concentration, is easy, effective in a healthy body (nerve cells affect mental functions and vitamins B1 & B12 help -whole grains, nuts, milk help better focus of attention and concentration).Exercising focus of attention, concentration as follows safely improves attention and concentration: (Sophisticated breathing techniques to deprive the brain of oxygen to force greater alpha-rhythm by increased carbon-dioxide retention, by some suggested, are known sometimes to have even upset one's automatic breathing, and should never be attempted.) 1. The simplest, easiest attention and concentration exercise is for 3 minutes a day to sit 5 feet away from a black spot 2 inches in diameter on a wall trying to focus attention, to concentrate, to see nothing but that. 2. Another attention and concentration exercise is studying carefully for a few minutes a picture or postcard of something unfamiliar to one (this must never be the picture of a person, nor a place where there may have been or can be expected to be any persons or animals ~and, it must be an unfamiliar scene-e.g. an artist's from imagination painted picture of mountains, fields; the same one always); then, after focusing attention, concentrating on it, one tries to recall the details of it -this daily increases success in focusing attention, concentration.3. Depending on one's time and interest, to exercise attention and concentration, one, in one's imagination, may expand a spot to a circle on a blank wall learning daily to more easily focus attention and concentrate.

Later by focusing attention, concentration, add in imagination a square around it; when you can do that easily proceed in imagination by attention and concentration to pull toward you the centre of that circle to form a cone; as gets easier your focus of attention, concentration, then a pyramid - daily improved attention and concentration will enable to easily change their colour and to paint them in imagination in many different colours. (It is possible to so improve one's attention and concentration as to place a piece of silver foil no bigger than a pin-head on a mirror and be able at will immediately to so focus attention as to concentrate, see absolutely nothing but just that - learnable is focus of attention, concentration.)

Concentration, focus of attention, it is generally agreed by science, can be improved.

Even the simplest and easiest of focus of attention and concentration exercises improve effective focus of attention and concentration on issues in life situations and in the true sense of attention and concentration one's intelligent success or grater success in all matters important to one. Power and intelligence is the ability to focus attention, concentration.

FORMATION OF MATHEMATICAL CONCEPTS

ABSTRACTING AND CLASSIFYING

Abstracting

Invariant properties of examples are abstracted: These memories persist longer in the memory than particular instances an activity by which we become aware of similarities among our experiences product of abstraction — concept

Classifying

Similarities of an instance with a class are noted: collecting together our experiences on the basis of these similarities

Abstraction

$$C_1\ C_2\ C_n\ C_3\ C\ C'\ C''\ Ch$$

Classification

- Naming an object classifies it.

- We then know how to behave in relation to it.
- Once classified, less open to other classifications.

Concept

- Requires for its formation a number of experiences which have something in common.
- Everyday concepts come from everyday experience.
- Process involved:
  - Generalization
  - Discrimination

NAMING: A CONCEPT AND ITS NAME

- Example given by Vygotsky:

Children were told that in a game a dog would be called 'cow'. The following is a typical sequence of questions and answers:

'Does a cow have horns?'

'Yes.' 'But don't you remember that the cow is really a dog? Come now, does a dog have horns?'

'Sure, if it is a cow, if it's called cow, it has horns. That kind of dog has got to have little horns.'

Another example: A peasant who, after listening to two students of astronomy talking about the stars, said that he could understand that with the help of instruments people could measure the distance from the earth to the stars and find their positions and motion. What puzzle him was how in the devil they found out the names of the stars.

NAMING

A concept is an idea; the name of a concept is a sound, or a mark on paper, associated with it.

This association can be formed after the concept has been formed, or in the process of forming it.

The use of a name help classifying object e.g. This is a kind of bottle opener useful and sometimes essential in the formation of new concepts — different names heard together.

Communication of Concept

Can a concept be communicated by simply verbally

defining it? Two ways to describe 'red':

Red is the colour we experience from light of wavelength in the region of 0.6 microns pointing to various objects and say 'This is a red tie', 'This is a red tie', ...

Two Kinds of Concept

Primary concepts: those which are derived from our sensory and motor experiences of the outside world, such as red, motor car, heavy,...

Secondary concepts: those which are abstracted from other concepts, such as ....

Of higher order means abstracted from (directly or indirectly) more abstract means ' more removed from experience of the outside world'.

Concepts of a higher order than those which people already have cannot be communicated to them by a definition but only by collecting together, for them to experience, suitable examples.

Use of Definitions

A way of adding precision to the bounaries of a concept, once formed, stating explicitly its relation to other concepts.

Communicate new concepts of lower order, e.g., " It is a colour, between red and blue, rather more blue than red".

The criterion for having a concept is not being able to say its name but behaving in a way indicative of classifying new data according to the similarities which go to form this concept.

Ways to Evoke a Concept

- Encountering an example of the concept — recognition.
- Hearing, reading or otherwise making conscious the name, or other symbol, for the concept — naming
- The ability to isolate concepts from any of the examples enable the formation of new concepts of greater abstraction. If we cannot detach concepts from the experience (using language).
- Each individual has to form their own concepts

directly from the environment.

- without language, the primary concepts cannot be brought together to form concepts of higher order.
- Concepts of the past not available.

Power of Conceptual Thinking

- Ability to combine and relate many different experiences and classes of experience. The more abstract the concepts, the greater their power to do this.
  - "Don't worry me with theory – just give me the facts"?
  - Appropriate theory enables us to explain, predict and control a great number of particular events in the classes to which it relates.
- Learning by using abstract symbols is meaningless to most students.

LEANING OF MATHEMATICAL CONCEPTS

- The particular problem (but also the power) of mathematics lies in the great abstractness and generality, achieved by successive generations of particularly intelligent individuals each of whom has been abstracting from, or generalizing, concepts of earlier generations.
- Mathematics cannot be learnt directly from the everyday environment, but only indirectly from other mathematicians, in conjunction with one's own reflective intelligence.

PRINCIPLES OF LEARNING MATHEMATICAL CONCEPTS

- Concepts of a higher order than those which people already have cannot be communicated to them by a definition, but only by arranging for them to encounter a suitable collection of examples
- Since in mathematics these examples are almost invariably other concepts, it must first be ensured

that these are already formed in the mind of the learner.

Learning and Teaching

Although we have to create all the concepts in our own minds, we are only able to do this by using the concepts arrived at by past mathematicians.

Very dependent on good teaching.

To know mathematics.

To communicate it to those at a lower conceptual level.

FACTORS INFLUENCING THE LEARNING OF MATHEMATICS

As the science of didactics of mathematics evolves, it is fragmenting into more and more subfields. Although research in each subfield has the common element of investigating questions related to mathematics learning, in each case the research focus is directed intensively at different aspects. This is having the unfortunate consequence that deep expertise gained – and results discovered – within each specialist subfield are too seldom communicated to others outside that subfield. This state of affairs persists even at large conferences in which several specialist subfields are represented.

The conference "The Future of Mathematics Education and Learning Mathematics" will consider the mathematical learning process from the most important perspectives and discuss the relationship to mathematics teaching. Two leading world-experts working in each of these perspectives will be invited to present a review of state-of-the-art research in their field, and they will discuss connections to the other approaches.

The conference's central goal is to promote interdisciplinary discussion of scientific viewpoints underpinning the various subfields, as well as discussion of interrelations between the subfields.

It is certainly impossible to address all the factors that influence the learning process. Nevertheless, presenting a somewhat broader view can provide the opportunity for researchers to glimpse the state of the art in the other fields, and this will help cross-fertilize research across the entire spectrum of didactics of mathematics.

MOTIVATION OF LEARNING OF MATHEMATICS

Mathematics is a universal subject, so much a part of life that anyone who is a participating member of society must know basic mathematics. Students' mathematical achievement, however, is ultimately determined and limited by the opportunities they have had to learn. Mathematics is not restricted to a select group of students. "All students must learn to think mathematically, and they must think mathematically to learn".

The Mathematics Study Panel also emphasized the importance of mathematics. Furthermore, the panel declared that it is essential that students develop math proficiency. No Child Left Behind Act are directed that research about effective practices be a guide in changing the way mathematics is taught so that high standards are met leading to an improvement in achievement.

Motivation Math incorporates research-based strategies and pedagogically sound principles for teaching and learning. This product is designed to support and enhance the best practices for teaching the TEKS. *Motivation Math* is founded on the modeling of "Active Teaching," which is teacher-directed instruction that proceeds in small steps.

Research indicates that this approach is associated with higher levels of student achievement. Students are guided through the learning process and are afforded opportunities for success which include:

- Introduction to skills
- Guided practice
- Independent practice

Assessment:

- Critical thinking activities
- Homework with parent activities

Hiebert and Wearne reported that a critical attribute in regards to student learning in mathematics, is the nature of the learning task in which to engage students. Students need mental engagement in challenging and worthwhile mathematical tasks that emphasize the conceptual aspects of the topic and promote the formation of mathematical connections. This type engagement is a prerequisite to learning skills with meaning and being able to apply those skills to solve problems. Students must receive direct encouragement to think and persist with the mathematical task at hand.

Grouws and Cebulla state that teaching mathematics with a focus on number sense encourages students to become problem solvers in a wide variety of situations and to view mathematics as a discipline which thinking is important. "Number sense" is an intuitive feel for number size and combinations, as well as the ability to work flexibly with numbers in problem situations in order to make reasonable judgments.

The processes of mentally computing, estimating, sensing number magnitudes, moving between representation systems for numbers, and judging the reasonableness of numerical results must be flexibly used. This type of instruction requires teachers to have a deep understanding of mathematics and how students learn mathematics. More specifically, teachers will encounter difficulty in teaching number sense without a working knowledge of number sense themselves.

The experiences, discussions, and review of the literature convinced the Mentoring Minds Product Development Team that resources for mathematics needed a change. Thus, the format for a Student Edition was designed to help move mathematics forward so that teachers could incorporate the teaching of TEKS in mathematics on a higher level and develop within students the confidence they need to succeed.

This study focuses on students' motivation in solving mathematical problems. Objectives of the study are to identify students' level of effort, self efficacy and worry in solving mathematical problems based on gender, current cumulative grade point average and year of study (ii) students' level of motivation in solving mathematical problems based on gender, current cumulative grade point average (CGPA) and year of study.

Establish relationship between levels of motivation and students' mathematics achievement. The subscales used in the measurement of motivation are effort, self-efficacy, and worry. Data was gathered through a descriptive survey using questionnaires. Overall, students' motivations was found to be high and majority of the respondents were in the high level for effort but were only moderate for self efficacy.

Significant difference was established in overall motivation scores between the female and male respondents, but not for the subscales effort, self-efficacy and worry. Respondents with higher CGPA obtained higher overall scores for motivation. Significant positive correlations were established between effort, self-efficacy, and overall motivation with students' overall academic achievement. Likewise, significant positive correlations were established between effort, self-efficacy, worry, and overall motivation with students' average mathematics achievement. Keywords: Motivation, mathematical problem solving, self-efficacy, effort, worry.

INTRODUCTION

Motivation refers to "a student's willingness, need, desire and compulsion to participate in, and be successful in the learning process" viewed motivation as reasons individuals have for behaving in a given situation. A more comprehensive definition was provided by Ames (1992) who stated that motivation exists as part of one's goal structures, one's beliefs about what is important and it determines whether or not one will engage in a given pursuit. Skinner and Belmont explained that students who are motivated to engage in school "select tasks at the border of their competencies, initiate action when given the opportunity, and exert intense effort and concentration in the implementation of learning tasks; they show generally positive emotions during ongoing action, including enthusiasm, optimism, curiosity, and interest" Motivation contributes to the ability to solve problems.

Based on several problem solving models, O'Neil & Schacter (1997) developed the CRESST model of problem solving that incorporates four elements; content understanding, problem solving strategies, metacognition and motivation. In their model, motivation comprises of three components; self efficacy, effort and worry. Several researches showed that high worry is associated with low cognitive performance. On the other hand, studies such as Wigfield and Meece (1988) showed that there is no relationship between worry and achievement.

Although worry can trigger negative effects on learning, depending on the degree of worry, it could also contribute to positive antecedent to high achievement. It may trigger positive outcomes, in terms that it will drive students to work harder if their worries drive as a challenge to exhibit better performance. Effort is synonym to motivation.

An individual who shows greater effort is considered to be motivated, whilst one who is motivated will also show greater effort. In Miller, Behrens, Greene, and Newman's study findings with respect to self-regulation and academic achievement, they confirmed that self-regulated learning comprised of several components, such as cognitive strategies and effort. Bandura and Schunk posited that effort is directly influenced by self-efficacy and directly affecting skill or performance.

Bandura defines self-efficacy as people's beliefs about their capabilities to produce designated levels of performance that exercise influence over events that affect their lives. Similar to Bandura's definition, Garcia et al.defined self-efficacy as self-appraisal of one's ability to accomplish a task and one's confidence in possessing the skills needed to perform that task. Several researches have shown that self-efficacy has a high positive correlation with test performance outcomes. Self efficacy is a continuous process throughout life. According to Bandura (1992), the growth of self-efficacy does not end during youth, but continues to evolve throughout life as people acquire new skills, experiences, and understanding.

Bandura characterizes individual with a strong sense of

self-efficacy as one who (i) view challenging problems as tasks to be mastered, (ii) develop deeper interest in the activities in which they participate, (iii) form a stronger sense of commitment to their interests and activities, and (iv) recover quickly from setbacks and disappointments.

Bandura added that people with a weak sense of self-efficacy (i) avoids challenging tasks, (ii) believes that difficult tasks and situations are beyond their capabilities, (iii) focuses on personal failings and negative outcomes, and (iv) quickly loses confidence in personal abilities. Bandura (1993) posited that "self-efficacy beliefs contribute to motivation in several ways: They determine the goals people set for themselves, how much effort they expend, how long they persevere in the face of difficulties, and their resilience to failures"

PERCEPTION IN MATHEMATICS

Teacher perceptions of students. While much has been written about teacher perceptions, surprisingly little concerns teacher perceptions of their students and the implications of these judgments, and even less deals with teacher perceptions of mathematics learning and Aboriginal students. The literature discusses how teacher perceptions of curriculum alter the way it comes to be implemented in classrooms and of the impact of teacher beliefs about the administration of a school on its successful organisation. Writings about teacher perceptions of students occur largely in assessment theory where discussions tie perceptions to student achievement and, in particular, how knowledge about students become part of what Wyatt-Smith (1995) described as the "teacher knowledge files" utilised when teachers are making assessment judgments.

Some studies do deal with teacher perceptions generally, examining the various different perceptions that teachers have of their students. A study by Uhlenberg and Brown (2002), for example, looked at teacher perceptions as the reason for the black-white achievement gap in the United States. Of interest to this study is that while black teachers tended to lay the blame at the doorstep of schools and educational systems, white teachers tended to focus on students, parents and home environments.

A further study by Drame (2002) collected data from 63 teachers to determine the extent to which socio-cultural variables affected teacher perceptions of classroom behaviour. The study concluded that teacher perceptions, particularly of learning disabilities and academic performances, affected teachers' instructional patterns and their dealing with students. A study conducted across four countries – India, Nigeria, United Kingdom and the United States – into dropout prevention discovered that reversing negative teacher perceptions about m children was one of the factors essential in keeping at-risk students in the education system. A further study found that rather than teacher perceptions of students being the primary determinant in affecting their behaviour in the classroom, it was in fact their own sense of behaviour and control that determined their treatment of students. While few studies have been conducted into teacher perceptions of Australian Aboriginal students, Green (1982) did examine the influence of the classroom teacher on the performance of Aboriginal children.

In this study, a group of 15 white teachers were asked to list the major differences between teaching Aboriginal and non-Aboriginal students. The teachers were drawn from classrooms where the Aboriginal school population varied from between 5-60%.

The responses of the teachers were separated into five separate categories. All of the categories developed worked out of a deficit model whereby Aboriginal students were seen as having some form of 'insufficiency' that caused their low academic performance. Of the 80 responses coded, 48 of them felt that the students themselves were deficient - lacking interest and language skills, and not having proper behavioural skills, adequate nutrition and proper school socialisation skills. Eleven of the responses blamed familial difficulties including low parental expectations, little parental support and a transient lifestyle as being the cause of the school problems experienced by Aboriginal students.

Six responses suggested that there was a cultural gap between Aboriginal and non-Aboriginal students and that this gap made it difficult for the students to assimilate into the schooling system, while four of the responses believed that the schools could be effective in teaching Aboriginal students if they received more assistance from government agencies. Few teachers saw the school as having any responsibility.

ATTITUDE AND APTITUDE IN MATHEMATICS

ATTITUDE EVALUATION

Attitudes affect everything that you attempt.

They affect your relations with other people and your openness to new experiences. If your attitude toward a task is positive, you will most likely enjoy the process of doing it and look for opportunities to do it. If your attitude is negative, you will most likely avoid or delay the occasion of doing it and, if you must do the task, you will probably not enjoy it or do well at it.

Your attitude toward mathematics affects how well or how often you do it, and how much enjoyment you derive from it. Many students taking mathematics courses in college have a negative attitude toward mathematics that can be described as "math anxiety" or "math avoidance." Math anxiety is a state of such tension or fear that the learning process in mathematics is blocked or interrupted. Math avoidance usually occurs because this fear or tension causes a person to react negatively to mathematical situations and therefore avoid them as much as possible.

The math anxious or avoidant student has difficulty doing well in mathematics. But this difficulty is not related to ability but rather is related to the attitudes that are held about math. Researchers have found that one of the traits of mathematical problem solvers is a low level of anxiety.

If you feel you have this fear of mathematics, it is important to recognize that you can change the attitudes that cause fear and prevent mathematical competency. Identify the negative statements that you make that are self-defeating and that cause you to do poorly merely because you "expect" to do poorly. You can stop making those negative statements and practice making positive ones about mathematics and your ability regarding it.

Use the following statements to explore your attitudes toward mathematics. Decide whether you agree or disagree with the statements.

1. *I never was good at math:* I just don't have a math mind.
2. *Math is cut and dried:* You are either right or wrong.
3. Sometimes I get the answer right, but I know I do it the wrong way.
4. I can do "easy" math, it's the "hard" math that I can't do.
5. When I take a math class or test, it seems that everyone else understands it, but I don't.
6. I should be taking a college level math course now, I'll never catch up.
7. People who are good in math do things quickly and do a lot of work "in their heads."
8. I am afraid of math.
9. I hate math.
10. I feel that I am never going to understand math.

You can probably see that these are all negative statements about math, and about a person's ability to perform in it. If you recognize that these are statements that you make to yourself or others, then that is a first step in overcoming negative attitudes.

Statement 1 illustrates a common myth about mathematics. There is no such thing as a "math mind" as there is no such thing as an "English mind" or a "history mind." People have different talents. You may not have the ability to become a concert pianist, but you can learn to play the scales, or learn the connection between a written note and the proper key on the piano.

Similarly, you can function mathematically even though you may not become another Einstein. By making statement 1, you are excusing yourself from making any effort in mathematics. Do not use your present negative attitude as an excuse; instead take responsibility for your learning.

Statements 2 and 7 illustrate other mathematical myths. There is much more to the mathematical process than "getting the answer." Very often we must perform a complicated mathematical process to help us make a logical decision that is different from the result of the computation.

At other times we may only be looking for an approximate or reasonable answer. Performing computations is important, but is not the only thing that we do in mathematics. Many people believe that math is done quickly, but often the mathematical process requires time and thought that spans several work sessions. You cannot always expect the "answer" to be achieved at one sitting, sometimes you have to go away from the problem and come back to it later. Speed is achieved when you are familiar with the material. Do not hesitate to write things down and use diagrams or any other tools that help you carry out the mathematical processes.

Statements 3 through 6 illustrate some common negative statements that students make about their math ability. Instead of giving themselves credit for being able to do certain mathematical processes, they dismiss what they can do as "not real math." You were not born with any knowledge of mathematics. You have a certain level of expertise in math and you achieved that level through study and practice. Give yourself credit for what you can do and believe that you can learn new material by moving in an orderly way through the levels of mathematics. Finally, do not believe that you are alone in your fears; other students share them as well. If possible, work with other students, sharing insights.

Some of the statements are statements of feelings, and feelings are neither "right" nor "wrong." Though a combination of honest attempts and successful experiences with mathematics during your courses here at OCCC, those of you who agreed with the statements will begin to disagree with them because your negative feelings about mathematics have changed.

DIVERGENT THINKING IN MATHEMATICS

Previous studies have provided evidences supporting the view that the role of domain general cognitive factors such as divergent thinking is not as critical to creativity as previously thought. Based on this evidence, some creativity researchers have argued that creativity is domain-specific rather than domain-general and that domain-specific knowledge and skills are more important than domain-general creative thinking abilities for creative performance in a given domain.

However, few past studies have examined the direct effects of domain knowledge and skills on creative performance. In addition, past studies have not systematically investigated the possible effects of domain-specific motivational factors, such as interest, on the relationships among domain knowledge, divergent thinking, and creative performance.

The purpose of the current study was to investigate and compare the effects of domain knowledge, divergent thinking, and different types of interest (i.e., individual interest and situational interest) on creative performance in art and math, as well as the hypothesized moderating and mediating effects of different types of interest on the relationships among domain knowledge, divergent thinking, and creative performance. 221 Korean eighth grade students from two public middle schools in Korea participated in the present study. A series of hierarchical multiple regression analyses were conducted to test the main effects of the variables of the study as well as the hypothesized moderating and mediating effects of the two types of interest. Regarding the main effects, divergent thinking did have statistically significant main effects on creative performance both in art and math. Domain knowledge also had statistically significant main effects on creative performance both in art and math.

The main effects of the two types of interest on creative performance in art and math were not statistically significant except that there was a statistically significant main effect of situational interest on creative performance in math. Regarding the moderating and mediating effects, the hypothesized moderating and mediating effects of the two types of interest were not statistically significant.

The theoretical implications and limitations of the study were discussed and suggestions for future studies were made, especially with respect to linking the relative importance of the main effects of the variables found in this study to the different domain structures of the art and math domains.

The present investigation was conducted to examine the role of problem discovery in the divergent thinking and creative performance of adolescents. Three divergent thinking tests were administered to a group of adolescents. Each test contained three presentedproblems and one discovered problem. The discovered problem allowed the adolescents to think of a problem and then to provide solutions. Comparisons indicated that the adolescents generated significantly more responses to the discovered problems than the presented problems. Most important was that the unique variance of the discovered problems (controlling the variance shared with scores from the presented problems) was reliable and significantly related to five indices of creative performance. These results support the componential theory of divergent thinking and creativity, and are consistent with the developmental view of problem finding.

CREATIVE THINKING IN MATHEMATICS

Creative thinking in philosophy is possible, because philosophical questions are open questions: an investigation into the nature of the problem is the start of the enterprise and the way followed is often much more interesting than the final results.

This enables children to be equal partners of grown-ups: their lack of knowledge is compensated by their openness.

Quite different: Most people would tend to think - is the situation in mathematics.

Mathematical problems are well-defined, they have strict solutions, and - at least for school mathematics - the way to success is clear and unilinear for the initiated. And because the standard solutions to problems of mathematics and calculation on paper look identical for sets of problems, it is easily assumed that what goes on or has to go on in the head of the learner, the child, is uniform too. Whoever thinks that for the child there is only one way to solve a mathematical problem and that creative originality has no place in elementary mathematics should read Selter's and Spiegel's book, which well merits an English translation.

Let us begin with an example.

A seven year old boy - Rohit - has to add the following numbers:

9 12 10 11 8 10 9 8 12 11 10 12

He comes up with this answer:

119 121 121 122 120 120 119 117 119 120 120 122

and asks the teacher if it is right. It is! However, it will take the reader some time to find out what Rohit exactly did.

By this we can show that children calculate differently:

than we do;

than we assume;

than other children do;

than they did before.

In the second chapter they give examples to illustrate these four points of view. In the next chapter they describe children's methods to handle several specific problems.

Chapter four consists of extensive transcripts of interviews with children, which are subsequently partly analysed - some analysing being left to the reader. The authors end with a chapter devoted to methodological questions concerning interviews with children. I will not go into every detail of the book, but concentrate on several points which seem to me particularly interesting or instructive for those engaged in doing philosophy for children.

The authors start from the assumption that - even if the thinking steps of children are sometimes difficult to understand or reconstruct - a rational thinking process underlies even their errors. "Errors should not be considered as flaws which should be eradicated as soon as possible or - even better - nipped in the bud. Instead, we should understand them as integrating part of a constructive learning process."

"We are of the opinion that one can considerably disrupt children's thought if one immediately tries to correct them."

This is particularly clear in one of the experimental sequences, where children are asked to solve 'impossible' word problems - 'impossible', because there is no solution Word problems are problems of the type: "At the start of a sea voyage the captain has one and a half times the combined age of his two members of crew.

After a voyage of five years they return and on return the age of the captain is exactly the combined age of his members of crew. How old is the captain on return?" Instead, the children have to solve problems like: "A shepherd has 19 sheep and 13 goats. How old is the shepherd?" In the fourth class 60% of the children 'solve' this kind of problem, whereas in the first class only 10% do so. Obviously - the authors conclude - the attitude of the children towards the problems was shaped by school instruction and, moreover, they had learned that mathematical problems have very little to do with reality and have to be solved, no matter how.

The authors and their student collaborators make use of the so-called 'clinical' method coined by Piaget, of which the aim is to reconstruct the thinking process of the children interviewed - which is not to say the authors underline Piaget conclusions. Even a transcript of the most sensitive interview requires, however, an interpretation and the authors explicitly warn for the many mistakes the investigator can make here.

Their purpose, of course, is research into thinking processes by means of interviews – a situation very different from classroom discussions in a community of inquiry -, but the amount of detailed observations and reconstructions makes the commentary on the interviews nevertheless highly instructive for philosophers.

Particularly treacherous is the fact that children not only think differently, but create their own terminology - and in mathematics even their own notation - to express their thought. The details of their analyses here are very instructive for those engaged in philosophy for children too. Not only instructive, but also amusing in this respect is a part of the book which would not be easy to translate into English. In German (and also in Dutch) for numbers between 20 and 100 the units are expressed before the tens; so 21 is pronounced as one-and-twenty, where the 'and' is reduced to a barely perceptible 'n'. The hundreds, however, come first. So 102 is pronounced as 'hundred two', but 121 as 'hundred

CAUSES FOR SLOW LEARNING IN MATHEMATICS

According to Paiget (1949, 1958), children learn primarily by manipulating objects until the age of 12. If children are not taught math with hands-on methods, between years 1 and 12, their ability to acquire math knowledge is disturbed at the point when hands-on explorations were abandoned in favour of abstractions. This clearly sets them up for mathematical disabilities in the next developmental period of formal propositional operations.

Brain lateralization, or hemisphere specialization, takes place earlier in girls than in boys. Because of girls' social development away from spatial tasks, the maximum spatial capability of the right hemisphere is fixed in a premature stage of development. Research shows that girls are overspecialized in left-hemisphere functioning, and must talk through spatial-visualization tasks, resulting in slow, unnatural performance.

Psychologist, Julia Sherman, believes that earlier female verbal and reading development leads females to prefer verbal and reading teaching and learning approaches to non-verbal right-hemisphere problem solving approaches. Other researchers see spatial visualization as essential to all levels of math learning. These skills exist on a continuum from low-level, requiring no image transformation, to high-level, involving the visualization and mental manipulation of 3-dimentional figures. Research on athletes suggests that spatial visualization skills can be learned.

Gerstman Syndrome symptoms include acalculia, right-left disorientation, finger anomia, and agraphia. "The concurrence of these four findings in a right-handed patient strongly predicts pathology in the left parietal lobe, particularly the left supramarginal gyrus." Test calculation by asking the patient to subtract backwards from 100 by sevens (the "serial sevens test"), or, in the less well educated subject, to make change from a dollar. To test right-left orientation, ask the patient to show you his left (or right) hand, to show you your left (or right) hand, and to place his right hand on your left hand. To test for finger anomia, ask the patient to name the thumb, index finger, or little finger. Accept synonyms for the index finger, such as "pointer".

Problems in math processing are attributed to anomalies in specific regions of the brain. Gerstmann's syndrome of dysgraphia, dyscalculia, finger agnosia, and right-left disturbance involves the left parietal lobe. Anosognosia involves the right parietal lobe. Right-left disturbance involves the left hemisphere.

The right hemisphere of the brain contributes the ability to perceive shapes, remember musical phrases, think holistically, face recognition, and the reproduction of designs. The usually dominant left hemisphere, which controls the right side of the body, specializes in speech, the sequential tasks involved in reading, and numerical tasks. When the right hemisphere is malfunctioning, patients are able to read and write, but have difficulty recognizing faces and remembering geographical locations. The ladder are common symptoms co-morbid with dyscalculia.

GENETIC AND SOCIAL FACTORS

As with all abilities, math aptitude can be inherited or an inborn disposition. Studies of identical twins reveal close math scores. Research into exceptionally gifted individuals shows high levels of math knowledge in early childhood, unexplained by external influences. Family histories of mathematically "gifted" and "retarded" individuals, revealed common aptitudes in other family members.

Even the most "mathematically gifted" individual can be hindered by inadequate math education. Likewise, a "mathematically retarded" individual will not attain competency in math despite intensive systematic training.

On the social side, Cohn explains that having a disability

in math is socially acceptable. He asserts that math ability is regarded more as a specialized function than a general indication of intelligence. As long as one can read and write, the stigma and ramifications of math failure can be diminished and sufficiently hidden.

Sharma concurs- explaining that in the West, it is common to find people with high IQ's who shamelessly accept incompetency in math. At the same time, they find similar incompetence- in spelling, reading, or writing- totally unacceptable. Prevailing social attitudes excuse math failure. Parents routinely communicate to their children that they are "no good at math."

Sharma asserts that gender differences in math skills are due more to social forces than to gender-specific brain construction and function. He believes that gender differences can be eliminated by equalizing the activities and experiences of both boys and girls at every level of development. Sharma contends that it is the social forces- that direct a child's experiences and activities- which lead to the differences in the neurological sophistication of boys and girls.

For example, most studies show that girls do better than boys in math until the age of 12. Then boys dominate the subject. This difference can be explained by analyzing the gender-specific development of math prerequisite spatial orientation skills. The main reason for this is the methodology of teaching in pre-school and elementary grades, where focus is on fine-motor skill development.

Boys and girls are given ample opportunities to play with blocks, Legos, board games, and various materials requiring fine-motor coordination. Naturally, girls have better fine-motor skills early in their development. And the learning environment, at this point, exercises these skills.

But as the children age, social biases preclude boys and girls from choosing to play with certain things and in certain ways. At this point of divergence, objects and activities acquire definite gender appropriateness. Blocks, Legos, tree climbing, outdoor activities, and ball sports become "boy" activities. Dolls, playing house, dressing up, talking, cooking, reading, sewing, crafting, and planning social activities become "girl" activities. By avoiding intricate mechanical manipulations and "rough and tumble" physical activities, girls loose ground in spatial organization abilities.

Girls' more sedentary activities offer few exercises in space/motion judgement, symmetry, part-to-whole constructions, and development of visualization, muscle memory, and geometric principles. Meanwhile, boys are gaining ground in all of these areas- and their improving spatial organizational abilities better prepare them for mathematics tasks.

SCHOLASTIC FACTORS

Cambridge College dean, Mahesh Sharma, asserts that math outcomes are terrible for a number of reasons. Our mathematics curriculums are not reflecting what we know about how children learn mathematics. Typical math curriculums are guided by chronological age. Math is presented in a pile up fashion. Each year, more math concepts are added to the pile of previously presented concepts. This is a tragic approach.

Sharma believes that teacher trainers are not bringing all the known aspects of math learning into the teacher preparation curriculum. New math teachers have not been taught the latest developments in learning theory and math conceptualization, and do not know how to use technology as a learning tool.

In the end, teachers teach as they were taught. Their teaching style reflects their own learning style. (It is natural to believe that everyone thinks like you do.) Teachers need to realise that if students are experiencing difficulty, they should ask themselves the following questions: Is my teaching style excluding students with certain learning styles? Are the methods and materials I am using appropriate for and compatible with the student's cognitive level and learning style? Has the student mastered requisite skills and concepts?

Recent studies show that student achievement is strongly influenced by teacher levels of expertise. An expert teacher's students perform 40% better than students of a novice teacher. Presently, the average K-8 teacher has taken only 3 or less math or math education classes in college. Not even 50% of 8th grade math teachers have taken a single class on math teaching at this level, and 28% of high school math teachers lack a major or minor in math.

REMEDIAL MEASURES

The mathematical development of children with Down syndrome is largely uncharted territory and yet the experience of parents and teachers reminds us that children with weak syndrome can and do learn mathematics. In the 1970s, few children with DS had access to schooling and authorities in the field were still arguing whether education was possible! Three decades later, the specific area of mathematics education for DS children remains an emerging field.

In 2008, many children with DS in Australia attend their local school and are included in classrooms with their age peers. At present, little research information is available to guide teachers to provide the best opportunities for the children to learn mathematics. Some suggestions are provided in the resource list at the end of this article.

Down syndrome is one of the most common congenital chromosomal variations present in all populations, occurring approximately once in 700 births. Down syndrome results almost universally in intellectual impairment, although the extent of the disability varies. People with Down syndrome have been part of many research studies and a great deal is known about how they learn, their physical development and their acquisition of language. However, very little is known about their acquisition of mathematical concepts.

Against this background of limited DS research, there is a stark contrast with the burgeoning interest in the mathematical development of children in general early childhood settings in Australia. A number of Australian states have undertaken major projects to assess and provide early intervention in mathematics (some states focussing on Number) such as the Early Numeracy Project (Victoria), Count

Me In Too, Year 2 Net and First Steps. Through these projects, a considerable amount of data on the mathematical development of Australian children has been obtained

INTERVIEWING THE CHILDREN

In making decisions about the staging of the interviews, we were mindful of research that demonstrated the diminished performance of children when they were interviewed in clinical settings by researchers they did not know. Therefore, children were interviewed in a familiar setting in the presence of a parent. On one occasion, a teacher observed as well and, in another, a teacher aide was present.

Time was spent at the start of the interview chatting to the parent and the child. This allowed the interviewer the opportunity to become accustomed to the style of communication of the child. Some of the children appeared nervous at the start, although most were clearly excited.

SUGGESTION TO TEACHERS

It is exciting to see the study unfolding. There is an enormous amount of data resulting from the video taped interviews and conversations with parents to be analysed. The small sample allows us to study individual cases in detail. It is early days in the analysis of our data but we believe our suggestions may be helpful and further investigation will follow.

Taking a visual approach to number concept development

Young children with Down syndrome will come to school varying greatly in their language development. Many children will be using signing to support their developing spoken language. Even so, many already will be reading! Using methods proposed by authors such as Oelwein, children are taught to read using sight words and for many this has been observed as a first language, with speaking coming second and enhanced as a result. We believe this well researched approach to teaching reading (Buckley, 2000) can underlie an alternative approach to teaching counting.

Usually young children learn the oral count words first

and many typically developing children arrive at school being able to say long strings in the counting word sequence. For children with DS, this may not have occurred due to difficulties with oral language.

Our research suggests this does not mean they are unable to count. It may be that some of the children who are as yet unable to say the count word sequence are able to order numbers and so would appear to have some aspects of the number concepts.

Learners with DS are likely to have a relative strength in the visual learning mode. This can be used to support the development of the oral and symbolic aspects of number concept development: emphasis the visual by teaching the symbols (numerals) and the connection to the word. Oelwein advocates the approach of 'match, select and name' sequence.

Unit V

Methods and Teaching Aids

INDUCTIVE METHOD OF TEACHING

Inductive reasoning works the other way, moving from specific observations to broader generalizations and theories. Informally, we sometimes call this a "bottom up" approach (please note that it's "bottom up" and *not* "bottoms up" which is the kind of thing the bartender says to customers when he's trying to close for the night!). In inductive reasoning, we begin with specific observations and measures, begin to detect patterns and regularities, formulate some tentative hypotheses that we can explore, and finally end up developing some general conclusions or theories.

These two methods of reasoning have a very different "feel" to them when you're conducting research. Inductive reasoning, by its very nature, is more open-ended and exploratory, especially at the beginning. Deductive reasoning is more narrow in nature and is concerned with testing or confirming hypotheses. Even though a particular study may look like it's purely deductive (e.g., an experiment designed to test the hypothesized effects of some treatment on some outcome), most social research involves both inductive and deductive reasoning processes at some time in the project.

In fact, it doesn't take a rocket scientist to see that we could assemble the two graphs above into a single circular one that continually cycles from theories down to observations and back up again to theories. Even in the most constrained experiment, the researchers may observe patterns in the data that lead them to develop new theories.

In the process of induction, you begin with some data, and then determine what general conclusion(s) can logically be derived from those data. In other words, you determine what theory or theories could explain the data. For example, you note that the probability of becoming schizophrenic is greatly increased if at least one parent is schizophrenic, and from that you conclude that schizophrenia may be inherited. That is certainly a reasonable hypothesis given the data.

Note, however, that induction does not prove that the theory is correct. There are often alternative theories that are also supported by the data. For example, the behaviour of the schizophrenic parent may cause the child to be schizophrenic, not the genes. What is important in induction is that the theory does indeed offer a logical explanation of the data. To conclude that the parents have no effect on the schizophrenia of the children is not supportable given the data, and would not be a logical conclusion.

Deduction and induction by themselves are inadequate for a scientific approach. While deduction gives absolute proof, it never makes contact with the real world, there is no place for observation or experimentation, no way to test the validity of the premises. And, while induction is driven by observation, it never approaches actual proof of a theory. The development of the scientific method involved a gradual synthesis of these two logical approaches.

INDUCTIVE AND DEDUCTIVE REASONING

"Deductive reasoning" refers to the process of concluding that something must be true because it is a special case of a general principle that is known to be true. For example, if you know the general principle that the sum of the angles in any triangle is always 180 degrees, and you have a particular triangle in mind, you can then conclude that the sum of the angles in your triangle is 180 degrees.

Deductive reasoning is logically valid and it is the fundamental method in which mathematical facts are shown to be true.

"Inductive reasoning" (not to be confused with

"mathematical induction" or and "inductive proof", which is something quite different) is the process of reasoning that a general principle is true because the special cases you've seen are true.

For example, if all the people you've ever met from a particular town have been very strange, you might then say "all the residents of this town are strange". That is inductive reasoning: constructing a general principle from special cases. It goes in the opposite direction from deductive reasoning.

Inductive reasoning is *not logically valid*. Just because all the people you happen to have met from a town were strange is no guarantee that all the people there are strange. Therefore, this form of reasoning has no part in a mathematical proof.

However, inductive reasoning does play a part in the *discovery* of mathematical truths. For example, the ancient geometers looked at triangles and noticed that their angle sums were all 180 degrees. After seeing that every triangle they tried to build, no matter what the shape, had an angle sum of 180 degrees, they would have come to the conclusion that this is something that is true of every triangle. Then they would have looked for a way to prove it using deductive reasoning; that is, deduce it as a consequence of other known general properties of triangles.

In summary, then: inductive reasoning is part of the discovery process whereby the observation of special cases leads one to suspect very strongly (though not know with absolute logical certainty) that some general principle is true. Deductive reasoning, on the other hand, is the method you would use to demonstrate with logical certainty that the principle is true.

Both are necessary parts of mathematical thinking. If you just started with the known properties of triangles and played around with them aimlessly using deductive reasoning, it is unlikely you would discover the fact that the angle sum is always 180 degrees (though if you did happen to discover it that way, you'd know it for certain). However, by noticing that it's true in all the examples you've ever seen, inductive reasoning leads you to suspect that this fact is true. Then, once your suspicions have given you a target and a direction for your deductive reasoning, you construct your rigorous logical proof using deductive reasoning.

The deductive reasoning, inductive reasoning, and hypothetic-deductive or hypothesis testing are the three scientific methods, which are referred to by the generic name of the scientific method.

The first thing which caught my attention was the fact that the first two *scientific methods* have a problem as the name is difficult to distinguish, given that in a language context they can represent just one concept with two statements: *reasoning* in one direction or the other, from general to specific, or vice versa.

Logically, the problem derives from the conceptual difficulty of clearly separating the elements of a scientific reasoning from the other; obviously, the chosen terms do not help retain these two concepts of scientific method or scientific reasoning in the memory. The first name of the *third scientific method* does not help much either.

Both deductive reasoning and inductive reasoning can go from general to specific and vice versa, in one direction or the other. Both use logic and arrive to a conclusion. As a last resort, they always have philosophic substratum elements. Both tend to be susceptible to empirical testing.

Although the deductive reasoning or deductive logic is more appropriate of the formal sciences and the inductive reasoning of the empirical sciences, nothing prevents the indiscriminate application of a scientific method, or any other method, to a particular theory.

In my opinion, without trying to create a controversy on this subject, the fundamental difference of the *deductive method and the inductive method* is that the first aims to indicate, through pure logic, the conclusion in its entirety based on a few premises. So that the veracity of the conclusions is guaranteed; that is, if the applied logic is not invalidated. It is about the axiomatic model proposed by Aristotle as the *ideal scientific method*.

On the contrary, the inductive method creates laws based

on the observation of the facts, by generalizing the observed behaviour; actually, what achieves is a type of generalization without obtaining a demonstration of the aforementioned laws or set of conclusions through logic.

Such conclusions could be false and, at the same time, the partial application of logic carried out could maintain its validity. For that reason, the *inductive method* needs an additional condition; its application would be valid if there is no case that does not fulfill the proposed model.

The *hypothetical-deductive method,* or the hypothesis testing, does not raise any problems in principle, given that its validity depends on the results of the appropriate empirical testing.

The *hypothetical-deductive method* tends to be used to improve or clarify previous theories according to new knowledge where the model's complexity does not allow logical formulations. Therefore, it has a predominantly intuitive character and needs, not only in order to reject a theory but also to impose its validity, the contrasting of its conclusions.

One could suggest the deductive reasoning, intuitive reasoning, and hypothesis testing as denominations for the three main variants of the scientific method, or for that matter, any set of words that refer to their fundamental differences or elements and do not raise any problems for the linguistic memory. However, in the exposition I will stick to the nomenclature generally used.

The *General Theory of the Conditional Evolution of Life* fits in perfectly with a theory based on the hypothetical-deductive, or hypothesis testing method.

Darwin's theory of evolution, on the other hand, would fit in the inductive reasoning; but despite finding opposing examples, the scientific community does not invalidate it but adapted to square off any triangle. *Why would it be*?

As was previously mentioned, every theory should be able to withstand refutation; however, a theory that does not allow refutation by any conceivable fact is not scientific. The impossibility of disproving a scientific theory is not a virtue but a defect.

DEDUCTIVE METHOD OF TEACHING

Deductive reasoning works from the more general to the more specific. Sometimes this is informally called a "top-down" approach. We might begin with thinking up a *theory* about our topic of interest. We then narrow that down into more specific *hypotheses* that we can test. We narrow down even further when we collect *observations* to address the hypotheses. This ultimately leads us to be able to test the hypotheses with specific data — a *confirmation* (or not) of our original theories.

In the process of deduction, you begin with some statements, called 'premises', that are assumed to be true, you then determine what else would have to be true if the premises are true. For example, you can begin by assuming that God exists, and is good, and then determine what would logically follow from such an assumption.

You can begin by assuming that if you think, then you must exist, and work from there. In mathematics you can begin with some axioms and then determine what you can prove to be true given those axioms. With deduction you can provide absolute proof of your conclusions, given that your premises are correct. The premises themselves, however, remain unproven and unprovable, they must be accepted on face value, or by faith, or for the purpose of exploration.

SYNTHETIC METHOD

A type of method of "treating at, and working at, scientific cognitions", opposed to the analytic method. The synthetic method goes from principles to consequents, from the simple to the composite. Also called the progressive method.

A straightforward heuristic-oriented method for stream tearing is proposed in this work. It does not use the traditional methods of evolutionary process-cycle analysis. First, an edge (stream) weighted *spanning-tree* is constructed from the *process graph* using weights based on the 'in' and 'out' degrees of the process digraph vertices. Second, a *directed acyclic graph* (*DAG*) is constructed such that it is the maximum edge (stream) acyclic sub-set of the process digraph. The *DAG* is constructed by adding ('put-back'), where possible, directed edges (streams) not already in the spanning-tree. A hierachial ordering based on the same preferential weighting system as the *spanning-tree* determines the sequence of the 'put-back' trials.

The remaining edges which cannot be 'put-back' into the *DAG* form a tear set. The weighting system used formed a *minimal cardinality* tear set in all of the examples tested. Pre-partitioning of the network into strongly connected components is not required and a node computational order is easily derived. Further, the method is extended to produce tear sets which minimise another set of stream weights, in this case the variables per stream. While the scheme proposed in this paper is heuristic-oriented, most of its methods are contained in classical graph theory and are consequently easily reproduced with efficient algorithms.

A synthetic estimator is one of the simplest estimators for a small area, and it has several variants. In this paper, a ratio-synthetic estimator is proposed and compared with the existing synthetic estimator (Ghangurde & Singh, 1977) and it is observed that the gain due to stratification in the case of a synthetic estimator reduces proportional to the domain coverage.

HEURISTIC METHOD

The first heuristic suggests that we make it a habit to purposefully pause and notice things because we know that our automatic perception processes miss a great deal of what goes on around us. The importance of learning to perceive the world in a fresh way is clearly a part of the generally accepted theory of creative thinking. If creative thinking is the novel association of existing concepts in memory, then it follows naturally that it is useful to create a storehouse of concepts. When you pause and notice, you are not looking for anything in particular.

A rule of thumb, simplification, or educated guess that reduces or limits the search for solutions in domains that are difficult and poorly understood. Unlike algorithms, heuristics do not guarantee optimal, or even feasible, solutions and are often used with no theoretical guarantee.

Heuristic is the art and science of discovery and a rule of thumb, simplification, or educated guess that reduces or limits the search for solutions in domains that are difficult and poorly understood. Unlike algorithms, heuristics do not guarantee optimal, or even feasible, solutions and are often used with no theoretical guarantee. 2. (algorithm) approximation algorithm. The word comes from the same Greek root as "eureka", meaning "to find". A heuristic is a way of directing your attention fruitfully.

The mathematician George Polya brought heuristics into popularity in the twentieth century in his book How to Solve It. He learned mathematical proofs as a student, but didn't know how mathematicians think of proofs, nor was this taught. How to Solve It is a collection of ideas about heuristics that he taught to math students: ways of looking at problems and casting about for solutions that often lead somewhere fruitful very quickly.

In computer science, a heuristic is an algorithm or procedure designed to solve a problem that ignores whether the solution is provably correct, but which usually produces a good solution or solves a simpler problem that contains or intersects with the solution of the more complex problem.

A heuristic is not guaranteed always to solve the problem, but often solves it well enough for most uses, and often does so more quickly than a more complete solution would.

More formally, a *heuristic* is a function, defined on the nodes of a search tree, which serves as an estimate of the cost of the cheapest path from that node to the goal node. Heuristics are used by informed search algorithms such as Greedy Best-first search and A* to choose the best node to explore.

Greedy Best-first search will choose the node that has the lowest value for the heuristic function. A* will expand nodes that have the lowest value for, where is the (exact) cost of the path from the initial state to the current node.

When h(n) is admissible - that is if never overestimates the costs of reaching the goal - A* is provably optimal.

The classical problem involving heuristics is the n-puzzle. Commonly used heuristics for this problem include counting the number of misplaced tiles and finding the sum of the manhattan distances between each block and its position in the goal configuration.

HEURISTIC PROBLEM SOLVING

Many heuristics are extremely clever, taking great advantage of the particular structure of the problem to be solved (by the way, I make a distinction between *problems* and *instances*. A problem is a set of instances. Generally, we will look at heuristics for problems, though sometimes a particular instance is important enough to justify heuristics for itself. Furthermore, heuristics for an individual instance can often be generalized to a larger problem).

But it is equally important to find general methods of creating heuristics. These provide quick and dirty solutions to many problems. Although the solution quality may not be the best, often they work well enough. In this section, we will examine some general heuristic techniques. These are random, greedy and exchanging methods. The first two are *solution generation* methods, while the last is a *solution improvement* method. Again, I will illustrate these ideas with the traveling salesman problem, but these are very general heuristic techniques. I will illustrate the heuristics using the example in figure.

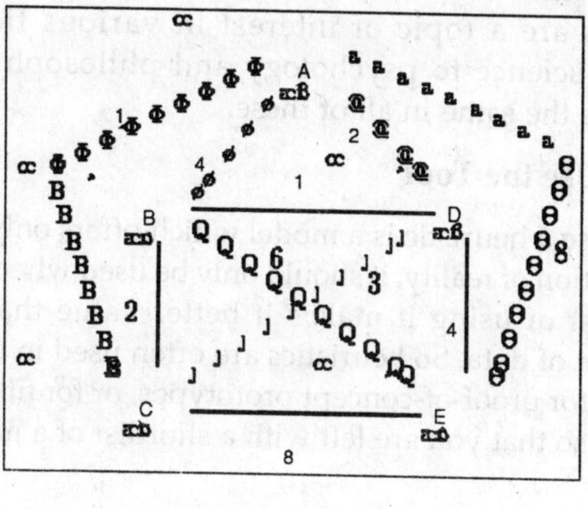

HEURISTIC METHOD

Most of us use "rules of thumb" in all sorts of areas of our daily lives. "When the needle on the fuel level indicator gets to the red, I know it'll last at least another 20 miles", for example, or "Software with a user interface that's anything other than grey or blue hardly ever gets through the user acceptance testing."

These rough rules, based on experience, are invaluable because they help us to make decisions without further detailed fact-finding: Drivers know they don't need to divert immediately to find a fuel station, and the software designer can save him or herself rework later by making the interface blue or grey in the first place.

But no one expects these rules to be 100% accurate: If the car ran out of fuel in 18 miles, the driver wouldn't be particularly surprised, and if testing showed that users actually liked an application that had a tasteful green interface, the developer might raise an eyebrow, but that would be all.

This is because rules of thumb are only used in situations where the risks associated with using a "good enough" approximation are acceptable. No one would use a rule of thumb such as this fuel usage one for a F1 racing car: They'd do a detailed analysis of the exact amount required to cover the race distance.

The formal term for these rules of thumb is "heuristics". Heuristics are a topic of interest in various fields from computer science to psychology and philosophy, but the principle is the same in all of these.

When to Use the Tool

Because a heuristic is a model which offers only a limited representation of reality, it should only be used when the speed or low cost of using it makes it better value than using a detailed set of data. So heuristics are often used in calculating estimates, for proof-of-concept prototypes, or for filtering a set of options so that you are left with a shortlist of a manageable size.

Constructing a Heuristic

Heuristics need to be formalized if they are to be most useful. This raises them above the level of "gut instinct", and it also means that they can be shared with other people.

When you find yourself using your experience to make a judgment, try to work out the rule of thumb that you've just invoked. If possible, add this to your procedure manual, or talk about it with a colleague so that your experience is validated and passed on.

A typical example in a car breakdown call centre might be, "25% of all reported breakdowns are caused by running out of fuel, so always start by asking the driver to check this before you schedule a mechanic."

In this case, using the heuristic allows a certain proportion of breakdowns to be "fixed" immediately, which means that the limited number of mechanics can focus on the real breakdowns. Heuristics can also be created specifically to solve a problem. For example, creating a diagram or straw man showing a possible solution will help you identify where your basic idea doesn't work, or is lacking some important feature, so that you can refine it more easily.

Another heuristic approach is to take a solution to another problem, and adapt it to solve yours. TRIZ is a systematic and highly developed approach for doing this.

Heuristic Checklists

Whether heuristics are used to filter a large number of options down to a manageable number, or whether you want to make an early "go/no go" decision, you will usually need to draw up a checklist of heuristics, rather than simply use an individual rule of thumb.

For example, in the food industry, the following heuristics might help the product development team decide whether it's worth investing in taking a new pie to the test marketing stage:

Does the pie look appetizing in its packaging?

Can it be packaged so that it won't be damaged in transit?

Can it be cooked in under 20 minutes, so that busy people will buy it?

Is its shelf life at least 5 days from manufacture to "use by" date?

Does it maintain its integrity when sliced (or will the pastry topping fall apart when being transferred to a plate)?

This type of list will have been developed based on experience of previous products, and from market research. Of course, there's no guarantee that a pie that meets all these criteria will prove to be a success: it might not taste as good as rival products, and so not attract repeat sales, or the mix of filling ingredients might make it too expensive. However, the heuristic checklist will help the development team quickly and cheaply weed out "non-starters".

Key Points

Heuristics or "rules of thumb" are models based on experience. When you use heuristic, it's important to remember that these models have their limitations, and so heuristics should not be applied in situations where there is a high degree of risk associated with making the wrong choice.

The term "heuristic methods" can be used to describe any problem solving or creativity technique that involves creating a basic model as a starting point for further experimentation or refinement. Heuristic methods are trial-and-error approaches.

ROLE OF HEURISTIC METHOD IN "DIFFERENTIAL DIAGNOSES" IN STRUCTURING CLINICAL DECISIONS

Designers of computer-based diagnosis programmes often view the physician's primary decision-making task as one of 'differential diagnosis." This term refers to a type of analytical task wherein the decision maker is confronted with a fixed set of diagnostic alternatives. His job is to determine whether sufficient data are available to make a decision among elements of this set and if not, to obtain whatever additional data may be required to make a decision.

Over the past two decades, a large number of specialized procedures have been developed to assist the physician in the differential diagnosis of a variety of well defined clinical problems. These have been extensively reported in the medical and computing literature. In addition, algorithms to deal with a host of common medical problems, expressed by means of detailed flowcharts, have increasingly found their way into the leading textbooks of medicine.

Many different techniques have been used in structuring these clinical algorithms. In some cases, special programmes have been formulated to capture the logic involved in the workup of particular classes of clinical problems. In other cases, generalized procedures have been adopted that are tailored to a particular application by specification of certain parameters; for example, many diagnostic programmes have been developed to use the normative models of statistical decision theory.

Evaluative studies frequently show that these programmes, whatever their basis, generally perform as well as experienced clinicians in their respective domains, and somewhat better than the non-specialist. It is interesting, therefore, to speculate on the reason that such programmes have not had greater impact on the practice of medicine.

Resistance in the medical community is sometimes attributed to the natural conservatism of physicians, or to their sense of being threatened by the prospect of replacement by machine. Some have argued that this can be resolved only on the basis of education and training, and that the next generation will be more comfortable with computer-based decision aids as these become routinely introduced into the medical school curriculum.

A very different explanation of the failure of acceptance of these systems has been voiced by Feinstein, who argues rather forcefully that the real reason that physicians have not adopted computer-based decision aids is that these have often been based on unrealistic models, which fail to deal with the physicians' real problems. Fein stein delivers a harsh indictment, which is close to the mark:

Mathematical enthusiasts could make substantial contributions to clinical medicine if the efforts now being expended on Bayesian and decision-analytic fantasies were directed to the major challenges of algorithmically dissecting clinical judgment, based on the way the judgments are actually performed. Instead, however, the enthusiasts usually become infatuated with the mathematical processes and with the associated potential for computer manipulations, so that the basic clinical challenges become neglected or evaded....

Perhaps the most shocking aspect of all this ethereal model-building is that the model-builders (and the editors of influential medical journals) have begun to confuse the difference between clinical reality and abstract imagery. In the customary standards of science, a model that failed to fit reality was rejected and the model-builder was sent back to the drawing board. Today, however, in the Procrustean era made possible by confusion about modern technology, a model-builder can avoid the constraints of reality and demand, instead, that reality adapt itself to fit the model.

I believe that the real issue is that the models underlying use of most diagnostic programmes require that the physician know—*a priori*—which is the correct differential diagnosis. While this is often the case, such well structured tasks generally do not constitute situations in which the physician requires diagnostic consultative assistance. The cases where expert assistance is really needed are those that entail diagnostic quandaries, where the physician is unsure as to the structure of his diagnostic problem.

There are many reasons why the physician might experience difficulty in formulating an appropriate differential diagnosis. It may be that the case involves a rare disease or unusual presentation. Often, such difficulties arise in clinical problems where two or more disease processes are at work, generating a plethora of abnormal findings that can be interpreted in a great variety of ways.

It might be argued that patients rarely have two or more significant diseases to be diagnosed. However, even in the case of an uncomplicated instance of disease, there are invariably some discrepant findings that arise due to misrepresentation by the patient or his family, the residual effects of a prior disease episode, or the occurrence of false positive laboratory results. Not uncommonly, apparent discrepancies can be attributed to an incomplete knowledge of the disease on the part of the physician and/or the biomedical community. Thus the process of sorting patient data into even two partitions (the relevant and the "red herrings") is often difficult for the physician. Where there is the potential for multiple concurrent diseases, this partitioning becomes ever more difficult.

Although these ubiquitous sources of error often make it problematic to determine whether or not one is actually working on the right problem, studies of human cognition have often revealed a strong bias towards the maintenance of initial problem formulations, even in some cases in the face of overwhelming evidence to the contrary. Thus it is not surprising that even skilled physicians sometimes need assistance in drawing out the full range of alternative formulations of a diagnostic problem.

What renders current computer-based consultation programmes less than useful to the medical community is their failure to deal with this creative aspect of the "art" of medical reasoning.

Modeling the "Art" of Diagnostic Reasoning

Physicians often refer to their clinical decision making process as more art than science, and suggest that while computers might be programmemed to deal with the scientific, analytical aspect of their work, they will never be able to capture the "art" of a skilled clinician.

The question of what it is that distinguishes the expertise of an accomplished clinician has been investigated by a variety of techniques both in our laboratory and elsewhere. One nearly universal finding is that the physician responds to cues in the clinical data by conceptualizing one or more diagnostic tasks which then play an important role in the subsequent decision making process. This conceptualization then governs to some extent the acquisition of additional data and the range of alternatives considered in the eventual diagnostic decision making process. One mark of an expert is his ability to formulate particularly appropriate differential diagnostic tasks on the basis of sometimes subtle hints in the patient record.

Recent studies of clinical cognition shed some light on the role of problem formulation in medical reasoning. While these studies typically show that physicians employ strategies of information gathering that are organized in response to a set of well structured differential diagnostic tasks, these analyses also show that physicians generate tasks early in the patient encounter, long before definitive data are available to ensure that the hypothesized task is indeed an appropriate one to pursue in the case at hand. It appears that the cognitive benefits of having a concrete task as a focus for the patient workup significantly outweigh the occasional need to reconceptualize, discarding one line of attack and invoking another.

In their analysis of the tape recorded behaviour of experienced physicians engaged in "taking the present illness" from a simulated patient, Kassirer and Gorry have observed:

The most striking aspect of the history-taking process revealed by the protocols is the sharp focus of the clinicians problem-solving behaviour. The subjects generated one or more working hypotheses early in the history-taking process when relatively few facts were known about the patient.... The process of hypothesis activation dominated the early part of the diagnostic session as the physicians searched for a context in which to proceed.... Identifying a context through the process of hypothesis activation appears to be one of the critical features of the diagnostic process. When a hypothesis was activated, the physician appeared to use this context—that is, his concept of a disease, a state, or a complication as a model with which to evaluate new data from the patient Such a model provides a basis for expectation; it identifies the relevant clinical features that should prove fruitful for farther investigation.

Similar patterns of behaviour have also been discovered by Elstein *et al.* in their study of medical problem solving. Quoting from the summary of their observations of physicians engaged in the analysis of clinical problems:

Diagnostic problems are solved through a process of

hypothesis generation and verification. Hypotheses are consistently generated early in a workup when only a very limited data base has been obtained. While any early formulation may be revised or discarded if subsequent data fail to confirm it, there is a high probability that at least some of the formulations of experienced physicians will be correct. Hypotheses serve as organizing rubrics in working memory. They help to overcome limitations of memory capacity and serve to narrow the size of the problem space that must be searched for solution. Since it would be impossible to conduct an efficient inquiry without some hypothetical goal that would tell the inquirer when to stop, hypotheses serve to transform an open medical problem

The early generation of diagnostic problem formulations would appear to be a major strategy that is used by physicians to determine the regions of the potential problem space that are most likely to yield a solution. In sum, we may propose that a set of problem formulations defines the dimensions of the functional problem space in which a physician's search for a diagnosis is conducted.

Dependent Strategies for Clinical Decision

The physician's concept of a diagnostic task establishes a context for a number of clinical decisions. For example, if he believes that the diagnostic task consists of selecting one of (X? or Y? or Z?) and he is able to rule out X and Y as possibilities, then (if his premises are correct) it follows that Z must be the case. This form of reasoning-by a process of elimination-is a powerful decision making strategy. By bounding the set of alternatives, then invoking procedures to gather additional information in order to eliminate candidates from the postulated decision set it is often possible to reach a positive conclusion concerning the remaining alternative without the need for definitive confirmatory evidence. This can be important to the patient, particularly when the clinching data would be costly to obtain or entail unnecessary risk of complications.

In some cases, the context of questioning can even turn

otherwise nonspecific findings into information items of diagnostic importance. For example, a finding of hepatitis B surface antigen in the blood does not ordinarily carry with it an implication of disease, because a fair portion of the population are unaffected carriers of the virus. In a setting of significant liver disease, however, where the physician's differential diagnosis encompasses various forms of inflammatory liver involvement, the finding of hepatitis B antigen might very well be considered definitive evidence as to the etiology of the illness. Similarly, in any task setting where there are but two alternatives (X? or Y?) if there is some abnormal finding that is a sine qua non for X which is found to be normal in the patient, this normal finding becomes diagnostic for concluding Y. Such reasoning is often at work in deciding between organic and functional (or psychosomatic) etiologies of an illness.

Perhaps the most important consequence of the physician's conceptualization of a diagnostic problem is the role that such a problem solving context plays in determining the strategy to be used for information acquisition: What questions should be asked of the patient and his family? What tests should be run? What therapeutic trials might provide useful information? What invasive procedures are absolutely necessary because of the importance of the data that only they can reveal? What data can safely be ignored?

Often, once the right questions have been asked and the right data obtained, the diagnostic decision becomes obvious to even the least experienced medical trainee. What distinguishes an expert is his ability to sense important omissions in the data that can often be filled in simply by asking the right questions. (The value of an item of information is not always well correlated with the cost of obtaining it.) When he does seek information that entails significant cost or danger to the patient, the expert clinician often has a good idea what the outcome will be, and is mainly seeking confirmation of his diagnosis. The real challenge in dealing with difficult medical problems is to identify and elicit those few critical findings that will clinch the case.

In considering the value of information, the physician often is concerned with an additional dimension, namely the reliability of the source. To what extent, for example, should a physician accept a patient's recollection of hospitalization twenty years previously, as opposed to a careful review of the day-to-day patient record that now resides in some musty archive. Clearly, the patient's recollection can be faulty and based on misconceptions: yet, unless there is reason to question the validity of such "hearsay" testimony, the physician dealing with the present illness rarely finds it necessary to go back to the source.

If, as most studies of clinical cognition seem to suggest, physicians make decisions concerning the acquisition of data and thereby determine diagnostic judgments on the basis of hypothesized problem contexts, it is clear that a potential exists for serious error due to the influence of the rationalization processes described above. For such context dependent decision strategies as the "process of elimination" to be effective, the physician's concept of the diagnostic task must either be correct at the outset or capable of transformation into the right task definition as additional evidence is developed and the case unfolds. Otherwise, physicians misled by inappropriate problem formulations may screen out and dismiss what might have been seen to be extremely important findings if viewed from another perspective; more likely, they are apt to neglect to inquire about those items of history and physical exam that might have corrected the context, if they were known.

Consultation with other specialists when evaluating difficult clinical problems helps to restore a breadth of perspective to ensure that reasonable alternatives to the primary physician's conceptualization of the problem will not be overlooked. Such formative support is not provided by most existing diagnostic consultation programmes, which-as noted earlier-deal primarily with the process of decision making in well structured situations where the differential diagnosis is given a priori. These programmes provide little if any assistance with respect to the more challenging business of formulating the differential diagnostic tasks that constitute the clinician's decision making context.

Structure of Ill Structured

A standard posture in artificial intelligence work, and in theorizing in this field, has been to consider only the idealized problems, and to leave the quality of the approximation and the processes for formulating that approximation to informal discussion outside the scopes both of the theory and of the problem solving programmes.

He defends this strategy as being "common to many fields of intellectual endeavor," but acknowledges:

It encourages allegations that the "real" problem solving activity occurs while providing a problem with structure, and not after the problem has been formulated as a WSP.

After pointing out that even within a well structured task environment, problem solvers can be repeatedly challenged by a sequence of tasks that do not require any reformulation of the problem space, Simon concludes:

Nevertheless, there is merit to the claim that much problem solving effort is directed at structuring problems, and only a fraction of it at solving problems once they are structured.

To show that the process of ill structured problem solving is not totally beyond the methods of artificial intelligence, Simon then proceeds to consider a number of problems that would generally be regarded as ill structured (e.g., composing a fugue and designing a house) and suggests a model that might be used to describe the reasoning process involved.

I should like to quote at some length from what Simon has to say concerning this class of ill structured problems in order to highlight what I find to be a compelling analogy between his characterization of the creative reasoning process of the artist, and what I understand of the reasoning process of the diagnostician. In both cases, the decision maker is engaged in an underconstrained endeavor that often requires the imposition of plausible (though not necessarily essential) constraints so that well understood decision strategies might be applied. The difficulty of starting off with a blank sheet of paper is well appreciated in all such endeavors.

It will generally be agreed that the work of an architect—in designing a house, say—presents tasks that lie well toward the ill structured end of the problem continuum. Of course this is only true if the architect is trying to be "creative"—if he does not begin the task by taking off his shelf one of a set of standard house designs that he keeps there.

The design task (with this proviso) is ill structured in a number of respects. There is initially no definite criterion to test a proposed solution, much less a mechanizable process to apply the criterion. The problem space is not defined in any meaningful way, for a definition would have to encompass all kinds of structures the architect might at some point consider.... even if we were to argue that the problem space can really be defined—since anything the architect thinks of must somehow be generated from or dredged from, his resources of memory or his reference library—some of this information only shows up in late stages of the design process after large amounts of search; and some of it shows up, when it does, almost accidentally.

Hence, the problem is even less well defined when considered from the standpoint of what is actually known at any point in time than when considered from the standpoint of what is knowable, eventually and in principle.

Simon then characterizes the progressive development of an architectural design, as additional data are developed and additional constraints imposed.

We can imagine a design process that proceeds according to the following general scheme. Taking the initial goals and constraints, the architect begins to derive some global specifications from them-perhaps the square footage or cubic footage of the house among them. But the task itself, "designing a house," evokes from his long-term memory a list of other attributes that will have to be specified at an early stage of the design: characteristics of the lot on which the house is to be built, its general style, whether it is to be on a single level or multi-storied, type of frame, types of structural materials and of sheathing materials, and so on. Design alternatives can also be evoked in component-by-component fashion. The subgoal of designing the beating system may lead the architect to consider various fuels and various distribution systems. Again, the source of these generators of alternatives is to be found in his long-term memory and reference facilities (including his access to specialists for helping design some of the component systems).

The whole design, then, begins to acquire structure by being decomposed into various problems of component design, and by evoking, as the design progresses, all kinds of requirements to be applied in testing the design of its components. During any given short period of tame, the architect will find himself working on a problem which, perhaps beginning in an Ill structured state, soon converts itself through evocation from memory into a well structured problem.

My observation of the diagnostic reasoning process suggests that the physician, like the architect, may at any one time be observed to be working on a problem, which though initially ill structured has been converted into a well structured task through the evocation and imposition of constraints that progressively bound the set of possible decisions. There is, however, a significant difference between these task domains in that for the architect, there is no one correct solution to the design problem. When the architect imposes an arbitrary constraint-though this reduces the degrees of freedom concerning the range of possible designs-one can generally be assured that the outcome will be a structure that meets at least some minimum set of requirements. If the physician invokes arbitrary constraints, however-so as to make his solution space more manageable-the outcome can be quite seriously compromised.

This is what makes it especially important that the medical decision maker be provided some means for assessing the consequences of alternative problem structuring constraints, a consideration that may or may not be of concern to the architect

General Model

In order to account for the creative, problem finding aspect of the ill structured problem solving process, Simon envisions a conceptual framework within which methods for the evocation and synthesis of problem structure would alternate with problem solvers of familiar kinds in the progressive definition, refinement, and eventual solution of such problems. Figure illustrates the interplay between the synthetic and analytic components of the process.

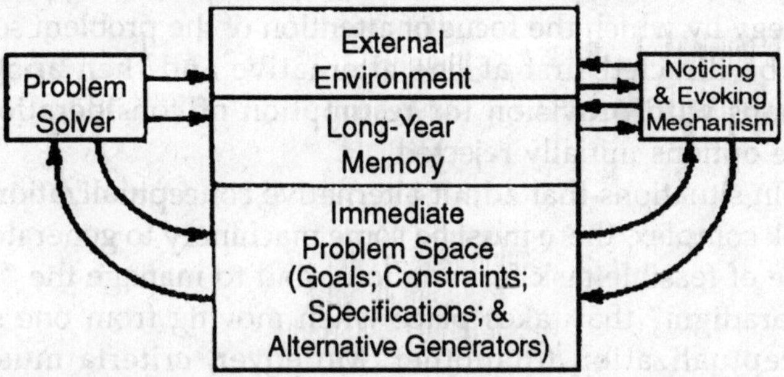

Fig. Schematic Diagram of a System for Ill Structured Problems. It Shows the Alternation between a Problem Solver Working on a Well Structured Problem, and a Recognition System Continually Modifying the Problem Space.

This model distinguishes two major facets of the reasoning process: a problem solver, which in a typical AI application might consist of a theorem prover or heuristic problem solving programme such as GPS [6], and a noticing and evoking mechanism, which monitors what is going on in working memory and modifies the problem space by fetching from long term memory (and/or the external environment) new constraints, new subgoals, new specifications, new generators of solution alternatives.

In order to characterize a particular ill structured reasoning system in terms of this general model, there are a number of features that must be specified more fully. One of the main things that needs to be defined is the mechanism by which elements of task structure are to be evoked from the system's long term memory. Depending upon the strategy chosen for this purpose, there must then be a determination of the goals and constraints that govern the selection and assembly of these structural fragments into complete (perhaps partial or multiple) task definitions.

Attention must also be given to the design of a problem solver that can be applied to the various complexes of tasks that might emerge.

A particularly important aspect of the overall design is what in the terminology of artificial intelligence programmeming is referred to as the "control regime," or strategy by which the focus of attention of the problem solver will be directed first at one alternative and then another, perhaps with provision for resumption of consideration of those options initially rejected.

In situations that admit alternative conceptualizations of a task complex, there must be some machinery to generate the space of feasible task formulations, and to manage the "shift of paradigm" that takes place when moving from one such conceptualization to another. Moreover, criteria must be developed by which to judge the various formulations of the task so as to guide the search process towards that task characterization which is actually correct. In addition, there must be some means of determining when this meta goal of the problem formulation process has been achieved.

Structuring of Medical Diagnostics

The model presented in the preceding section can be used as a basis for characterizing and contrasting a number of approaches to computer aided diagnosis that have been developed over the past two decades. The primary features distinguishing these diverse approaches include:

- The nature of the decision problem being dealt with.
- The procedure employed in the "problem solver" module.
- The allocation of responsibility to the user and to the computer for various aspects of the overall process, particularly with respect to the functions of "noticing and evoking," and the control strategy.

Degenerate Cases

The great majority of diagnostic programmes fall into a degenerate category, in that the entire computer-based procedure consists of the single module labeled "problem solver." The premise underlying use of such procedures is that the clinical problem can be encompassed by a fixed differential diagnosis; i.e., there is a given set of diagnostic possibilities, and it is a presupposition in using the programme that the patient has one and only one of the listed disorders. Another way of saying this is that the list of diagnostic possibilities is exhaustive and mutually exclusive, a necessary condition for the application of many statistical decision making strategies, notably Bayes' rule.

That part of the overall process that Simon refers to as "noticing and evoking," which deals with the evocation or formulation of diagnostic tasks in response to cues in the data, must be performed by the physician user of such a system without benefit of computer assistance. There are alternative approaches to the design of diagnostic programmes in which the computer plays a more active role in the generation of diagnostic tasks. The two principal methods that have been employed for computer-assisted evocation of diagnostic tasks are discussed in the following sections.

An interesting study was completed recently by Sherman, in which be compared the performance of two algorithms, one patterned after the MIT/Tufts Present Illness Programme (PIP), the other using the problem structuring and decision making strategies of INTERNIST-I. The former uses a decision strategy consistent with a binary choice task structure, while the latter employs a differential diagnostic strategy. Both algorithms were provided access to the same knowledge base of birth defects, and were run on the same set of diagnostic decision problems. Sherman's findings tend to corroborate the thesis advanced in the preceding discussion concerning the relative power of these two models of diagnostic decision making.

Perhaps the most troublesome aspect of employing a binary choice task structure for clinical decision making is the difficulty of interpreting the output of such a diagnostic procedure in cases where multiple diagnostic decisions are possible. Because disease hypotheses are not organized into decision sets by such a procedure, there is no guidance provided to the user concerning the assembly of a diagnostic complex; i.e., when the programme prints out a list of possibilities with associated scores, there is no indication whether they are to be considered conjunctive or disjunctive sets, or some combination thereof.

Thus in complex cases—where decision support is presumably most needed—diagnostic procedures based on binary choice decision strategies offer little assistance in shaping the physician's decision making context.

Direct Evocation of Differential Diagnostic Tasks

There is an alternative approach to the structuring of medical decisions that directly yields differential diagnostic task structures. In its most elementary form, this method would have the "noticing and evoking" mechanism of the decision making programme consider every abnormal finding encountered during the patient workup, and for each, create the task of determining the disease or pathological condition that is responsible for causing this abnormality.

For example, an observation of "fever" would evoke a differential diagnostic task encompassing a large number of diagnostic possibilities, including infections of all types, many forms of cancer, blood abnormalities, cardiovascular disorders, and a variety of diseases associated with abnormal immunity.

As this example suggests, the set of disease entities comprising a differential diagnosis tend to be aggregated-often on the basis of some common characteristic or similarity of presentation-into general diagnostic categories. One reason for such grouping is so that entire subcategories may be ruled in or ruled out on the basis of particularly discriminating questions. In the example of fever given above, one might narrow the range of diagnostic possibilities considerably by inquiring whether the patient had experienced shaking chills. An affirmative answer would usually serve initially to constrain the physician's differential diagnosis to some form of infectious process. Through a combination of training and experience, the clinician acquires a rich network of associations that serve to partition the space of possible diagnoses. These knowledge structures enable the clinician to develop his conceptualization of a clinical problem by working from what are initially broad descriptive characterizations through a succession of refinements until eventually specific disease entities are considered and assessed. This serves to limit the number of decision alternatives that need to be dealt with in the context of any particular evoked task.

Another factor serving to limit the apparent magnitude of the cognitive task associated with a differential diagnosis is that physicians invariably exploit the truism that "common things are common," which argues for consideration of diseases in the differential diagnosis on the basis of their prevalence, or frequency of occurrence in the population. Thus, while the complete differential diagnosis associated with a particular finding may encompass hundreds of diseases, only a few of the more common possibilities on this list are likely to occur to the physician when first encountering this complaint. The remaining alternatives hover in the background, to be brought into view only when the major contenders fall from favour for one reason or another.

The main problem with the direct evocation of differential diagnostic tasks, as outlined above, is that there would be as many diagnostic tasks to deal with as there are abnormal findings in the data. Although each such task has prima facie validity since every finding has to be explained in one way or another, no physician would seriously consider himself to be confronted with twenty diagnostic tasks in a patient with as many findings. Instead, he would most likely consider most of these data to be manifestations of the same underlying cause, and initially at least, proceed as though faced with but one diagnostic task.

This suggests that it might be useful to structure differential diagnostic procedures around certain combinations of findings, which, when they occur together in a patient, may be presumed to be part of the same underlying process. This approach has been investigated by Patrick *et al.* [14], who suggested use of "activation rules" that would be employed to evoke selected differential diagnostic tasks on the basis of patterns of findings.

There are difficulties with this approach to the structuring of diagnostic algorithms, which in certain respects are more serious than those discussed previously. In the case where a differential diagnostic procedure is designed to deal with a single abnormal finding, one can at least be assured that all possible explanations of that abnormality are potentially accessible to die algorithm: i.e., the differential diagnosis constitutes an exhaustive enumeration of all known causes of die given finding.

When algorithms are designed to be invoked on the basis of patterns of clinical or laboratory findings, however, many potential diagnoses become inaccessible: namely, those that fail to account for all of the data in the evoking pattern. Thus there is the danger that plausible explanations of a clinical problem that might involve alternative partitionings of the input data, with corresponding differences in the patterns of task evocation, will not be brought into "conscious" consideration.

Another way to attack this problem would be to maintain the discrete task definitions associated with each individual finding, but provide for the tentative merging or "synthesis" of multiple elementary task definitions into a single unified task, for purposes of guiding the workup and focusing the acquisition of additional information, The essential mechanism involved in the construction of such a "synthesized" differential diagnosis would be that of set intersection.

If some basis can be found for focusing on a particular subset of the data, then the differential diagnosis lists associated with each of the selected findings can be intersected to derive a much narrower list of prospective diagnoses, each capable of explaining that entire subset of the data.

Whenever the problem solver invokes an attention focusing maneuver aimed at narrowing in on the most probable region of the problem space, it must then set about to acquire additional evidence that will clinch the case. In this setting, the acquisition of additional information can be undertaken to serve two purposes. As in any case of a decision among elements in a decision set, information may be sought to help discriminate among these alternatives and to narrow the focus even further by eliminating elements from the set In addition, the premises underlying the choice of the selected decision problem may be put to the test by eliciting additional information that might help in either confirming or rejecting the problem focus as a whole.

It is important to keep in mind that the principle of parsimony, while often a useful heuristic guide to pursue in narrowing the focus of attention, is not in itself a valid basis for making final clinical judgments. Therefore, any diagnostic programme that permits narrowing of the problem solver's focus on the basis of purely heuristic maneuvers must make provision for those maneuvers to be undone. This means that a diagnostic problem structuring and solving procedure, which incorporates heuristic task combination methods, must also adopt the type of sophisticated control strategy often found necessary in other artificial intelligence programmes that rely on heuristic methods.

One aspect of our study has been investigation of knowledge structures that can be used to aggregate or "chunk" elements in a differential diagnosis. We have explored two conceptual frameworks that are commonly used to organize medical knowledge, both of which can be exploited to derive categories for classifying the alternatives in a diagnostic decision set.

One of these is the "causal graph," in which the concept of causality or pathophysiology is used to define a network of interrelated pathological states that might arise in the course of a disease. The other type of structure used to aggregate disease entities is the taxonomy of disease, also called a "nosology," which is used to classify disease entities on the basis of anatomical locus, etiological agent, or other discriminating characteristic.

The first programmes developed in our laboratory

employed an elaborate causal network to structure elements in a differential diagnosis: given a set of abnormal findings, a search procedure was used to scan the causal network, seeking opportunities to "synthesize" unifying hypotheses. For reasons that will be discussed presently, this approach encountered serious computational barriers to the process of task synthesis: i.e., the combining of multiple discrete tasks into unified task formulations. In subsequent developments, the incorporation of explicit causal mechanisms was dc-emphasized and an alternative approach to task structuring based on the use of nosologies. or taxonomies of disease categories, was pursued. This led to more efficient formulation of complex, synthesized task definitions, but proved deficient in the precision with which the attribution of findings to particular diseases could be assessed.

As our experience with both approaches to the structuring of medical knowledge has identified problems with each taken separately, current work on CADUCEUS is aimed at investigating the conceptualization of differential diagnostic problems in both causal and taxonomic terms.

To give somewhat more substance to the concepts being discussed, the following section provides some specifics concerning the implementation of the task structuring and decision making methods employed in the original INTERNIST-I system. This system constituted the point of departure for the investigation of issues in artificial intelligence and the representation of medical knowledge that has led to the general model of diagnostic reasoning presented in the preceding section. We shall return to consideration of the general model after sharpening the issues with a concrete case analysis and critique of INTERNIST-I.

Although not strictly interpretable as a measure of probability, for reasons that will be discussed presently, this weighting factor can be viewed as somewhat analogous to a posterior probability because it describes the relative likelihood of disease entities evoked on the basis of a single observation. As suggested by this analogy, the ordering of a differential diagnosis provided by evoking strength tends to reflect the a priori probability or prevalence of disease in the population.

The inverse of the EVOKES relation is also recorded explicitly in the knowledge base. By means of the MANIFESTS data structure, each disease entity is profiled with an associated list of manifestations known to occur in that disease, recorded along with an estimate (in this case recorded on a scale of 1-5) of the frequency of occurrence. Although it is not employed in the usual way to calculate posterior probabilities (the actual calculus used in combining these weights will be sketched in the following section), this weighting factor is strictly analogous to the conditional probability of a manifestation given a disease.

Other relations are defined on the set of disease entities to record the causal, temporal, and other patterns of association by which the various disease entities and distinguished pathological states are interrelated; these relations also incorporate weighting factors analogous to the evoking strength and frequency weights mentioned above.

The extent of pathophysiology represented in this fashion has been deliberately limited, however, because of the difficulties—alluded to earlier—which are encountered when the process of combining multiple elementary task definitions into unified task constructs requires search of a detailed causal graph. Thus, for the most part, the INTERNIST-I knowledge base has been structured so that abnormal findings evoke disease hypotheses directly without calling for consideration of any intermediate pathological condition.

Conceptually, this can best be thought of as the result of embedding information concerning the manifestations of the various pathological states associated with each disease within the profile of that disease. There are exceptions, however, as certain important syndromes and pathological states have been recorded in the INTERNIST-I knowledge base as separate entities (e.g., "ascites," "portal hypertension," " heart failure," "nephrotic syndrome") because of their well established clinical significance as points of departure for differential diagnosis.

The INTERNIST-I knowledge base also contains a nosologic hierarchy of disease categories, organized primarily around the concept of organ systems, having at the top level such categories as "liver disease," "lung disease," "kidney disease," etc. Each of these areas is divided into more specific categories, which may in turn be further subdivided any number of times until the terminal level representing individual disease entities is reached.

There are also several auxiliary relations defined on the class of manifestations to record properties of interest, such as the type of a manifestation (history, symptom, sign, or one of three designations of laboratory finding that reflect progressively greater cost and/or danger to the patient), its global importance (a measure of how important it is to account for that manifestation in a final diagnosis, recorded on a scale of 1-5), and its relation to other manifestations (such as the derivability of one from another).

Problem-Formation Method

The heuristic problem structuring procedure of INTERNIST-I is invoked repeatedly during the course of a diagnostic consultation in order to deal sequentially with the component parts of a complex clinical problem.

The process is as follows. First, during the initial input phase, patient data consisting of both positive findings and pertinent negative findings may be entered in any order and any amount. Each positive finding is used to evoke an elementary differential diagnostic task that may contain a mixture of individual disease nodes and higher level nodes of the disease hierarchy. Where a manifestation evokes one of the higher level category nodes, it is because that finding can be explained by all subnodes of the given category.

In order to detect the possibility of combining multiple tasks, each associated with a single abnormal finding, the INTERNIST-I programme uses a scoring procedure that awards credit to disease hypotheses on the basis of the number and the importance of elementary tasks that are unified by those hypotheses. In this scoring process, the evoking strength and importance of manifestations explained by a disease are counted in its favour; frequency weights count against those disease hypotheses in which the corresponding manifestations are expected but not found present.

Given a ranked list of disease hypotheses, a synthesized task definition is then formulated on the basis of the most highly rated of these items, using the following heuristic criterion: two disease entities are considered to be alternatives to one another (hence part of the same task definition) if, taken together, they explain no more of the observed findings than are explained by one or the other separately.

The set of alternatives so determined, with scores within a fixed range of the top ranked disease hypothesis on the list, are then composed into a differential diagnostic task, which becomes the focus of problem-solving attention.

The programme then selects questions that will help to discriminate among entities in the problem set. There are three major strategies that may be employed in selecting questions to be asked and identifying tests to be performed. When the set of decision alternatives contains five or more elements, a RULEOUT strategy is invoked, whereby the programme seeks negative findings that will help to disconfirm one or more elements in the set. If the decision set contains between two and four elements, the programme fixates on the leading two contenders and seeks information that will help separate them in score; this is referred to as a DISCRIMINATE information acquisition strategy. When only one alternative remains in the decision set, the programme embarks on a PURSUING strategy, whereby it seeks confirmatory data that will extend the separation of the leading contender from its nearest competitor above a given threshold value.

Once the programme has inquired about the selected information items and acquired additional positive or negative patient data, it then re-evaluates all diseases evoked (whether in or out of the current problem focus) on the basis of new information obtained, and then reformulates the differential diagnosis. Depending on which disease entity emerges as most highly rated on successive iterations of the process, the focus of attention may shift from one diagnostic task to another—but at any one time, there is a single problem under active consideration.

Whenever a diagnostic task becomes solved, its result is entered into a list of concluded diagnoses, all manifestations explained by that disease are marked "accounted for," and the process recycles until all problems present in the case have been uncovered and solved.

Because of causal, temporal, or other interrelationships, certain combinations of disease entities are more likely to occur than others. This fact is recognized in INTERNIST-I by the scoring algorithm, which, on each iteration of the process, gives additional weight to any disease entity that is in any way linked to some already concluded disease.

In the course of gathering additional information, it sometimes happens that the programme runs out of questions deemed useful for the strategy being pursued. If this happens while engaged in a PURSUING strategy, the programme renders a peremptory conclusion even though the desired threshold of separation has not been achieved.

If the programme exhausts its list of useful questions during a DISCRIMINATE or RULEOUT phase, however, it performs what we refer to as a "deferral." At this point, the set of findings used to define the current differential diagnostic task are set aside for the time being (as though a positive decision had been made that some unknown member of that decision set is actually correct) so that some other decision problem might be brought into consideration.

The hope, often borne out in practice, is that by solving a second—possibly related—decision problem, the programme might then go back to the deferred differential diagnostic task and make somewhat more progress in its resolution.

By virtue of this deferral mechanism, INTERNIST-I exhibits a limited capability for concurrent problem-formation and problem-solving, an important characteristic of human diagnostic behaviour about which more will be said later in the critique of INTERNIST-I performance.

Key Elements of INTERNIST Logic

Based on our observation of clinicians interacting with this model of diagnostic logic, we have come to understand what are the most important features of the model. The following elements have been found to affect in significant ways both the diagnostic behaviour of the system and its potential acceptability to the intended user community.

The scoring mechanism does not always lead to an appropriate task definition, however. as the procedure can be sensitive to the preponderance of data as well as the more relevant measures of specificity and importance. Thus it sometimes happens that important, specific data are "disregarded" by INTERNIST's problem focusing heuristic while less significant facts of the clinical problem are selected for investigation on the basis of a large volume of data, much of which might be of limited importance.

This brings us to consideration of the second most significant aspect of the INTERNIST-I logic, namely:

The only difficulty with this approach is that in complex cases, the programme often begins its analysis by considering wholly inappropriate tasks, on which it may spend an inordinate amount of time. This rarely leads to a false conclusion, but does prolong the sessions of terminal interaction unnecessarily. This phenomenon also dictates the use of a very conservative approach to the patient workup, as more aggressive strategies might seek costly items of information pertaining to an ill-advised initial conceptualization of a clinical problem.

Although it has the capacity to deal with multiple concurrent problems in due course, because of its sequential task formulation and decision making strategy, INTERNIST-I is generally not conscious at the outset of evidence concerning any problem other than the one initially formulated. This phenomenon is exemplified by the first few rounds of task definition in the preceding case analysis. Most clinicians reviewing the initial data would probably characterize the case as an acute febrile illness having hepatic, renal and systemic involvement. Given the further observation that the patient had recently been exposed to small wild animals, it is highly probable that most experienced physicians would "put it all together" and consider the possibility of leptospirosis involving multiple organ systems from the outset.

Unfortunately, one of the things that limits INTERNIST-I to the sequential formation and consideration of problems is also one of the features of the system most responsible for its robust behaviour, namely:

The reason for this is that under the heading "cholestasis" are recorded only those disease entities whose predominant mode of presentation is cholestatic. Other diseases that may present variously with some degree of cholestasis are scattered throughout the "liver disease" subtree and other regions of the hierarchy; e.g., alcoholic hepatitis resides under "hepatocellular inflammation" (its predominant facet), primary biliary cirrhosis is classified under "hepatic fibrosis," infectious mononucleosis and toxoplasmosis are structured under "infectious lymphadenopathies," etc.

As the INTERNIST-I hierarchy requires that each disease be recorded in one and only one place, the partitioning procedure was devised to group diagnoses when the basis for aggregation is other than the one used in structuring the hierarchy. Thus, whenever it postulates a differential diagnostic task, INTERNIST-I often gathers together disease entities from throughout the hierarchy, without regard for the a-priori groupings recorded there.

The main difficulty with this decision strategy is that the programme does not, and cannot in its present implementation. consciously question the validity of the postulated problem focus in the context of which its decision making process is being carried out. As mentioned previously, the programme often generates incorrect task definitions at the outset, but the relative ease and frequency with which the problem focus is reformulated generally guarantees that eventually an appropriate decision problem will emerge. There is nothing in the logic to ensure that this will happen, however, and this sometimes leads to incorrect diagnostic results.

The reason that the problem cannot be dealt with

effectively within the INTERNIST-I framework is the ephemeral nature of the task conjectures employed there. These *ad hoc* constructs have no substance outside the context of the particular case in which they emerge. Although clinicians viewing a decision problem formulated by INTERNIST-I may have no difficulty attaching an appropriate clinical label, and may even have very specific ideas about the proper way to work up such a problem—INTERNIST-l has no access to such problem-specific advice.

The only way to make such clinically relevant knowledge available to the programme would be to incorporate new knowledge structures containing explicit information about well structured differential diagnostic tasks, the disease entities they comprise, criteria useful in ruling alternatives either in or out, and specific advice where useful concerning die decision process that is to be followed relative to the postulated diagnostic task.

Inability to Test Conditional Attributions in the Associative Knowledge Structure of INTERNIST-I. Finally, there is a fairly serious problem that derives from the fact that in the INTERNIST-I knowledge base, much of the detail has been "compiled out," especially concerning the mechanisms by which particular abnormal findings happen to occur in the various diseases with which they are associated. It is not uncommon, therefore, to find within the same disease profile references to manifestations that indicate presence of a particular pathological condition, and also references to findings that might be expected to occur in the given disease only if that pathological state obtains. For example, the profile of "sinusoidal portal hypertension" includes the finding of "esophageal varices" (a type of abnormal vasculature in the walls of the esophagus), and also the finding of "hematemesis" (vomiting of blood), which can be explained by the portal hypertension only if the patient does indeed have varices.

This is a serious problem for several reasons. At times, it can cause the programme to give inordinate weight to a disease hypothesis because of a presumption concerning its ability to explain data, which a careful pathophysiological analysis would show to be incorrect. This can lead to inaccurate decisions. Moreover, even when it does not foster an erroneous result, mistaken attribution can prevent INTERNIST-I from pursuing additional diagnoses because it "thinks" everything has been adequately explained, when in fact this is not the case.

Another problem that results from the commingling of manifestations from many sources in a master disease profile is that this prevents the incorporation in INTERNIST-I of an effective time line, for assessing the fit of a patient's illness with the temporal pattern of a disease.

For adequate characterization of many disease processes, it is essential to be able to express temporal constraints with respect to the various facets of the illness; e.g., those elements comprising the prodrome should precede those of the active stage of the disease, otherwise the pattern does not fit.

To enforce such conditions on the attribution process would require the ability to make judgments concerning clinical and pathological descriptors which can be said to be true of the patient at certain points in time.

The problem with the INTERNIST-I representation is that there is not a convenient way to make the attribution of a finding to a disease conditional on the occurrence (or time of occurrence) of an intermediate state, without making the latter an explicit node in the causal graph.

But as we have already seen, the incorporation of additional intermediate states tends to obscure the potential for discovering unifying hypotheses, because of the sequential nature of the INTERNIST-I problem formulation and problem solving procedure.

We shall return to this point in more detail in the following sections, but for now the experience with INTERNIST-I in this regard can be summed up in the following somewhat paradoxical observation: a diagnostic reasoning programme must have access to detailed pathophysiological knowledge in order to permit the test of hypothesized attributions; however, if the programme is forced into consideration of the detailed pathophysiology, there is the danger that unifying gestalts may fail to emerge.

Towards a More Highly Structured Knowledge Base

One of the major lessons learned from our experience with INTERNIST-I is that it is necessary for the programme to be able to make decisions with respect to descriptors that partially constrain the space of alternatives; these decision points constitute loci of well structured sub-problems about which special procedures and other advice concerning decidability, significance, treatability, and other such matters may be organized.

In particular, it should be possible for the programme to establish milestones in the workup of a clinical problem by making judgments concerning nosological categories into which the illness falls. Also, as is presently the case in a somewhat limited form, the programme should be able to make judgments concerning pathological descriptors.

The design of a successor to INTERNIST-I that would deal with these issues has been under investigation for some time. In Pople [17], the general outline of an approach was provided. The idea proposed there was to exploit what came to be called "constrictor" relationships in the data that allow decisions to be made with respect to pathological and nosological descriptors, thereby setting in motion a number of parallel or concurrent differential diagnostic analyses.

Initially, it was hoped that the necessary constrictor patterns could be extracted from the original INTERNIST-I knowledge structure using heuristic mapping rules. This has not proved to be the case, however, because of two reasons: use of a strict hierarchy in INTERNIST-I for defining categories of diseases, which has served to make diffuse what would otherwise be strong constrictor relations; and elimination of pathophysiological detail which cannot be restored without a considerable investment of medical expertise. Both of these call for major revision to the structure of medical knowledge underlying the INTERNIST programme.

In this section, we review the major knowledge structures employed in clinical reasoning. We consider first a pure "causal" model of medical knowledge, detailing both the benefits provided by such a structure and the problems encountered in using this for conceptualizing the overall picture of what might be happening in a complex case.

We then consider a nosological structure, which provides for better general characterization of a clinical problem but, as noted previously, fails to provide sufficient detail of pathophysiology to enable critical evaluation and justification of hypotheses. Finally, we show how these two approaches can be combined to achieve a synergistic blend, yielding much of the benefit provided by each of the knowledge structuring principles. Using this combined knowledge structure, a general approach to the problem of task synthesis is then provided.

The Causal Network

In a typical pathophysiological model, manifestations of disease are organized on the basis of the pathological states giving rise to such observations, and these states are in turn organized into a causal network (a fragment of such a network is illustrated in figure.

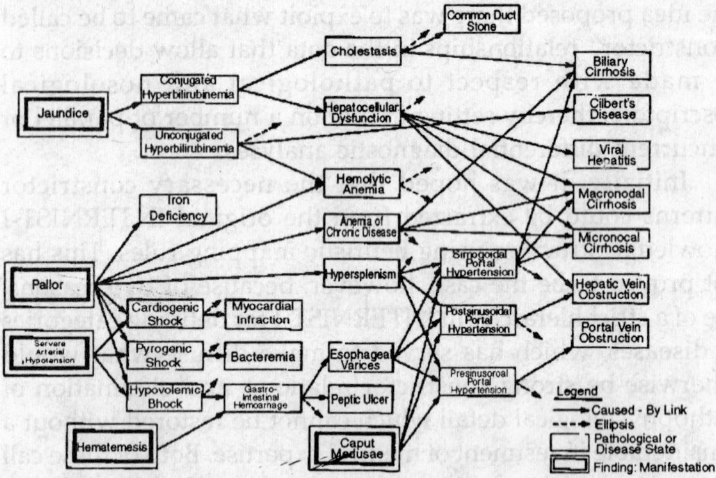

Fig. A portion of a causal network, which depicts the attribution pathways by which manifestations of disease can be accounted for in pathophysiological terms.

In this graph, arcs (links) are marked by arrowheads in the "caused-by" direction; thus, the links emanating from the node "jaundice" indicate that jaundice can be caused by either conjugated or unconjugated hyperbilirubinemia (a condition characterized by elevated levels of bilirubin in the blood). In order to emphasize the incompleteness of the graph, most of the nodes have dashed arrows coming from them which are to be interpreted as "and so forth." In the few cases where such ellipses are not shown, it should be understood that the set of causes explicitly shown constitutes an exhaustive set; e.g., in the case of "jaundice," and of "caput medusae.[16]

Nodes in the network having no successors in the "caused-by" relation represent specific disease entities (e.g., "common duct stone," "hepatitis," "micronodal cirrhosis," etc.); Those having no predecessors (e.g., "jaundice," "pallor," "caput medusae," etc.) stand for possible findings: symptoms, signs, abnormal lab values, etc. in between these extreme points of the network lie chains of nodes representing syndromes, various pathological derangements, and other entities that are significant facets of the disease process.

One of the major uses of such a knowledge structure is as a basis for aggregating elements in a differential diagnosis, thereby reducing the apparent number of alternatives to be considered at any one decision point. We refer to a differential diagnosis comprising pathological descriptors, which in turn point to more underlying causal diagnoses as a "refined" differential. This is in contrast to the "raw" differential diagnosis, which for any finding can be found by compiling a list of all disease entities that appear as terminal nodes anywhere to the right of the point of entry of the finding into the causal graph.

Thus, the raw differential diagnosis for "jaundice," based on the simplified graph of Figure 2, would encompass the set of alternatives: ("common duct stone"? or "biliary cirrhosis"? or "Gilbert's disease"? or "hemolytic anemia"? or "viral hepatitis"? or "macronodal cirrhosis"? or "micronodal cirrhosis"? or "hepatic vein obstruction"?) However, the "refined" differential, based on descriptors of the causal graph, would encompass only the two items ("conjugated hyperbilirubinemia"? or "unconjugated hyperbilirubinemia"?).

The advantage of such a refined differential diagnosis is the opportunity it provides for establishing milestones in a diagnostic workup. The presence of pathological states represented by many of the nodes in the network can often be suggested and even confirmed on the basis of fairly commonplace clinical data. This is typically not true of the more remote (i.e., less observable) disease entities that inhabit the far reaches of the causal net, which often require for their confirmation some definitive, often costly procedure such as biopsy, arteriography, CAT scan evaluation, etc.

In dealing with the pathological descriptors of a causal network, it is often the case that manifestations which are not diagnostic as to the decision among a subset of disease entities, are nonetheless sufficient to permit conclusions concerning intermediate pathological states. We refer to such one-to-one associations between manifestations and nodes of the network representing partial descriptions of a patient's illness as "constrictor" relationships, as they serve to constrict the range of alternatives in a decision set that will need to be pursued further.

For example, if a patient is observed to be jaundiced, the initial decision suggested by the graph would be to choose between conjugated and unconjugated hyperbilirubinemia. This can generally be decided by determining the so-called indirect to direct ratio, which if it is elevated suggests a preponderance of unconjugated bilirubin in the blood, or if low the converse. Assume that the result of this test indicates that the patient's jaundice is due to an excess of conjugated bilirubin in the blood. Then a new decision problem arises: to make a choice between "cholestasis" and "hepatocellular dysfunction" as cause of the conjugated hyperbilirubinemia. For this purpose, assays of liver enzymes (simple laboratory values often obtained on routine blood screening) may be able to settle the issue.

As this example shows, the confirmation of an intermediate node of the network often signals the resolution of one (refined) differential diagnostic task, and the initiation of another: namely, the task of identifying which of the disease entities or pathological states causally linked to the concluded node is actually responsible for the pathological condition that has been decided.

Such decisions can become "propagated" through the network by means of a sequence of choices among the immediate causes of each concluded pathological state. By proceeding in this systematic fashion, the search for an underlying cause can often be progressively constrained on the basis of relatively easy to acquire clinical or paraclinical data. This sequential decision making process can often serve to postpone the necessity for undertaking costly, invasive procedures in the search for pathognomonic data until the set of diagnostic alternatives has been reduced to a small number.

An example may help clarify the issue. Consider again the graph of figure and assume that a patient has been observed to exhibit both pallor and jaundice. Here, chains of causal links emanating from "jaundice" and "pallor" come together at the node "hemolytic anemia"; other chains of links converge on the three "cirrhosis" nodes, and on "hepatic vein obstruction."

Note that the nodes representing possible underlying causes of the observed findings are as many as five links removed from the point of entry of the findings in this simplified graph; in a more complete causal graph the distance could be a dozen links or more.

In order to discover the potential to combine differential diagnoses on the basis of common causal nodes that are far removed from the starting nodes, a programme would have to incorporate a search procedure that would scan the subgraphs emanating from each of the nodes selected as starting differential diagnoses, looking for points of convergence of the causal chains arising there. The problem with this is that the discovery procedure would entail multiple exponential searches of the causal network, which—depending on the level of resolution of the graph—could be extremely costly in terms of computation time, and the expenditure of other scarce resources such as physician waiting time.

In the following section, we turn our attention to

consideration of an alternative knowledge structure, which can also serve to refine the elementary differential diagnoses associated with individual findings, but without complicating the discovery of synthesis

Through analysis of these shortcomings, we have come to a new design for the medical knowledge to be incorporated in the successor system, now renamed as CADUCEUS. This new knowledge representation provides multiple nosologic structures, by which disease entities may be classified in as many descriptive ways as appropriate.

In addition, there is provision for a representation of detailed pathophysiology, by means of a causal graph having no restriction as to level of resolution. These basic structures are supplemented by a set of generalized links—a subset of the transitive closure of the causal graph—which provides for as rapid convergence on tentative unifying hypotheses as in INTERNIST-I, while at the same time enabling access-via a sub-path instantiation mechanism—to as much detail as is available in the underlying causal graph.

This result has been facilitated by means of a path unification algorithm used to combine elementary task definitions into unified complexes. As application of this synthesis operator cannot be considered irrevocable, it is necessary to envelop these heuristic maneuvers within a sophisticated control regime. Thus we have discovered within the task environment of medical diagnosis a core problem, the solution of which requires some of the most powerful methods available in the armamentarium of artificial intelligence.

It soon becomes apparent to anyone who sets about to study the medical reasoning process that there is a considerable intellectual component to medical expertise. Outstanding practitioners of the art exist, and they are known for their ability to converge rapidly on the essential nature of a diagnostic task, sensing "instinctively" the variety of ways in which the pieces of a complex puzzle can fall into place. A review of the record of clinical pathology conferences, where experts are asked to structure and solve difficult clinical problems, often reveals virtuoso performance in this creative endeavor. In view of this richness of human behaviour in diagnostic reasoning, it should come as no surprise that the simple algorithmic approach to computer aided diagnosis has proved unsatisfactory.

What has misled many investigators is the undeniable prominence of the differential diagnosis as a primary structuring feature of the reasoning process. As has been demonstrated many times, this aspect of diagnostic reasoning does not require artificial intelligence methods. What I have tried to show in this chapter is that there is, indeed, an intellectually challenging aspect of clinical reasoning generally overlooked in the design of algorithmic diagnostic procedures. This is the meta level problem involved in the structuring of medical diagnostics: the heuristic search for the right task formulation.

PROBLEM SOLVING METHOD

Problem Solving is very important but problem solvers often misunderstand it. This report proposes the definition of problems, terminology for Problem Solving and useful Problem Solving patterns.

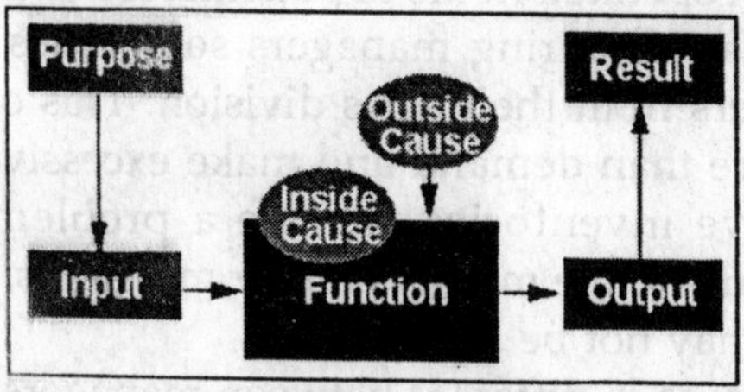

We should define what is the problem as the first step of Problem Solving. Yet problem solvers often forget this first step.

Further, we should recognize common terminology such as Purpose, Situation, Problem, Cause, Solvable Cause, Issue, and Solution. Even Consultants, who should be professional problem solvers, are often confused with the terminology of Problem Solving. For example, some consultants may think of issues as problems, or some of them think of problems as causes. But issues must be the proposal to solve problems and problems should be negative expressions while issues should be a positive expression.

Some consultants do not mind this type of minute terminology, but clear terminology is helpful to increase the efficiency of Problem Solving. Third, there are several useful thinking patterns such as strategic thinking, emotional thinking, realistic thinking, empirical thinking and so on. The thinking pattern means how we think. So far, I recognized fourteen thinking patterns. If we choose an appropriate pattern at each step in Problem Solving, we can improve the efficiency of Problem Solving.

This report will explain the above three points such as the definition of problems, the terminology of Problem Solving, and useful thinking patterns.

DEFINITION OF PROBLEM

A problem is decided by purposes. If someone wants money and when he or she has little money, he or she has a problem. But if someone does not want money, little money is not a problem.

For example, manufacturing managers are usually evaluated with line-operation rate, which is shown as a percentage of operated hours to potential total operation hours. Therefore manufacturing managers sometimes operate lines without orders from their sales division. This operation may produce more than demand and make excessive inventories. The excessive inventories may be a problem for general managers. But for the manufacturing managers, the excessive inventories may not be a problem.

If a purpose is different between managers, they see the identical situation in different ways. One may see a problem but the others may not see the problem. Therefore, in order to identify a problem, problem solvers such as consultants must clarify the differences of purposes. But oftentimes, problem solvers frequently forget to clarify the differences of purposes and incur confusion among their problem solving projects. Therefore problem solvers should start their problem solving projects from the definition of purposes and problems

TERMINOLOGY OF PROBLEM SOLVING

We should know the basic terminology for Problem Solving. This report proposes seven terms such as Purpose, Situation, Problem, Cause, Solvable Cause, Issue, and Solution.

Purpose

Purpose is what we want to do or what we want to be. Purpose is an easy term to understand. But problem solvers frequently forget to confirm Purpose, at the first step of Problem Solving. Without clear purposes, we can not think about problems.

Situation

Situation is just what a circumstance is. Situation is neither good nor bad. We should recognize situations objectively as much as we can. Usually almost all situations are not problems. But some problem solvers think of all situations as problems. Before we recognize a problem, we should capture situations clearly without recognizing them as problems or non-problems.

Without recognizing situations objectively, Problem Solving is likely to be narrow sighted, because problem solvers recognize problems with their prejudice.

Problem

Problem is some portions of a situation, which cannot realise purposes. Since problem solvers often neglect the differences of purposes, they cannot capture the true problems. If the purpose is different, the identical situation may be a problem or may not be a problem.

Cause

Cause is what brings about a problem. Some problem solvers do not distinguish causes from problems. But since problems are some portions of a situation, problems are more general than causes are. In other words causes are more specific facts, which bring about problems. Without distinguishing causes from problems, Problem Solving can not be specific.

Finding specific facts which causes problems is the essential step in Problem Solving.

Solvable Cause

Solvable cause is some portions of causes. When we solve a problem, we should focus on solvable causes. Finding solvable causes is another essential step in Problem Solving. But problem solvers frequently do not extract solvable causes among causes. If we try to solve unsolvable causes, we waste time. Extracting solvable causes is a useful step to make Problem Solving efficient.

Issue

Issue is the opposite expression of a problem. If a problem is that we do not have money, the issue is that we get money. Some problem splvers do not know what Issue is. They may think of "we do not have money" as an issue. At the worst case, they may mix the problems, which should be negative expressions, and the issues, which should be positive expressions.

Solution

Solution is a specific action to solve a problem, which is equal to a specific action to realise an issue. Some problem solvers do not break down issues into more specific actions. Issues are not solutions. Problem solvers must break down issues into specific action.

THINKING PATTERNS

This report lists fourteen thinking patters. Problem solvers should choose appropriate patterns, responding to situations. This report categorized these fourteen patterns into three more general groups such as thinking patterns for judgements, thinking patterns for thinking processes and thinking patterns for efficient thinking. The following is the outlines of those thinking patterns.

Thinking Patterns for Judgements

In order to create a value through thinking we need to

judge whether what we think is right or wrong. This report lists four judging patterns such as strategic thinking, emotional thinking, realistic thinking, and empirical thinking.

Strategic Thinking

Focus, or bias, is the criterion for strategic thinking. If you judge whether a situation is right or wrong based on whether the situation is focused or not, your judgement is strategic. A strategy is not necessarily strategic. Historically, many strategists such as Sonfucis in ancient China, Naplon, M. Porter proposed strategic thinking when they develop strategies.

Emotional Thinking

In organizations, an emotional aspect is essential. Tactical leaders judge whether a situation is right or wrong based on the participants of emotional commitment. They think that if participants can be positive to a situation, the situation is right.

Realistic Thinking

- Start from what we can do.
- Fix the essential problem first.

These two criteria are very useful. "Starting" is very important, even if we do very little. We do not have to start from the essential part. Even if we start from an easier part, starting is a better judgement than a judgement of not-starting in terms of the first part of realistic thinking. Further, after we start, we should search key factors to make the Problem Solving more efficient.

Usually, 80 % of the problems are caused by only 20 % of the causes. If we can find the essential 20 % of the causes, we can fix 80 % of problems very efficiently. Then if we try to find the essential problem, what we are doing is right in terms of the second part of realistic thinking.

Empirical Thinking

When we use empirical thinking, we judge whether the situation is right or wrong based on our past experiences. Sometimes, this thinking pattern persists on the past criteria too much, even if a situation has changed. But when it comes to our daily lives, situations do not change frequently. Further, if we have the experience of the identical situation before, we can utilize the experience as a reliable knowledge data base.

THINKING PATTERNS FOR THINKING PROCESSES

If we can think systematically, we do not have to be frustrated when we think. In contrast, if we have no systematic method, Problem Solving frustrate us. This reports lists five systematic thinking processes such as rational thinking, systems thinking, cause & effect thinking, contingent thinking, and the Toyota®fs five times WHYs method.

Rational Thinking

Rational thinking is one of the most common Problem Solving methods. This report will briefly show this Problem Solving method.

- Set the ideal situation.
- Identify a current situation.
- Compare the ideal situation and the current situation, and identify the problem situation.
- Break down the problem to its causes.
- Conceive the solution alternatives to the causes.
- Evaluate and choose the reasonable solution alternatives.
- Implement the solutions.
- We can use rational thinking as a Problem Solving method for almost all problems.

Systems Thinking

Systems thinking is a more scientific Problem Solving approach than the rational thinking approach. We set the system, which causes problems and analyse them based on systems®f functions. The following arre the system and how the system works.

System

- Purpose
- Input

- Output
- Function
- Inside cause (Solvable cause)
- Outside cause (Unsolvable cause)
- Result

In order to realise Purpose, we prepare Input and through Function we can get Output. But Output does not necessarily realise Purpose. Result of the Function may be different from Purpose. This difference is created by Outside Cause and Inside Cause. We can not solve Outside Cause but we can solve Inside Cause. For example, when we want to play golf, Purpose is to play golf.

If we can not play golf, this situation is Output. If we can not play golf because of a bad weather, the bad weather is Outside Cause, because we can not change the weather. In contrast, if we cannot play golf because we left golf bags in our home, this cause is solvable. Then, that we left bags in our home is an Inside Cause. Systems thinking is a very clear and useful method to solve problems.

Cause and Effect Thinking

Traditionally, we like to clarify cause and effect relations. We usually think of finding causes as solving problems. Finding a cause and effect relation is a conventional basic Problem Solving method.

Contingent Thinking

Game Theory is a typical contingent thinking method. If we think about as many situations as possible, which may happen, and prepare solutions for each situation, this process is a contingent thinking approach.

Toyotafs Five Times WHYs

At Toyota, employees are taught to think WHY consecutively five times. This is an adaptation of cause and effect thinking. If employees think WHY and find a cause, they try to ask themselves WHY again. They continue five times. Through these five WHYS, they can break down causes into a very specific level. This five times WHYs approach is very useful to solve problems.

THINKING PATTERNS FOR EFFICIENT THINKING

In order to think efficiently, there are several useful thinking patterns. This report lists five patterns for efficient thinking such as hypothesis thinking, conception thinking, structure thinking, convergence & divergence thinking, and time order thinking.

Hypothesis Thinking

If we can collect all information quickly and easily, you can solve problems very efficiently. But actually, we can not collect every information. If we try to collect all information, we need so long time. Hypothesis thinking does not require collecting all information.

We develop a hypothesis based on available information. After we developed a hypothesis, we collect minimum information to prove the hypothesis. If the first hypothesis is right, you do not have to collect any more information. If the first hypothesis is wrong, we will develop the next hypothesis based on available information. Hypothesis thinking is a very efficient problem-solving method, because we do not have to waste time to collect unnecessary information.

Conception Thinking

Problem Solving is not necessarily logical or rational. Creativity and flexibility are other important aspects for Problem Solving. We can not recognize these aspects clearly. This report shows only what kinds of tips are useful for creative and flexible conception. Following are portions of tips.

- To be visual.
- To write down what we think.
- Use cards to draw, write and arrange ideas in many ways.
- Change positions, forms, and viewpoints, physically and mentally.

We can imagine without words and logic, but in order to

communicate to others, we must explain by words and logic. Therefore after we create ideas, we must explain them literally. Creative conception must be translated into reasonable explanations. Without explanations, conception does not make sense.

Structure Thinking

If we make a structure like a tree to grasp a complex situation, we can understand very clearly.

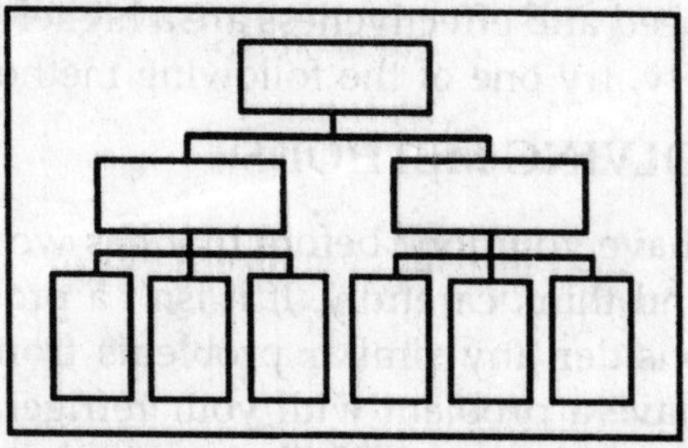

Upper level should be more abstract and lower level should be more concrete. Dividing abstract situations from concrete situations is helpful to clarify the complex situations. Very frequently, problem solvers cannot arrange a situation clearly. A clear recognition of a complex situation increases efficiency of Problem Solving.

Convergence and Divergence Thinking

When we should be creative we do not have to consider convergence of ideas. In contrast, when we should summarize ideas we must focus on convergence. If we do convergence and divergence simultaneously, Problem Solving becomes inefficient.

Time Order Thinking

Thinking based on a time order is very convenient, when we are confused with Problem Solving. We can think based on a time order from the past to the future and make a complex situation clear.

Want some problem solving methods that are easy-to-use

and effective? There may be a hundred good creative techniques out there, like challenging assumptions, brainstorming crazy ideas, or using a modifying word list. Many of these are really powerful if you want to invent something new or exercise that creativity.

Sometimes, however, you just need a fast effective solution to a real-life problem. In that case, it may be time to try some less-creative problem solving methods. With that in mind, when speed and effectiveness are a higher priority than radical creativity, try one of the following methods.

PROBLEM SOLVING METHODS

1. What have you done before that has worked?

Ask this and think carefully. If it isn't a problem you've had before, consider any similar problems from your past. Suppose you have a problem with your refrigerator. Should you fix it, or buy a new one? We'll suppose that you haven't had one break before, so you aren't sure which route makes more sense. Your most similar problem in the past was when a clothes dryer that broke. You recall that you went online and found a clear diagram showing how to replace the belt, which fixed the problem. You immediately go online and find from the symptoms find that you can get the refrigerator fixed for half of what a new one would cost.

2. How have others have solved the problem?

This is the next quick question to ask yourself. For example, Bob has a problem with cats coming into his yard and making a mess all over. Looking at number two on this list of problem solving methods, he recalls that his neighbour doesn't seem to have the same problem, so he calls her. She buys cat urine in a spray bottle she explains, and sprays the entry points to her yard every few weeks or so. Cats think the territory is marked by another cat and so they don't enter.

This is an interesting, even creative solution. Bob, however, just had to ask a question to get this solution. Simply ask others who have had similar problems. You can also ask those who don't have the problem, but should. See what they are they doing. You can do this online too.

3. Sleep on the problem.

Allen needs to create a new product for his craft business, something related to the hand-carved walking sticks he is selling. It might be a new kind of walking stick, or something related. After running through all the problem-solving and idea-generating techniques he knows, he doesn't like any of the ideas he had. Then he sees the number three problem solving method here and decides to sleep on it.

Before he falls asleep, he imagines himself telling someone about his new product. "What is it," the person asks, and he replies, "I'll let you know in the morning." His unconscious mind is now set to go to work for him as he sleeps. He wakes up in the morning and realizes that in a dream he was explaining a his new invention to someone. He reviews the dream.

His new product is a walking stick with two thin metal bars recessed in it. They pull out to make a tripod, and on top is a camera-holder. It can be used as normal walking stick, and then when the hiker wants to take a photo, he doesn't need to try balancing the camera on a rock or log. He just opens up his tripod.

Ask how you've solved a problem before, ask how others have solved it, or just sleep on it, and see if a solution comes. These aren't the most creative problem solving methods, but sometimes a simple and easy way is all you need.

ACTIVITY BASED LEARNING

The aim of Activity-Based Learning (ABL) is to change the teacher from an authority in knowledge to a facilitator for the student to discover knowledge. When anyone experiences interest in something, whether it is a subject, sport or activity, nothing will stop him or her from learning all they can about it. Academic subjects can also be introduced from an interesting perspective, where fun is a gateway for learning.

The teacher changes from authority to facilitator by finding ways to present a syllabus that is based on fun. Many types of games and activities can be modified for school use and once children understand and enjoy the games, they will create games for themselves and other classes. Whether through play or through games created for learning, children automatically remember the subject involved. Just because children and teachers are enjoying the games does not mean that the subject matter gets lost; on the contrary, the subject matter is the starting point.

In 1944, towards the end of the Second World War, an Englishman called David Horsburgh came to India as part of the Royal Air Force. He was posted somewhere in Bengal, in what is now part of Bangla Desh. He fell in love with the complexity of the culture, the openness of the people and the beauty of the countryside. When the war was over, he went back and enrolled in courses in Indian history and culture and studied Sanskrit and Hindi. He came back to India to teach and worked in Rishi Valley School and Blue Mountain School for some years. He joined the British Council and worked in Madras and Bangalore for twenty years. Taking retirement voluntarily, he located a 7- acre site in Kolar District and opened his school, Neel Bagh. For him, the school was the fulfillment of a dream. Neel Bagh constituted the nucleus for a host of creative methods in teaching and a vast quantum of well-planned learning materials.

David was a charismatic leader and a born teacher. With his wife Doreen and his son Nicholas, David developed a diverse curriculum, which included music, carpentry, sewing, masonry, gardening, as well as the usual school subjects, English, mathematics, Sanskrit, and Telugu. He had vertical grouping in the classroom and the children worked on the material on cards, at their specific level. These pedagogic materials were systematically planned, with sketches and drawings and an occasional touch of humour. Fresh materials on cards would be added frequently, to emphasize that the sources for lessons were not finite. David endowed Neel Bagh with a magnificent library that was accessible to teachers and students.

As one example of what the curriculum contained, we may consider music. Children were taught to sing melodiously and in harmony. They were taught folk and classical songs from different cultures and in different languages. It was a treat to the ears. And what is more, the music period would be the first one every morning. Like music, drama also was an important feature of the curriculum. The Horsburghs had talent in theatre, acting, direction and production and scenes from Shakespeare or the Panchatantra would be staged, with the acting and production by the Neel Bagh children, from Rayalpad.

ACTIVITY-BASED LEARNING IN TAMIL NADU

In Tamil Nadu, the initiative, which has drawn upon several resources, we have the possibility of a system which can succeed in keeping children motivated and fully occupied, while they are mastering the fundamentals. Ideally, every classroom should have a teacher. However, even if all the vacant teaching positions are not filled, the lessons can proceed.ABL offers solutions to two major problems: multi-grade classes and inadequate staffing.

It provides the learning material for several children to be working on, while the teacher is busy with one group. ABL appears to be a system where the teacher can facilitate learning, without dominating the classroom or intimidating the children. Since the child learns in a self-directed way, from the systematic materials provided, teacher absence or occasional unavailability may not be a tragedy. This report traces the long history of the method and delineates the main aspects of the ABL. Suggestions for its improvement and strengthening are also made at the end.

OPENING SCENE

A visitor walks into a Corporation school in Chennai. The children sit in groups on four or five mats on the floor. Each child is engaged in some academic task. The teacher is also at the floor level, with seven or eight children around her. She is looking into the notebook of one of the children and checking the written work. There are several blackboards at the level of the children. The shelves are neatly stacked with colourful materials for learning and children's drawings and paintings, suspended on high strings across the room, flutter colourfully. The children do not shout "Vanakkam" in unison or even take much notice of the passing visitor.

The visitor talks to a 9- year old boy and asks him if he can read Tamil.

When the boy nods confidently, he takes the current Tamil newspaper, Dinamani, and hands it to the child. The boy reads the headlines clearly, without errors, and returns the paper. The visitor asks him how he learned to read. He hears the boy say that he has studied in the same school for the last four years and he has gone step by step on the Learning Ladder.

How did the children learn to read? Who taught them? What is the ladder? Where can one find out more about the system? Why cannot all our schools follow this method

ACTIVE LEARNING METHOD

INTRODUCTION

The past decade has seen an explosion of interest among college faculty in the teaching methods variously grouped under the terms 'active learning' and 'cooperative learning'. However, even with this interest, there remains much misunderstanding of and mistrust of the pedagogical "movement" behind the words. The majority of all college faculty still teach their classes in the traditional lecture mode.

Some of the criticism and hesitation seems to originate in the idea that techniques of active and cooperative learning are genuine alternatives to, rather than enhancements of, professors' lectures. We provide below a survey of a wide variety of active learning techniques which can be used to supplement rather than replace lectures. We are not advocating complete abandonment of lecturing, as both of us still lecture about half of the class period. The lecture is a very efficient way to present information but use of the lecture as the only mode of instruction presents problems for both the instructor and the students. There is a large amount of research attesting to the benefits of active learning.

"Active Learning" is, in short, anything that students do

in a classroom other than merely passively listening to an instructor's lecture. This includes everything from listening practices which help the students to absorb what they hear, to short writing exercises in which students react to lecture material, to complex group exercises in which students apply course material to "real life" situations and/or to new problems. The term "cooperative learning" covers the subset of active learning activities which students do as groups of three or more, rather than alone or in pairs; generally, cooperative learning techniques employ more formally structured groups of students assigned complex tasks, such as multiple-step exercises, research projects, or presentations. Cooperative learning is to be distinguished from another now well-defined term of art, "collaborative learning", which refers to those classroom strategies which have the instructor and the students placed on an equal footing working together in, for example, designing assignments, choosing texts, and presenting material to the class.

Clearly, collaborative learning is a more radical departure from tradition than merely utilizing techniques aimed at enhancing student retention of material presented by the instructor; we will limit our examples to the "less radical" active and cooperative learning techniques. "Techniques of active learning", then, are those activities which an instructor incorporates into the classroom to foster active learning.

TECHNIQUES OF ACTIVE LEARNING

Exercises for Individual Students

Because these techniques are aimed at individual students, they can very easily be used without interrupting the flow of the class. These exercises are particularly useful in providing the instructor with feedback concerning student understanding and retention of material. Some (numbers 3 and 4, in particular) are especially designed to encourage students' exploration of their own attitudes and values. Many (especially numbers 4 - 6) are designed to increase retention of material presented in lectures and texts.

The "One Minute Paper"

This is a highly effective technique for checking student progress, both in understanding the material and in reacting to course material. Ask students to take out a blank sheet of paper, pose a question (either specific or open-ended), and give them one (or perhaps two - but not many more) minute(s) to respond. Some sample questions include: "How does John Hospers define "free will"?", "What is "scientific realism"?", "What is the activation energy for a chemical reaction?", "What is the difference between replication and transcription?", and so on. Another good use of the minute paper is to ask questions like "What was the main point of today's class material?" This tells you whether or not the students are viewing the material in the way you envisioned.

Muddiest (or Clearest) Point

This is a variation on the one-minute paper, though you may wish to give students a slightly longer time period to answer the question. Here you ask (at the end of a class period, or at a natural break in the presentation), "What was the "muddiest point" in today's lecture?" or, perhaps, you might be more specific, asking, for example: "What (if anything) do you find unclear about the concept of 'personal identity' ('inertia', 'natural selection', etc.)?".

Affective Response

Again, this is similar to the above exercises, but here you are asking students to report their *reactions* to some facet of the course material - i.e., to provide an emotional or valuative response to the material. Obviously, this approach is limited to those subject areas in which such questions are appropriate (one should not, for instance, inquire into students' affective responses to vertebrate taxonomy). However, it can be quite a useful starting point for courses such as applied ethics, particularly as a precursor to theoretical analysis.

For example, you might ask students what they think of Dr. Jack Kevorkian's activities, before presenting what various moral theorists would make of them. By having several views "on the table" before theory is presented, you can help students to see the material in context and to explore their own beliefs. It is also a good way to begin a discussion of evolutionary theory or any other scientific area where the general public often has views contrary to current scientific thinking, such as paper vs. plastic packaging or nuclear power generation.

Daily Journal

This combines the advantages of the above three techniques, and allows for more in-depth discussion of or reaction to course material. You may set aside class time for students to complete their journal entries, or assign this as homework. The only disadvantage to this approach is that the feedback will not be as "instant" as with the one-minute paper (and other assignments which you collect the day of the relevant lecture).

But with this approach (particularly if entries are assigned for homework), you may ask more complex questions, such as, "Do you think that determinism is correct, or that humans have free will? Explain your answer.", or "Do you think that Dr. Kevorkian's actions are morally right? What would John Stuart Mill say?" and so on. Or you might have students find and discuss reports of scientific studies in popular media on topics relevant to course material, such as global warming, the ozone layer, and so forth.

Reading Quiz

Clearly, this is one way to coerce students to read assigned material! Active learning depends upon students coming to class prepared. The reading quiz can also be used as an effective measure of student comprehension of the readings (so that you may gauge their level of sophistication as readers). Further, by asking the same sorts of questions on several reading quizzes, you will give students guidance as to what to look for when reading assigned text.

If you ask questions like "What colour were Esmerelda's eyes?" (as my high school literature teacher liked to do), you are telling the student that it is the details that count, whereas questions like "What reason did Esmerelda give, for murdering Sebastian?" highlight issues of justification. If your goal is to instruct (and not merely to coerce), carefully choose questions which will both identify who has read the material (for your sake) and identify what is important in the reading.

Clarification Pauses

This is a simple technique aimed at fostering "active listening". Throughout a lecture, particularly after stating an important point or defining a key concept, stop, let it sink in, and then (after waiting a bit!) ask if anyone needs to have it clarified.

You can also circulate around the room during these pauses to look at student notes, answer questions, etc. Students who would never ask a question in front of the whole class will ask questions during a clarification pause as you move about the room.

Response to a Demonstration or Other Teacher Centered Activity -

The students are asked to write a paragraph that begins with: I was surprised that... I learned that... I wonder about... This allows the students to reflect on what they actually got out of the teachers' presentation. It also helps students realise that the activity was designed for more than just entertainment.

QUESTIONS AND ANSWERS

While most of us use questions as a way of prodding students and instantly testing comprehension, there are simple ways of tweaking our questioning techniques which increase student involvement and comprehension. Though some of the techniques listed here are "obvious", we will proceed on the principle that the obvious sometimes bears repeating (a useful pedagogical principle, to be sure!).

The "Socratic Method"

Taking its namesake from the most famous gadfly in history, this technique in its original format involved instructors "testing" student knowledge (of reading assignments, lectures, or perhaps applications of course material to a wider context) by asking questions during the course of a lecture. Typically, the instructor chooses a particular student, presents her with a question, and expects an answer forthwith; if the "chosen" student cannot answer the question presented, the instructor chooses another (and another) until the desired answer is received.

This method has come under criticism, based on claims that it singles out students (potentially embarrassing them), and/or that it favors only a small segment of the class (i.e., that small percentage of the class who can answer any question thrown at them).

In addition, once a student has answered a question they may not pay much attention as it will be a long time before the teacher returns to them for a second question. In spite of these criticisms, we feel that the Socratic method is an important and useful one; the following techniques suggest variations which enhance this method, avoiding some of these pitfalls.

Wait Time

Rather than choosing the student who will answer the question presented, this variation has the instructor WAITING before calling on someone to answer it. The wait time will generally be short (15 seconds or so) - but it may seem interminable in the classroom. It is important to insist that no one raise his hand (or shout out the answer) before you give the OK, in order to discourage the typical scenario in which the five students in the front row all immediately volunteer to answer the question, and everyone else sighs in relief.

Waiting forces every student to think about the question, rather than passively relying on those students who are fastest out of the gate to answer every question. When the wait time is up, the instructor asks for volunteers or randomly picks a student to answer the question. Once students are in the habit of waiting after questions are asked, more will get involved in the process.

Student Summary of Another Student's Answer

In order to promote active listening, after one student has volunteered an answer to your question, ask another student to summarize the first student's response. Many students hear little of what their classmates have to say, waiting instead for the instructor to either correct or repeat the answer. Having students summarize or repeat each others' contributions to the course both fosters active participation by all students and promotes the idea that learning is a shared enterprise. Given the possibility of being asked to repeat a classmates' comments, most students will listen more attentively to each other.

The Fish Bowl

Students are given index cards, and asked to write down one question concerning the course material. They should be directed to ask a question of clarification regarding some aspect of the material which they do not fully understand; or, perhaps you may allow questions concerning the application of course material to practical contexts. At the end of the class period (or, at the beginning of the next class meeting if the question is assigned for homework), students deposit their questions in a fish bowl. The instructor then draws several questions out of the bowl and answers them for the class or asks the class to answer them. This technique can be combined with others.

Quiz/Test Questions

Here students are asked to become actively involved in creating quizzes and tests by constructing some (or all) of the questions for the exams. This exercise may be assigned for homework and itself evaluated (perhaps for extra credit points). In asking students to think up exam questions, we encourage them to think more deeply about the course material and to explore major themes, comparison of views presented, applications, and other higher-order thinking skills.

Once suggested questions are collected, the instructor may use them as the basis of review sessions, and/or to model the most effective questions. Further, you may ask students to discuss the merits of a sample of questions submitted; in discussing questions, they will significantly increase their engagement of the material to supply answers.

Students might be asked to discuss several aspects of two different questions on the same material including degree of difficulty, effectiveness in assessing their learning, proper scope of questions, and so forth.

IMMEDIATE FEEDBACK

These techniques are designed to give the instructor some indication of student understanding of the material presented during the lecture itself. These activities provide formative assessment rather than summative assessment of student understanding, Formative assessment is evaluation of the class as a whole in order to provide information for the benefit of the students and the instructor, but the information is not used as part of the course grade; summative assessment is any evaluation of student performance which becomes part of the course grade.

For each feedback method, the instructor stops at appropriate points to give quick tests of the material; in this way, she can adjust the lecture mid-course, slowing down to spend more time on the concepts students are having difficulty with or moving more quickly to applications of concepts of which students have a good understanding.

Finger Signals

This method provides instructors with a means of testing student comprehension without the waiting period or the grading time required for written quizzes. Students are asked questions and instructed to signal their answers by holding up the appropriate number of fingers immediately in front of their torsos (this makes it impossible for students to "copy", thus committing them to answer each question on their own). For example, the instructor might say "one finger for 'yes', two for 'no'", and then ask questions such as "Do all organic compounds contain carbon [hydrogen, etc.]?". Or, the instructor might have multiple choice questions prepared for the overhead projector and have the answers numbered, asking students to answer with finger signals.

In very large classes the students can use a set of large cardboard signs with numbers written on them. This method allows instructors to assess student knowledge literally at a glance.

Flash Cards

A variation of the Finger Signals approach, this method tests students' comprehension through their response to flash cards held by the instructor. This is particularly useful in disciplines which utilize models or other visual stimuli, such as chemistry, physics or biology. For example, the instructor might flash the diagram of a chemical compound and ask "Does this compound react with H_2O?". This can be combined with finger signals.

Quotations

This is a particularly useful method of testing student understanding when they are learning to read texts and identify an author's viewpoint and arguments. After students have read a representative advocate of each of several opposing theories or schools of thought, and the relevant concepts have been defined and discussed in class, put on the overhead projector a quotation by an author whom they have not read in the assigned materials, and ask them to figure out what position that person advocates.

In addition to testing comprehension of the material presented in lecture, this exercise develops critical thinking and analysis skills. This would be very useful, for example, in discussing the various aspects of evolutionary theory.

CRITICAL THINKING MOTIVATORS

Sometimes it is helpful to get students involved in discussion of or thinking about course material either *before* any theory is presented in lecture or after several conflicting theories have been presented. The idea in the first case is to generate data or questions prior to mapping out the theoretical landscape; in the second case, the students learn to assess the relative merits of several approaches.

The Pre-Theoretic Intuitions Quiz

Students often dutifully record everything the instructor says during a lecture and then ask at the end of the day or the course "what *use* is any of this?", or "what good will philosophy [organic chemistry, etc.] do for us?". To avoid such questions, and to get students interested in a topic before lectures begin, an instructor can give a quiz aimed at getting students to both identify and to assess their own views.

An example of this is a long "True or False" questionnaire designed to start students thinking about moral theory (to be administered on the first or second day of an introductory ethics course), which includes statements such as "There are really no correct answers to moral questions" and "Whatever a society holds to be morally right is in fact morally right". After students have responded to the questions individually, have them compare answers in pairs or small groups and discuss the ones on which they disagree.

This technique may also be used to assess student knowledge of the subject matter in a pre-/post-lecture comparison. The well-known "Force Concept Inventory" developed by Hestenes to measure understanding of force and motion is another good example of this.

Puzzles/Paradoxes

One of the most useful means of ferreting out students' intuitions on a given topic is to present them with a paradox or a puzzle involving the concept(s) at issue, and to have them struggle towards a solution. By forcing the students to "work it out" without some authority's solution, you increase the likelihood that they will be able to critically assess theories when they are presented later. For example, students in a course on theories of truth might be asked to assess the infamous "Liar Paradox" (with instances such as 'This sentence is false'), and to suggest ways in which such paradoxes can be avoided. Introductory logic students might be presented with complex logic puzzles as a way of motivating truth tables, and so forth.

In scientific fields you can present experimental data which seems to contradict parts of the theory just presented or use examples which seem to have features which support two opposing theories.

SHARE/PAIR

Grouping students in pairs allows many of the advantages of group work students have the opportunity to state their own views, to hear from others, to hone their argumentative skills, and so forth without the administrative "costs" of group work (time spent assigning people to groups, class time used just for "getting in groups", and so on). Further, pairs make it virtually impossible for students to avoid participating thus making each person accountable.

Discussion

Students are asked to pair off and to respond to a question either in turn or as a pair. This can easily be combined with other techniques such as those under "Questions and Answers" or "Critical Thinking Motivators" above. For example, after students have responded to statements, such as "Whatever a society holds to be morally right is in fact morally right" with 'true' or 'false', they can be asked to compare answers to a limited number of questions and to discuss the statements on which they differed.

In science classes students can be asked to explain some experimental data that supports a theory just discussed by the lecturer. Generally, this works best when students are given explicit directions, such as "Tell each other <u>why</u> you chose the answer you did".

Note Comparison/Sharing

One reason that some students perform poorly in classes is that they often do not have good note-taking skills. That is, while they might listen attentively, students do not always know what to write down, or they may have gaps in their notes which will leave them bewildered when they go back to the notes to study or to write a paper.

One way to avoid some of these pitfalls and to have students model good note-taking is to have them occasionally compare notes. The instructor might stop lecturing immediately after covering a crucial concept and have students read each others' notes, filling in the gaps in their own note-taking. This is especially useful in introductory courses or in courses designed for non-majors or special admissions students. Once students see the value of supplementing their own note-taking with others', they are likely to continue the practice outside of class time.

Evaluation of Another Student's Work

Students are asked to complete an individual homework assignment or short paper. On the day the assignment is due, students submit one copy to the instructor to be graded and one copy to their partner.

These may be assigned that day, or students may be assigned partners to work with throughout the term. Each student then takes their partner's work and depending on the nature of the assignment gives critical feedback, standardizes or assesses the arguments, corrects mistakes in problem-solving or grammar, and so forth. This is a particularly effective way to improve student writing.

COOPERATIVE LEARNING EXERCISES

For more complex projects, where many heads are better than one or two, you may want to have students work in groups of three or more. As the term "cooperative learning" suggests, students working in groups will help each other to learn. Generally, it is better to form heterogeneous groups (with regard to gender, ethnicity, and academic performance), particularly when the groups will be working together over time or on complex projects; however, some of these techniques work well with spontaneously formed groups. Cooperative groups encourage discussion of problem solving techniques ("Should we try this?", etc.), and avoid the embarrassment of students who have not yet mastered all of the skills required.

Cooperative Groups in Class

Pose a question to be worked on in each cooperative group and then circulate around the room answering questions, asking further questions, keeping the groups on task, and so forth.. After an appropriate time for group discussion, students are asked to share their discussion points with the rest of the class. (The ensuing discussion can be guided according to the "Questions and Answers" techniques outlined above.)

Active Review Sessions

In the traditional class review session the students ask questions and the instructor answers them. Students spend their time copying down answers rather than thinking about the material. In an active review session the instructor posses questions and the students work on them in groups. Then students are asked to show their solutions to the whole group and discuss any differences among solutions proposed.

Work at the Blackboard

In many problem solving courses (e.g., logic or critical thinking), instructors tend to review homework or teach problem solving techniques by solving the problems themselves. Because students learn more by doing, rather than watching, this is probably not the optimal scenario.

Rather than illustrating problem solving, have students work out the problems themselves, by asking them to go to the blackboard in small groups to solve problems. If there is insufficient blackboard space, students can still work out problems as a group, using paper and pencil or computers if appropriate software is available.

Concept Mapping

A concept map is a way of illustrating the connections that exist between terms or concepts covered in course material; students construct concept maps by connecting individual terms by lines which indicate the relationship between each set of connected terms. Most of the terms in a concept map have multiple connections. Developing a concept map requires the students to identify and organize information and to establish meaningful relationships between the pieces of information.

Visual Lists

Here students are asked to make a list—on paper or on the blackboard; by working in groups, students typically can generate more comprehensive lists than they might if working alone. This method is particularly effective when students are asked to compare views or to list pros and cons of a position. One technique which works well with such comparisons is to have students draw a "T" and to label the left- and right-hand sides of the cross bar with the opposing positions (or 'Pro' and 'Con'). They then list everything they can think of which supports these positions on the relevant side of the vertical line.

Once they have generated as thorough a list as they can, ask them to analyse the lists with questions appropriate to the exercise. For example, when discussing Utilitarianism (a theory which claims that an action is morally right whenever it results in more benefits than harms) students can use the "T" method to list all of the (potential) benefits and harms of an action, and then discuss which side is more heavily "weighted". Often having the list before them helps to determine the ultimate utility of the action, and the requirement to fill in the "T" generally results in a more thorough accounting of the consequences of the action in question. In science classes this would work well with such topics as massive vaccination programmes, nuclear power, eliminating chlorofluorocarbons, reducing carbon dioxide emissions, and so forth.

Jigsaw Group Projects

In jigsaw projects, each member of a group is asked to complete some discrete part of an assignment; when every member has completed his assigned task, the pieces can be joined together to form a finished project. For example, students in a course in African geography might be grouped and each assigned a country; individual students in the group could then be assigned to research the economy, political structure, ethnic makeup, terrain and climate, or folklore of the assigned country. When each student has completed his research, the group then reforms to complete a comprehensive report. In a chemistry course each student group could research a different form of power generation (nuclear, fossil fuel, hydroelectric, etc.). Then the groups are reformed so that each group has an expert in one form of power generation. They then tackle the difficult problem of how much emphasis should be placed on each method.

Role Playing

Here students are asked to "act out" a part. In doing so, they get a better idea of the concepts and theories being discussed. Role-playing exercises can range from the simple (e.g., "What would you do if a Nazi came to your door, and you were hiding a Jewish family in the attic?") to the complex. Complex role playing might take the form of a play (depending on time and resources); for example, students studying ancient philosophy might be asked to recreate the trial of Socrates. Using various sources (e.g., Plato's dialogues, Stone's The Trial of Socrates, and Aristophanes' The Clouds), student teams can prepare the prosecution and defence of Socrates on the charges of corruption of youth and treason; each team may present witnesses (limited to characters which appear in the Dialogues, for instance) to construct their case, and prepare questions for cross-examination.

Panel Discussions

Panel discussions are especially useful when students are asked to give class presentations or reports as a way of including the entire class in the presentation. Student groups are assigned a topic to research and asked to prepare presentations (note that this may readily be combined with the jigsaw method outlined above). Each panelist is then expected to make a very short presentation, before the floor is opened to questions from "the audience". The key to success is to choose topics carefully and to give students sufficient direction to ensure that they are well-prepared for their presentations. You might also want to prepare the "audience", by assigning them various roles. For example, if students are presenting the results of their research into several forms of energy, you might have some of the other students role play as concerned environmentalists, transportation officials, commuters, and so forth.

Debates

Actually a variation of #27, formal debates provide an efficient structure for class presentations when the subject matter easily divides into opposing views or 'Pro'/'Con' considerations. Students are assigned to debate teams, given a position to defend, and then asked to present arguments in support of their position on the presentation day.

The opposing team should be given an opportunity to rebut the argument(s) and, time permitting, the original presenters asked to respond to the rebuttal. This format is particularly useful in developing argumentation skills (in addition to teaching content).

Games

Many will scoff at the idea that one would literally play games in a university setting, but occasionally there is no better instructional tool. In particular, there are some concepts or theories which are more easily illustrated than discussed and in these cases, a well-conceived game may convey the idea more readily. For example, when students are introduced to the concepts of "laws of nature" and "the scientific method", it is hard to convey through lectures the nature of scientific work and the fallibility of inductive hypotheses.

Instead, students play a couple rounds of the Induction Game, in which playing cards are turned up and either added to a running series or discarded according to the dealer's preconceived "law of nature". Students are asked to "discover" the natural law, by formulating and testing hypotheses as the game proceeds.

APPLICATIONS

ACTIVE LEARNING IN STUDENT ENVIRONMENT

Learning by "doing" is a theme that many educators have stressed since John Dewey's convincing argument that children must be engaged in an active quest for learning and new ideas. Jean Piaget stressed the need for "concrete operations" in early childhood.

While few educators are unaware of Piaget's work, many incorrectly assume that active learning is important only in the education of young children. But Piaget makes it clear that this in not so: "Experience is always necessary for intellectual development ... the subject must be active....". Although Piaget's research was focused primarily on young children, a growing body of research indicates the efficacy of active learning for secondary and postsecondary students.

ACTIVE LEARNING IN SOCIAL STUDIES

While experimental research continues to show the usefulness of active learning, descriptive research indicates little application of active learning methods. Project SPAN (Social Studies Priorities, Practices, and Needs) described the current status of social studies and identified problems for social studies in the 1980s. The report showed that relatively little use is made of such active learning methods as inquiry, discovery, community-based learning, and simulations.

Similarly, in his eight-year study on schooling, Goodlad noted "a preponderance of classroom activity including listening, reading textbooks, completing workbooks and worksheets, and taking quizzes—with a paucity of activities requiring problem solving, the achievement of group goals, student's planning and executing a project, and the like".

While Goodlad's description is quite applicable to American schools in general, there are some particular areas where active learning is practiced to a greater degree than in the average school. Law-related education (LRE) is one of these areas. Mock trials engage students in role playing and simulation, in which students assume the roles of characters in a case, set up a mock trial courtroom, and conduct a simplified trial. LRE programmes also include case study analyses, opinion polls, surveys, and learning stations (Smith 1983).

Community-based education is also commanding increased attention. The 1984 NCSS Bulletin (72), *Citizenship And The Critical Role of The Social Studies*, presents a wide variety of action-oriented community-based approaches to teaching citizenship, including the following (Parker and Jarolimek 1984):

- Social-political action projects, such as becoming involved in political campaigns and working with legislators.
- Community projects, such as student work in health clinics and on youth hotlines.
- Student volunteer services, such as work in day care centers.
- Community study, such as surveys of attitudes on current issues.
- Internships in which a few hours per week are spent with community resources such as prosecutors, welfare workers, and artists.

Social studies educators can use the following methods to make the learning experience more active:

- Assess their own teaching methods and plan to incorporate at least one new technique that is more activity oriented than those being used at present.
- Provide students with at least one special, long-term learning experience each year that requires initiative and active participation.
- Focus on skills involving active acquisition of information, organizing and using information, and increasing interpersonal relationships and social participation.
- Take advantage of programmes that by their nature

invite the use of active learning, such as law-related education and local history projects.

- Involve students in recruiting and using community resource people.

Teachers introducing active learning methods for the first time will need to provide a lot of support and encouragement, extended periods of time for exploration, tasks of manageable complexity, and time for students to verify that their answers will be accepted.

IMPORTANCE OF TEACHING AIDS

Education should be a part of everyone's life. A good education offers something for everyone, whether it be on the simple level or a more complex one. Education should provide provide an opportunity for students to develop a strong sense of creativity, a high self esteem, and a life long respect for learning. Education should help students establish a strong sense of confidence in themselves. A teacher will be one factor that helps a student learn and progress along their way through life. Teachers combine their own ideas with other people's to be able to give a good education to their students.

The philosophy on education exists with my ideas combined with others. I agree with Rousseau in that children are neither good nor evil. They can be either. It's how they are brought up that determines that. Children should be in an environment that encourages a desire to learn and make moral choices. Rousseau also brought up the idea of one to one teaching with hands on experience, and I believe that is the best way for the students to learn.

1. First, people tend to not remember what they're told if they don't have a visual to remember it by (especially if it's information they aren't highly motivated to remember). The only parts of Chem 11 I can still remember are the concepts which were taught by demos.
2. Students who are not academically inclined automatically tune out when a teacher is standing in the front and droning on and on about a topic. When

there's something for them to watch, they end up paying attention and becoming engaged (in most cases).

3. Students who are not native speakers may have a very difficult time understanding scientific words, but if they have something visual to see, they can understand the concept and understand the new vocabulary faster.
4. Lastly, using demos allows students to see scientific equipment being used - some of which they may not have a chance to use themselves. Demos show students exactly how certain concepts were discovered (such as the above example of showing how we know the air is only made out of about 21% oxygen).

PROJECTED AIDS

Projected aids are those that require audiovisual equipment in order to be presented properly. Some of the aids included in this category are slides, filmstrips, overhead transparencies (vu-graphs), and motion pictures. It is important to remember that most nonpro- jected aids may be adapted for use as projected aids. A chart, for example, can be photographed and made into a slide.

Anything that can be photographed can be made into a slide. Slides are one of the best known projected aids. They are found in all types and levels of briefings, both informative and educational. Presentations utilizing 35-mm slides can be both informative and educational, while at the same time they can be relatively inexpensive to produce. Filmstrips are used primarily in an educational environment.

Each frame of the 35-mm filmstrip is related to others in such a way that an entire story or lesson can be contained in one strip. A major disadvantage of filmstrips is that they cannot be repaired (spliced) without information.

As used here, transparencies refer to large vu-graph transparencies projected with overhead projectors.

Depending on time factors, the information to be presented, and the quality of transparency desired, production methods may vary from typed information on clear plastic to complex illustrations on colored film. The standard size is 7-1/2 × 9 inches (19 × 23 cm).

KEY POINTS IN USING PROJECTED AIDS

- Preview the material to be projected (film, slide, transparencies, etc.) to insure proper handling of the material. Note the contents of the material in separate files for easy reference.
- Set up the equipments and screen to provide best vision to the screen.
- Check seating arrangements to prevent distorted image.
- Check lighting.
- Test the projection equipment and have an advance rehearsal.
- Always follow the instructions that accompany the equipment.
- Place 'keep out' signs on door to prevent people from entering during the shows.

SLIDE PROJECTOR

The slide projector is available with separate slide carriers.

How to Use

- Fix the slide carrier gently in the right position.
- Arrange the slides in a proper sequence.
- Insert the slide in an exactly "inverted position" to have the image projected in the right position on the screen. Follow the instruction "view from this side" given on the side of each slide to fix it rightly.
- Focus and centre the image on the screen.
- Project the first slide, second one and proceed smoothly in the proper sequence.

Salient Points

At the end of completion of your "slide" showing push

the switch to "fan" position and let it run for a few minutes to cool the lamp and projector. Then switch to "off" position.

Remove the slides from the projector after completion of projection. The slides should be numbered according to sequence, place them in the proper order with thumb marks on each slide on the upper right hand corner for easy handling. Keep the slides in the appropriate containers/boxes with labels for quick reference and prevent them from rolling off or sliding off, as the case may be.

OVER HEAD PROJECTOR

This projection equipment involves large apertures 7" × 7" or 10" × 10" in size. The instructional items must first be converted into transparencies. This is an inexpensive operation. Transparency once made may be used repeatedly.

How to Use[SH]

The extension worker can write directly on the transparency with a help of OHP pen as the object is being projected and at the end of the training, the pen marking may be removed from the transparency by wiping it with a clean cloth or with the help of special cleaner. Over head projector enables the extension officer to face his audience from the front of an illuminated room and project on the screen above and behind him. The extension officer can write, sketch and erase as he is presenting his talk. In addition, he can prepare the required numbers of transparencies in advance and use them at his discretion with no dual operation. The main advantage being that the extension officer facing his audience all the time can observe their reaction to his presentation.

OPAQUE PROJECTOR OR EPIDIASCOPE

Opaque materials like pictures, drawings and three-dimensional objects can be projected through opaque projector.

How to use

- Select proper material.

- *Prepare the material for use:* The actual projectable material should not exceed 10" × 10" and if possible cut into this size.
- For permanence, select a medium weight mounting cardboard.
- For dramatic effect, use coloured background that blend with the picture. Black mounting materials should never be used.
- Cut pictures straight from magazines, journals, or newspapers or from any other available source and mount them evenly and smoothly on the cardboard.
- If desirable, give brief title or explanation on the mount.

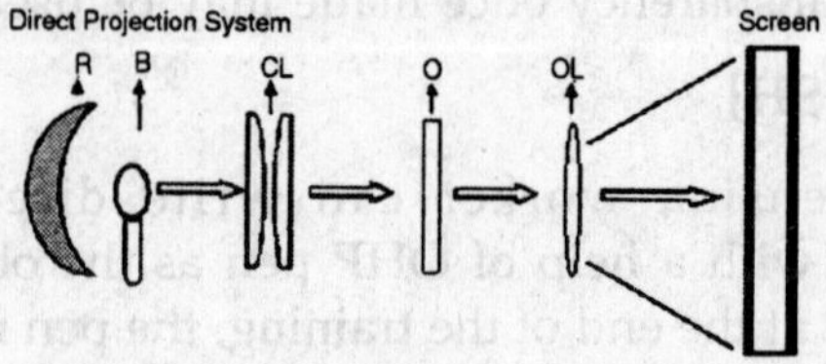

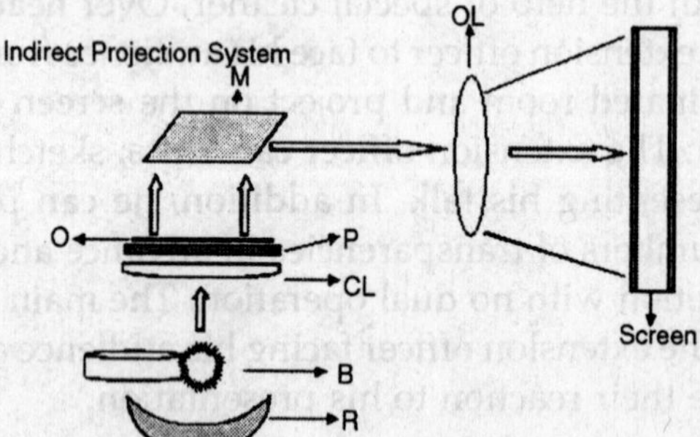

NON-PROJECTED AIDS

- Chalkboard and Whiteboard
- Flannelboard and Magnetboard
- Flipboard, Charts and Wall-Charts
- Posters and Pictorial Materials
- Realia and Models

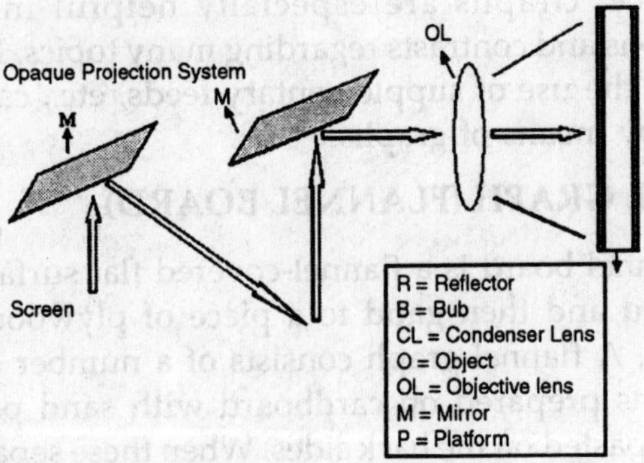

POSTERS

Posters either advertise and sell an idea or convey a message to educate. Posters are aimed towards masses. They are intended to motivate people to act by repeated reminders. Posters are always linked with a campaign in the villages. Five rules for the creation of posters.

- The theme idea
- Psychology of presentation
- Wording
- Composition of design
- Colour management.

CHARTS

Charts make learning experiences more vivid and long lasting. The purposes of charts are

- Present the materials symbolically
- Summaries information.
- Present abstract ideas in visual form.
- Show how something operates.
- Show the size and placements of parts.
- Make facts and figures clear and interesting.
- Show development of structures.
- Emphasise relationships.

GRAPHS

A good graph requires little explanation and tells its story at a glance. Graphs are especially helpful in depicting comparisons and contrasts regarding many topics. Production, growth in the use of supplementary feeds, etc., can easily be depicted by means of graphs.

FLANNEL GRAPH (FLANNEL BOARD)

A flannel board is a flannel-covered flat surface. Flannel is stretched and then gaud to a piece of plywood or heavy cardboard. A flannel graph consists of a number of separate illustrations prepared on cardboard with sand paper strips stapled or pasted on the back sides. When these separate pieces of the flannel graph are placed on the flannel, they stick to it. A flannel graph is a very handy aid for extension workers.

SELECTION OF TEACHING AIDS

Basic Teaching Aids are:

CHALKBOARD OR WHITEBOARD

A chalkboard or whiteboard will help you demonstrate and instruct. The best recommendation, if you need to decide between the two would be the whiteboard—they are cleaner than chalkboards by far.

POINTER

This wand-like teaching aid has many purposes. A pointer can help you with pointing out certain areas like cities, rivers etc. on large, classroom maps, on overhead projectors and on your whiteboard or chalkboard.

CLASSROOM MAPS

Using classroom maps for your teaching aids is a great thing to do.

Often textbooks will have maps in them, but they will be smaller and harder to read. Sometimes when you have the children look at a map in a book and ask them to find a certain area—not all the children will be able to find it right away and so they will miss out on the lesson while searching.

Very seldom will a student raise his or her hand to ask

where on the map the class is looking, either out of shyness or embarrassment.

OVERHEAD PROJECTOR

To have an overhead projector for the classroom is a wonderful teaching aid, you can even use overhead projectors as a substitute for large, hanging classroom maps. The maps can come in eight and a half by eleven or eight by ten sizes that can be projected into much, much larger maps onto your whiteboard or onto a white canvas in the front of the room.

These maps can often be drawn on by an erasable marker (the same you would use for a whiteboard). Thus, there would be no need to use a pointer or to have all those huge roll-up maps to deal with.

COMPUTERS

If it is within the budget of your school or learning institution, to have computers in the classroom or even just in a computer lab somewhere in the school as teaching aids is one of the best types of teaching aids you can offer your students.

Technology is growing every day—and the more children learn about the basics of—and even excel in school-related educational software programmes is almost a necessity these days.

There is also computer software for studying at home. Teaching aids that can be used in the home as tutorials for students who need help in one or more subjects.

There are lots of them out there, so you may want to research which ones will best help the children in your class who have fallen behind. If the software is too costly for the parents, perhaps the school could have this software installed for after-school tutoring.

MASS MEDIA IN TEACHING MATHEMATICS

Mass media is the method of communication used to reach large numbers of people at the same time - TV, newspapers, radio, magazines, films, books, the internet

CONCEPTS OF MEDIA STUDIES

1. All media messages are constructed.
2. Media messages are constructed using a creative language with its own rules.
3. Different people experience the same messages differently.
4. Media have embedded values and points of view.
5. Media messages are constructed to gain profit and/ or power.

Selective Perception

This perspective on how humans "see" the world is based on individual differences of upbringing, race, gender, socioeconomic status, life experiences. The result of these differences is that people perceive and interpret the world differently. Recognizing shared perceptions of the world is essential to understanding how individuals form communities.

Selective Exposure

Individuals are exposed to different experiences and influences—some profound (like nationality or gender) and some subtle (like bigtown/smalltown)—that help shape how they see and make sense of the world, people, issues, culture, society.

Selective Perception

As a result of these difference background and formative influences, individuals see and make sense of the world differently; we all create our own meanings of events around us, filtering information that reaches us through our own prejudices and prior knowledge, framing information so that it makes sense in our own context.

Selective Retention

Based on how we see the world, individuals tend to pay attention to different kinds of information that is more or less relevant and familiar to their own experience. Some information flies right past us; some sticks.

Gatekeeping

There are gatekeepers in any communication system—interpersonal, written, mass communication. These are elements that make constant decisions about what information is or isn't important enough to pass along—what information gets through the "gate" from the sender of a message to a receiver of that message.

Not only does gatekeeping occur in deciding the end message (e.g., what stories get into the newspaper), but also as a reporter decides what stories to cover, what sources to interview, what questions to ask, and what parts of her reporter's notebook are important enough to make it into the story.

So there is both "front-end" gatekeeping as a media message is created, and a "back-end" gatekeeping as an editor decides what stories to put in the paper, on what page, with what headline, and what part of the reporter's story gets edited out. Clearly, individual perceptions of the world and what things are important in it (selective perception) are in play in this process. The ultimate gatekeeper in the mass communication process is the news reader/viewer—what do they think is important/relevant enough to permit through the "gates" of their conscious minds? In this context (and under agenda-setting, below), the media do not reflect "reality"; they filter, shape and construct a "reality." (Remember the principles of media literacy.)

Agenda-Setting

This theory holds that although the mass media can't tell us what to think, the media are stunningly successful at telling us what to think about. That is, through their selection or de-selection of what is "news" (gatekeeping), the mass media serve to create an agenda for social discourse.

When there were only three major national TV networks, and some 70-80% of Americans watched them nightly, a very clear national agenda of what's most important was created. Even in such a monopolistic and dominated mass media system, the networks couldn't make people think in certain ways (because of individual selective perception), but they were and are able to focus attention of some issues while ignoring others. (The Project Censored story is an illustration of what stories did not make the public's agenda/consciousness.) Examples of how agenda-setting worked in society include: The OJ Simpson murder trial; the Clinton impeachment hearings following Zippergate; WMDs and the Iraq War/War on Terrorism. Consider the implications of agenda-setting for public policy debate and creation of laws. Another question: Who sets the agenda for the media agenda-setters?

Framing

This subset of agenda-setting concerns how news and information are "framed" or presented once through the news "gate" and on the public agenda. A media "frame" is the central organizing idea for a news story that supplies a context and emphasizes certain aspects of a story while minimizing or ignoring others.

As media literacy theory tells us, media messages are constructions or representations of "reality." It is impossible for a media message to be anything more than a summary or representation of the world. Thus, the question for message consumers is always: "What aspects of this story are not being told?"

"What information lies outside the 'frame' of this message?" and, perhaps most importantly, "What might be the intent (ideological, intentional or inadvertent) of the senders (gatekeepers) of this message?" So framing suggests that the bottom line in news coverage is not just what to think about (agendasetting), but how to think about it, based on how the story is presented. Framing is not a conspiracy to skew the news (although it can be done that way); individuals, based on their selective perceptions, not only select different things as important, but inevitably frame them in different ways to conform to how they see the world. But what is the effect of that framing on the receiver of those messages, and on the larger society?

Cultivation

The images and impressions and topics (and how they are framed) that appear in the mass media serve to "cultivate" in all of us certain impressions of the world. These messages and the way they are framed—if they are a stable set of images consistent over time—may serve to change our own individual perceptual frame of the world around us. The mass media build and maintain a stable set of images—stories about our culture, our society, who we are—that govern our lives and how we see the world, and influence the decisions we make. Ultimately, mass media messages in sufficient accumulation may influence our behaviour, attitudes, decisions and life choices. This has wide implications for both individuals and for societies. One example is

Gerbner's "mean world syndrome," in which research found that heavy viewers of news tended to perceive the world as a more dangerous and scarier place than light TV viewers. Based on the amount and kind of stuff we include in our mass media diets, we may over time start to "cultivate" new perceptions of people, ideas, issues, etc., with which we have little direct involvement. In short, the cultivate media "reality" may become more real to us over time than real reality. This has important implications for mass media producers and consumers, and for the society in which we live— advertising, consumerism, society anxiety, racism, sexism, etc.

Third Person Effect

Rather than examining media effects in terms of how media may effect the way individuals think about issues and people, TPE theory examines our beliefs about how media effects us and others. In other words—rather than taking the approach that media affect our perceptions, TPE considers how our perceptions shape our ideas about media effects. Research shows that most of us have the perception that media will not have its strongest impact on us—but on other people.

In other words, media will influence other people—but have little influence over me personally. One result of this attitude/perception, according to research, is that people who have this perception, tend to overestimate media's potential impact on others and underestimate potential impact on self.

GOALS

Professional study in the School of Education is based on a model that recognizes and prepares teachers as Professional Educators. The school is committed to providing challenging opportunities for a diverse learning community in a nurturing environment. It is the goal of the School of Education to prepare competent, reflective, and committed professional educators. Competent is the ability to function at a high level of performance within the educational setting of expertise.

Reflective is the ability to call upon the foundation of knowledge so as to make informed decisions within the educational setting.

Committed is the ability to dedicate oneself to providing students with the most effective educational experiences possible and is demonstrated in ones professionalism and willingness to pursue life-long learning.

These three dispositions form the foundation for the professional teacher, administrator, or counselor working in the school setting. The AUM School of Education recognizes that the development of a committed, reflective, and competent educator means the development of a Professional Educator.

Review of Dispositions and Outcomes

1. *Subject Matter Knowledge (Disposition: Competent):* The Professional Educator understands the central concepts tools of inquiry, and structures of the disciplines.
2. *Human Development (Disposition: Reflective):* The Professional Educator understands how people learn and develop.
3. *Diversity (Disposition: Reflective):* The Professional Educator understands how students different in their approaches to learning and creates instructional opportunities that are adapted to diverse learners.

4. *Planning (Disposition: Reflective):* The Professional Educator develops plans based on knowledge of subject matter, students, community, and curriculum goals.
5. *Learning Environment (Disposition: Competent):* The Professional Educator uses an understanding of individual and group motivation plus is responsible for managing and monitoring student learning.
6. *Instructional Strategies (Disposition: Competent):* The Professional Educator understands and uses a variety of instructional strategies.
7. *Communication (Disposition: Competent):* The Professional Educator uses knowledge of effective verbal, nonverbal, and media communication technologies.
8. *Assessment (Disposition: Competent):* The Professional Educator uses formal and informal assessment strategies to evaluate.
9. *Technology (Disposition: Reflective):* The Professional Educator is proficient in the use of technology to enhance teaching and learning.
10. *Professionalism (Disposition: Committed):* The Professional Educator is a reflected practitioner who evaluates the effects of his/her choices and actions on others, and seeks to grow professionally.

Unit VI

Evaluation and Statistic

DIFFERENT TYPES OF TESTS IN MATHEMATICS

MULTIPLE-CHOICE TESTS

Multiple-choice items can be used to measure both simple knowledge and complex concepts. Since multiple-choice questions can be answered quickly, you can assess students' mastery of many topics on an hour exam. In addition, the items can be easily and reliably scored. However, good multiple-choice questions are difficult to write.

TRUE-FALSE TESTS

Because random guessing will produce the correct answer half the time, true-false tests are less reliable than other types of exams. However, these items are appropriate for occasional use. Some faculty who use true-false questions add an "explain" column in which students write one or two sentences justifying their response.

MATCHING TESTS

The matching format is an effective way to test students' recognition of the relationships between words and definitions, events and dates, categories and examples, and so on.

ESSAY TESTS OR ASSIGNMENTS

Essay tests or assignments enable you to judge students' abilities to organize, integrate, interpret material, and express themselves in their own words. Research indicates that students study more efficiently for essay-type examinations than for selection (multiple-choice) tests: students preparing for essay tests focus on broad issues, general concepts, and interrelationships rather than on specific details, and this studying results in somewhat better student performance regardless of the type of exam they are given (McKeachie, 1986).

Essays also give you an opportunity to comment on students' progress, the quality of their thinking, the depth of their understanding, and the difficulties they may be having. However, because essay tests pose only a few questions, their content validity may be low. In addition, the reliability of essay tests is compromised by subjectivity or inconsistencies in grading.

A *variation of an essay test* asks students to correct mock answers. One faculty member prepares a test that requires students to correct, expand, or refute mock essays. Two weeks before the exam date, he distributes ten to twelve essay questions, which he discusses with students in class. For the actual exam, he selects four of the questions and prepares well-written but intellectually flawed answers for the students to edit, correct, expand, and refute.

The mock essays contain common misunderstandings, correct but incomplete responses, or absurd notions; in some cases the answer has only one or two flaws. He reports that students seem to enjoy this type of test more than traditional examinations. Such a design also allows you to focus on specific elements of understanding which provides a bit more structure for students taking the exam and in grading it.

SHORT-ANSWER TESTS

Depending on your objectives, short-answer questions can call for one or two sentences or a long paragraph. Short-answer tests are easier to write, though they take longer to score, than multiple-choice tests.

They also give you some opportunity to see how well students can express their thoughts, though they are not as useful as longer essay responses for this purpose.

PROBLEM SETS

In courses in mathematics and the sciences, your tests can include problem sets. As a rule of thumb, allow students ten minutes to solve a problem you can do in two minutes.

ORAL EXAMS

Oral exams are sometimes used for undergraduates in foreign language classes. In other classes they are usually seen as too time-consuming, too anxiety provoking for students, and too difficult to score unless the instructor tape-records the answers.

However, a math professor has experimented with individual thirty-minute oral tests in a small seminar class. Students receive the questions in advance and are allowed to drop one of their choosing. During the oral exam, the professor probes students' level of understanding of the theory and principles behind the theorems. He reports that about eight students per day can be tested.

PERFORMANCE TESTS

Performance tests ask students to demonstrate proficiency in conducting an experiment, executing a series of steps in a reasonable amount of time, following instructions, creating drawings, manipulating materials or equipment, or reacting to real or simulated situations. Performance tests can be administered individually or in groups. Performance tests can be useful in classes that require students to demonstrate their skills.

If you use performance tests,

- Specify the criteria to be used for rating or scoring (for example, the level of accuracy in performing the steps in sequence or completing the task within a specified time limit).
- State the problem so that students know exactly what they are supposed to do (if possible, conditions of a performance test should mirror a real-life situation).
- Give students a chance to perform the task more than once or to perform several task samples.

ALTERNATIVE TEST METHODS

Take-home Tests

Take-home tests allow students to work at their own pace with access to books and materials. Take-home tests also permit longer and more involved questions, without sacrificing valuable class time for exams. Problem sets, short answers, and essays are the most appropriate kinds of take-home exams. Be wary, though, of designing a take-home exam that is too difficult or an exam that does not include limits on the number of words or time spent. Also, be sure to give students explicit instructions on what they can and cannot do: for example, are they allowed to talk to other students about their answers?

A variation of a take-home test is to give the topics in advance but ask the students to write their answers in class. Some faculty hand out ten or twelve questions the week before an exam and announce that three of those questions will appear on the exam.

Open-book Tests

Open-book tests simulate the situations professionals face every day, when they use resources to solve problems, prepare reports, or write memos. Open-book tests tend to be inappropriate in introductory courses in which facts must be learned or skills thoroughly mastered if the student is to progress to more complicated concepts and techniques in advanced courses. On an open-book test, students who are lacking basic knowledge may waste too much of their time consulting their references rather than writing. Open-book tests appear to reduce stress but research shows that students do not necessarily perform significantly better on open-book tests. Further, open-book tests seem to reduce students' motivation to study.

A compromise between open- and closed-book testing is to let students bring an index card or one page of notes to the exam or to distribute appropriate reference material such as equations or formulas as part of the test.

Group Exams

Some faculty have successfully experimented with group exams, either in class or as take-home projects. Faculty report that groups outperform individuals and that students respond positively to group. For example, for a fifty-minute in-class exam, use a multiple-choice test of about twenty to twenty-five items.

For the first test, the groups can be randomly divided. Groups of three to five students seem to work best. For subsequent tests, you may want to assign students to groups in ways that minimize differences between group scores and balance talkative and quiet students. Or you might want to group students who are performing at or near the same level (based on students' performance on individual tests).

Some faculty have students complete the test individually before meeting as a group. Others just let the groups discuss the test, item by item. In the first case, if the group score is higher than the individual score of any member, bonus points are added to each individual's score. In the second case, each student receives the score of the group. Faculty who use group exams offer the following tips:

- Ask students to discuss each question fully and weigh the merits of each answer rather than simply vote on an answer.
- If you assign problems, have each student work a problem and then compare results.
- If you want students to take the exam individually first, consider devoting two class periods to tests; one for individual work and the other for group.
- Show students the distribution of their scores as individuals and as groups; in most cases group scores will be higher than any single individual score.

A variation of this idea is to have students first work on an exam in groups outside of class. Students then complete the exam individually during class time and receive their own score. Some portion of the test items are derived from the group exam. The rest are new questions. Or let students know in advance you will be asking them to justify a few of their responses; this will keep students from blithely relying on their work group for all the answers.

Paired Testing

For paired exams, pairs of students work on a single essay exam, and the two students turn in one paper. Some students may be reluctant to share a grade, but good students will most likely earn the same grade they would have working alone. Pairs can be self-selected or assigned. For example, pairing a student who is doing well in the course with one not doing well allows for some peer teaching. A variation is to have students work in teams but submit individual answer sheets.

Portfolios

A portfolio is not a specific test but rather a cumulative collection of a student's work. Students decide what examples to include that characterize their growth and accomplishment over the term. While most common in composition classes, portfolios are beginning to be used in other disciplines to provide a fuller picture of students' achievements.

A student's portfolio might include sample papers (first drafts and revisions), journal entries, essay exams, and other work representative of the student's progress; it should included a reflective essay explaining effects, outcomes, uses of ideas, skills and values documented in the portfolio. You can assign portfolios a letter grade or a pass/not pass. If you do grade portfolios, you will need to establish clear criteria.

MATHEMATICS ACHIEVEMENT

Math is a critical skill in the information age. We must improve achievement to maintain our economic leadership. While technology advances with lightning speed, stagnant math performance in schools shortchanges our students' future and endangers our prosperity and our nation's security.

Math achievement is improving slightly, but much more work must be done to ensure that our children receive a sound background in mathematics.

According to the 2000 National Assessment of Educational

Progress (NAEP), the average math scores of fourth- and eighth-graders, and twelfth-graders have improved only slightly.

However, only a quarter of our fourth- and eighth-graders are performing at or above proficient levels in math. Twelfth-grade math scores have not improved since 1996, and a closer look at those scores reveals that the biggest drop occurred at the lowest levels of achievement. These are the students who most need our help and who can least afford to lose any more ground.

No Child Left Behind creates Math and Science Partnerships to rally every sector of society to work with schools to increase math and science excellence.

- The National Science Foundation and the U.S. Department of Education will provide an estimated $1 billion over five years for results-oriented partnerships between local districts and universities to bring urgency, tested methods, and high level expertise to rebuilding math excellence.
- Partnerships will invite businesses, science centers, museums and community organizations to unite with schools to improve achievement.
- The programme rewards states for increasing participation of students in advanced courses in math and science and passing advanced placement exams.
- To ensure accountability, the Partnerships must report annually to the U.S. Secretary of Education on progress in meeting their set objectives, aligned to state standards.

  The president has called for increasing the ranks and pay of teachers of math and science.
- *No Child Left Behind* requires states to fill the nation's classrooms with teachers who are knowledgeable and experienced in math and science by 2005. The president supports paying math and science teachers more to help attract experience and excellence.

  Our nation must research the best way to teach math and science and measure students' progress in math.

- *No Child Left Behind* requires that federal funding go only to those programmes that are backed by evidence.
- Over the last decade, researchers have scientifically proven the best ways to teach reading. We must do the same in math. That means using only research-based teaching methods and rejecting unproven fads.
- The new law also requires states to measure students' progress in math annually in grades 3-8 beginning in 2005.

The number of research studies conducted in mathematics education over the past three decades has increased dramatically. Research findings indicate that certain teaching strategies and methods are worth careful consideration as teachers strive to improve their mathematics teaching practices. For the classroom implications of the research findings summarized here, please see the companion to this Digest, "Improving Student Achievement in Mathematics,

1. The extent of the students' opportunity to learn mathematics content bears directly and decisively on student mathematics achievement.

Opportunity to learn (OTL) was studied in the First International Mathematics Study (Husen, 1967), where teachers were asked to rate the extent of student exposure to particular mathematical concepts and skills. Strong correlations were found between OTL scores and mean student achievement scores, with high OTL scores associated with high achievement. The link was also found in subsequent international studies, such as the Second International Mathematics Study and the Third International Mathematics and Science study.

2. Focusing instruction on the meaningful development of important mathematical ideas increases the level of student learning.

There is a long history of research, going back to the work of Brownell (1945,1947), on the effects of teaching for meaning and understanding. Investigations have consistently shown that an emphasis on teaching for meaning has positive effects on student learning, including better initial learning, greater retention and an increased likelihood that the ideas will be used in new situations.

3. Students can learn both concepts and skills by solving problems.

Research suggests that students who develop conceptual understanding early perform best on procedural knowledge later. Students with good conceptual understanding are able to perform successfully on near-transfer tasks and to develop procedures and skills they have not been taught. Students with low levels of conceptual understanding need more practice in order to acquire procedural knowledge.

4. Giving students both an opportunity to discover and invent new knowledge and an opportunity to practice what they have learned improves student achievement.

Data from the TIMSS video study show that over 90% of mathematics class time in the United States 8th-grade classrooms is spent practicing routine procedures, with the remaining time generally spent applying procedures in new situations. Virtually no time is spent inventing new procedures and analyzing unfamiliar situations. In contrast, students at the same grade level in typical Japanese classrooms spend approximately 40% of instructional time practicing routine procedures, 15% applying procedures in new situations, and 45% inventing new procedures and analyzing new situations.

Research suggests that students need opportunities for both practice and invention. Findings from a number of studies show that when students discover mathematical ideas and invent mathematical procedures, they have a stronger conceptual understanding of connections between mathematical ideas.

5. Teaching that incorporates students' intuitive solution methods can increase student learning, especially when combined with opportunities for student interaction and discussion.

Student achievement and understanding are significantly improved when teachers are aware of how students construct knowledge, are familiar with the intuitive solution methods that students use when they solve problems, and utilize this knowledge when planning and conducting instruction in mathematics.

Structuring instruction around carefully chosen problems, allowing students to interact when solving problems, and then providing opportunities for them to share their solution methods result in increased achievement on problem-solving measures. These gains come without a loss of achievement in the skills and concepts measured on standardized achievement tests.

6. Using small groups of students to work on activities, problems and assignments can increase student mathematics achievement.

Davidson reviewed studies that compared student achievement in small group settings with traditional whole-class instruction. In more than 40% of these studies, students in the classes using small group approaches significantly outscored control students on measures of student performance.

In only two of the 79 studies did control-group students perform better than the small group students, and in these studies there were some design irregularities. From a review of 99 studies of cooperative group-learning methods, Slavin concluded that cooperative methods were effective in improving student achievement. The most effective methods emphasized both group goals and individual accountability.

7. Whole-class discussion following individual and group work improves student achievement.

Research suggests that whole class discussion can be effective when it is used for sharing and explaining the variety of solutions by which individual students have solved problems. It allows students to see the many ways of examining a situation and the variety of appropriate and acceptable solutions. Wood (1999) found that whole-class discussion works best when discussion expectations are clearly understood. Students should be expected to evaluate each other's ideas and reasoning in ways that are not critical of the sharer. Students should be expected to be active listeners who participate in discussion and feel a sense of responsibility for each other's understanding.

8. Teaching mathematics with a focus on number sense encourages students to become problem solvers in a wide variety of situations and to view mathematics as a discipline in which thinking is important.

"Number sense" relates to having an intuitive feel for number size and combinations, and the ability to work flexibly with numbers in problem situations in order to make sound decisions and reasonable judgments. It involves mentally computing, estimating, sensing number magnitudes, moving between representation systems for numbers, and judging the reasonableness of numerical results.

Markovits and Sowder (1994) studied 7th-grade classes where special units on number magnitude, mental computation and computational estimation were taught. They determined that after this special instruction, students were more likely to use strategies that reflected sound number sense, and that this was a long-lasting change. In a study of second graders, Cobb (1991) and his colleagues found that students' number sense was improved by a problem-centered curriculum that emphasized student interaction and self-generated solution methods. Almost every student developed a variety of strategies to solve a wide range of problems. Students also demonstrated increased persistence in solving problems.

9. Long-term use of concrete materials is positively related to increases in student mathematics achievement and improved attitudes towards mathematics.

In a review of activity-based learning in mathematics in kindergarten through grade 8, Suydam and Higgins (1977) concluded that using manipulative materials produces greater achievement gains than not using them. In a more recent meta-analysis of sixty studies (kindergarten through postsecondary) that compared the effects of using concrete materials with the effects of more abstract instruction, Sowell (1989) found that the long-term use of concrete materials by teachers knowledgeable in their use improved student achievement and attitudes.

10. Using calculators in the learning of mathematics can result in increased achievement and improved student attitudes.

Studies have consistently shown that thoughtful use of calculators improves student mathematics achievement and attitudes toward mathematics. From a meta-analysis of 79 non-graphing calculator studies, Hembree and Dessart (1986) concluded that use of hand-held calculators improved student learning.

Analysis also showed that students using calculators tended to have better attitudes towards mathematics and better self-concepts in mathematics than their counterparts who did not use calculators. They also found that there was no loss in student ability to perform paper-and-pencil computational skills when calculators were used as part of mathematics instruction.

Research on the use of graphing calculators has also shown positive effects on student achievement. Most studies have found positive effects on students' graphing ability, conceptual understanding of graphs and their ability to relate graphical representations to other representations. Most studies of graphing calculators have found no negative effect on basic skills, factual knowledge, or computational skills.

IMPORTANCE

Basic Skills Serve Equity

The lack of progress in computation skills has disproportionately affected African-American students. The black-white achievement gap expanded in every computation skill area in the 1990s. This is typical of what happens when basic skills are shortchanged. The students who pay the biggest price are those with the least to lose, those for whom the educational system has never worked very well. When basic skills are not taught, the least privileged in our society—those who cannot afford tutors, fancy computer programmes, or academic summer camps—suffer the biggest losses.

Basic Skills are Necessary to Advance in Math

Insisting that students master computation skills is not to advocate that they stop at the basics. Basic skills are a floor, not a ceiling. Students must learn arithmetic so that they can move on to more demanding mathematics—algebra, geometry, calculus. An emphasis on the basics should never be used as an excuse to straightjacket students or to slow their progress in the math curriculum.

Basic Skills Predict Adult Earnings

In recent years, a growing body of research has documented that the skills and knowledge students learn in school is correlated with success later in life. In their landmark study showing the impact of basic skills on adult earnings, Richard Murnane and Frank Levy conclude, "mastery of skills taught in American schools no later than the eighth grade is an increasingly important determinant of subsequent wages."

A final Word on the Controversy Surrounding Basic Skills

I am mystified when some analysts refer to a concern for arithmetic and computation skills as advocating "back to basics." Well, as an old elementary teacher, I am very concerned about American fourth graders learning arithmetic. A 50% proficiency rate is unacceptable. But I don't want to go back to anything.

I want to go *forward* on the basics. Back to basics implies there was a golden age when everyone learned essential skills. That age has never existed. To ensure that every fourth grader is proficient at whole number arithmetic means that we must go forward, not backward.

We must go forward on basic skills if a more equitable school system is a national goal; we must go forward if American students are to be prepared for higher level mathematics; we must go forward if young people are to master the skills correlated with middle class employment as adults.

Back to basics is a bad idea. There is nothing to go back to but mediocrity and failure. It is time to go forward as a nation on basic skills.

DIAGNOSTIC IN MATHS

The Diagnostic in Mathematics comprises of Module Tests which are primarily criterion-referenced based, as opposed to norm-referenced. Diagnostic Reading and Spelling Tests are norm-referenced tests. As the math tests are criterion-referenced, it means that they relate closely to an efficient mathematical curriculum outline of essential skills and understandings. In short, they follow an extensive and reliable mathematical scope and sequence. There is no strict time limit for each test, however, there is a set range of tests for particular age/year levels.

Being criterion-referenced, also means that essentially, students should be able to achieve a high degree of success with the tests assigned to their particular age/year level. Teachers may also need to read out the questions to students (without guiding them in how to answer). In particular, junior primary teachers may need to gauge the reading competency of their group and decide whether to have all the students complete the sections as they are read out.

Complex concepts are supported by lower order concepts in earlier tests. For example, children who have trouble telling the time need to understand foundation concepts such as recognizing numerals, understanding quantity and order, counting by ones, fives and tens, event sequencing, even understanding exactly what half and quarter actually mean. All these essential foundation skills are covered before clock-face time is introduced.

This is how all the tests have been designed to work and that is why they remain as popular as ever. Given these tests can be efficiently used on a group or one-to-one basis, they will quickly highlight student strengths and weaknesses. If used on a cross-school basis, student results can be recorded and compared year to year using the Maths subject section of School Express. Please note that Version 2 of School Data Express also allows for the automated graphing of student Math percentage results over time. Student results can be compared against the average results of any found group (or all records) in your school.

The following table has been reproduced from the Help section of School Data Express. This information is supplied in response to teachers wanting to know the approximate age levels for each test. An approximate Math's Age can be derived from the table. Many teachers have established the data via field use of the scope and sequence of each test,, over a 20 year period. Math test books currently selling have this table printed in the Introduction.

In the field, a year 3 student given test, at the start of their school year, should achieve highly (e.g. 90-100%). Furthermore, given the math tests follow a detailed and essential scope and sequence, no 'average' score below a high mark of achievement for any one test is acceptable. Hence the guide given below already establishes the 'average' tests for each age/year level. Therefore, if a year 3 student can not achieve a high success rate with test 9, yet obtains a high success rate with test 7, you can assume that the student has achieved beginning year 2 concepts and is operating approximately a year behind, that being middle year 2.

The maximum raw score is based on the total number of question sections. There may be two or more problem examples for each question section. It is up to individual teachers to decide how they score the tests. It is also important for teachers to make informed judgements about a student's understanding of particular concepts as well as their degree of applied skill.

This may not always be apparent on face value and may necessitate the teacher running brief student conferencing or allowing students time to revisit test items (particularly if they have overlooked items or failed to comprehend the direct meaning of a task in the first instant). It is recommended that a mark be given for a question section where more than half of the examples are answered correctly and/or demonstrate understanding by the student.

Therefore, question section 1 has 15 response examples. If the student answers 8 correctly, the teacher may give half a mark for question section 1. If the student answers 13 correctly, the teacher may give a full mark for that section. Once all the marks are added up, a student may score 17 out of 19 for Test 16. This approximate 90% success rate quickly demonstrates the time is right for the student to move onto harder skill learning phases and/or the next test.

A score of less than 17 means failed test sections would need to be revisited with appropriate learning opportunities. Unlike norm-referenced tests, students should be given their marked tests back so they can see evidence of their successes and failures. If the tests go in a school-home assessment/ communication folder/book, then parents also become valuable participants in their child's learning process.

PROGNOSTIC IN MATHEMATICS

The validity of a test depends on what the information (test result) is to be used for. For the kind of test discussed here it seems proper to talk about prognostic validity. This means that the analysis and interpretation of the results (i.e. the written test protocols) must be based on how well they may prognosticate academic performance in mathematics. The prognostic validity of the test may then be valued from the outcomes of this process, and is thus a function of such factors as design, selection of tasks, content specification, and rationale for protocol analysis In this paper, with prognostic validity in focus, a framework for the protocol analysis has been suggested consisting of ten factors that have been judged to be critical for future academic performance in mathematics.

In a traditional achievement score, which within a mathematics department has a considerable reliability and validity, according to the standards of the faculty, critical factors may implicitly be evoked. There is seldom, however, a stated 'general manual' for the correcting proce-dure. The validity and reliability of the markings are normally based on teacher experience and judgement only. A theory of how to find appropriate forms for analysing responses to an assessment situation is still lacking (Webb, 1992). One has to take into account not only the four components mentioned above 9 but also the interaction between them. This means that one must keep some kind of control of the whole assessment process, so that all its aspects are in alignment with the purpose of the assessment.One preliminary quantitative measure of the prognostic validity of the DP test is given by the correlation between the total score on the DP test and the total score on the university mathematics exams.

As can be seen from table 4, these ranged from.52 to.90 on the first calculus exam, and from.44 to.86 on the second. For the Y and D programmemes, this prognostic validity of the DP test was quite substantial. A fact that must be considered here is that the DP test and the first calculus exam both are written problem solving mathematics tests, given with a delay of only two months. Therefore a positive correlation between those tests was to be expected and explained maybe by the general cognitive ability factor *g* (cf. the factor analysis in table 3). However, the point made here is that the DP test, based on high school mathematics content only, was designed to have a strong correlation with the exams results, and it may well be the case that in basic university mathematics the *g* factor shows by its influence on the critical factors (cf Gustafsson, 1988).

More data will be needed to further evaluate the prognostic validity of the DP test.

CRITERION AND NORM REFERENCED EVALUATION

There are Two forms of grading exist:

- Criterion based.
- Norm reference based.
- Criterion and Norm-Referenced assessment refer to the 'type' of assessment, while summative and formative refer to the 'function' of the assessment (Brown, Bull, and Pendlebury, 1997).

A criterion-referenced assessment has set criteria to be achieved and therefore the pass-fail aspect of the assessment is the most important aspect. The driving test is a good example of a criterion-referenced assessment. In theory all students could pass the assessment or alternatively all students could fail the assessment.

A norm-referenced assessment expresses the candidates' scores in rank order, based on a distribution of scores. It is comparative, telling us that one student is better than another student. Normal distributions curves are often associated with norm-referenced assessment.

Letter grades appear in both forms on the academic transcript. Once on the transcript, neither form is distinguishable from the other.

The grade scale, which sets a predetermined numerical performance value equal to a letter grade, is criterion based. Perhaps the most frequently used scale sets 90% -100% as A, 80% - 89% as B, 70% - 79% as C, etc. This is the purest form of the "classic grading system." There is no predetermined class GPA. All students can, in theory, earn the grade of A. Reducing or watering down course content facilitates a large number of high letter grades. This practice is called dubbing down.

The class curve constitutes a norm reference based system. The class average may or may not be taken into account as a basis for assigning grades. A predetermined class GPA may or may not exist.

If so, this GPA may be set by the individual faculty member, or by the department, or even by the institution for all departments. If the class average GPA is not set in advance it can be expected to vary from class to class and course to course.

In either case, preset GPA or not, the real extent of course content mastery cannot be determined from the academic transcript. The transcript itself does not distinguish between criterion based and norm reference based evaluation.

Both forms of evaluation should now be combined into a single format in order to provide much improved clarity in presenting the actual level of content mastery that occurs course by course.

CRITERION BASED

Textbook content defines the appropriate level of learning to be achieved in most courses. This is criterion based. Course syllabi define the extent of in-class coverage of textbook content. Master syllabi define the content of course syllabi. This system provides a consistent standard against which the extent of learning is measured. Adoption of a strictly numerical approach to evaluation of learning provides the clearest depiction of the extent of learning accomplished.

NORM REFERENCED

Norm referenced evaluation is defined by relative standing in the class in relation to some standard or norm. When norm referenced evaluation adopts a totally numerical approach and assigns a rank of 0 to the class average, ranking is expected to produce a *normal* distribution commonly referred to as the bell shaped curve.

Such a ranking system removes the incentive to numerically inflate performance scores. Academic assessment procedures can be implemented to further discourage numerical inflation. Such a system then permits use of standard statistical procedures in calculating the variance and standard deviation. Further resolution can be attained through established statistical methods in use for hypothesis testing.

Use of the grade scale has led or is rapidly leading to a distribution of letter grades in which A's predominate. C has been called the "Mark of Cain." D & F are disappearing. This produces a distribution appropriate to describing the occurrence of random events. One random event simply occurs more frequently than the next, and so on down the line.

Letter grades are converted to a numerical value, the GPA which does permit calculations of variance and standard deviation. Upper end compaction skews the resulting distribution which no longer represents a balanced use of the entire letter grade spectrum. Tighter compaction around this elevated GPA compresses the variance and standard deviation making students appear increasingly identical. This compression defies the simple truth that all students are not the same and not all students are excellent in all disciplines. The end result is that grade inflation discriminates against higher education's better students by covering their hard earned academic achievements under an avalanche of high grades.

DIFFERENCE IN TWO TEST

Dimension	*Criterion-Referenced Tests*	*Norm-Referenced Tests*
Purpose	To determine whether each student has achieved specific skills or concepts. To find out how much students know before instruction begins and after it has finished.	To rank each student with respect to the achievement of others in broad areas of knowledge. To discriminate between high and low achievers.
Content	Measures specific skills which make up a designated curriculum. These skills are identified by teachers and curriculum experts. Each skill is expressed as an instructional objective.	Measures broad skill areas sampled from a variety of textbooks, syllabi, and the judgments of curriculum experts.
Item Characteristics	Each skill is tested by at least four items in order to obtain an adequate sample of student performance and to minimize the effect of guessing. The items which test any given skill are parallel in difficulty.	Each skill is usually tested by less than four items. Items vary in difficulty. Items are selected that discriminate between high and low achievers.
Score Interpretation	Each individual is compared with a preset standard for acceptable achievement. The performance of other examinees is irrelevant. A student's score is usually expressed as a percentage. Student achievement is reported for individual skills.	Each individual is compared with other examinees and assigned a score--usually expressed as a percentile, a grade equivalent score, or a stanine. Student achievement is reported for broad skill areas, although some norm-referenced tests do report student achievement for individual skills.

CONSTRUCTION OF ACHIEVEMENT TEST

GENERAL STEPS

- Identify and define the learning outcomes to be measured
- Prepare test specifications
- Construct relevant test items
- Review and edit the items
- Arrange the items in the test
- Prepare directions

Step 1

- Identify and Define Learning Objectives (Outcomes)
- State the General Objectives
- Develop 5 to 15 General Objectives
- Begin each General Objective with one of the six cognitive domain headings of Bloom's Taxonomy
- State the Specific Objectives
- For each G.O., develop 3-5 Specific Objectives
- Begin each S.O. with an action verb

Step 2

Preparing Test Specifications

- Select the Specific Outcomes to be tested
- Outline the subject matter by listing topic and subtopic areas in the lesson plan
- Make a two-way Table of Specifications

Step 3

Construct Relevant Test Items and Consider:

- Selecting the type of test items to use
- Selection Type Items (e.g., multiple choice, true-false, matching, interpretive exercises.
- Supply Type Items (e.g., short answer, essay (restricted response), essay (extended response)
- Matching items to Specific Objectives
- For each S.O., write one or more related items

Nature of Multiple-Choice Items

Parts of an Item:

- Stem - the question or incomplete sentence.
- Alternatives - the choices
- Distractors - the incorrect choices

Uses of Multiple-Choice Items

Knowledge Items

Measures the degree to which material is remembered

Comprehension Items

Measures the degree to which material is remembered and understood

Application Items

Measures the degree to which material is remembered, understood, and can be applied

Writing Multiple-Choice Items

General Rules

Nothing in the item should prevent an informed student from answering correctly

Nothing in the item should increase the probability that an uninformed student will answer correctly

True-False Items

Students identify whether a statement of fact is correct. Most effective when there are only two possible responses.

Variations of True-False Items

Supply-Type

For statements that are false, the student must underline the part of the statement that is false and change the false statement so it is true

Cluster-Type

The student judges whether a series of items based on a common stem are true or false.

Matching Items

- When the same alternatives are repeated in several multiple-choice items, combine in a matching item.

Parts of a Matching Item

Premises: A series of stems.
Responses: A series of alternative answers.

Interpretive Exercises

- An introductory paragraph, table, chart, graph, map or picture is provided and the student answers a series of items related to specific objectives

Types of Supply-Type Items

- Short-Answer Items
- Restricted-Response Essay.
- Extended-Response Essay.

Short-Answer Items

- Requires the student to supply the appropriate words, numbers or symbols to complete a statement.

Restricted-Response Essays

- The student supplies a response to a narrowly defined problem and directions.

Extended-Response Essays

- Student supplies a response to a problem with few boundaries.

Guidelines for Effective and Fair Grading

- Inform students of grading procedures
- Base grades on student achievement only
- Base grades on a variety of valid assessment data

- When combining scores, use proper weighting
- Select an appropriate frame of reference (i.e., absolute or relative)

STATICAL MEASURES

OVERVIEW

Currently, the Simulator class collects two Lists. One has the length of a session, the other has the maximum stake during a session. We need to create some descriptive statistics to summarize these stakes and session lengths.

ON STATISTICS

In principle, we could apply basic probability theory to predict the statistics generated by this simulation. Indeed, some of the statistics we are gathering are almost matters of definition, rather than actual unknown data. We are, however, much more interested in the development of the software than we are in applying probability theory to a relatively simple casino game. As a consequence, the statistical analysis here is a little off-base.

In spite of our problems, we will build a relatively simple-minded set of descriptive statistics. We will average two metrics: the peak stake for a session and the duration of the session. Both of these values have some statistical problems. The peak stake, for instance, is already a summary number. We have to be cautious in our use of summarized numbers, since we have lost any sense of the frequency with which the peaks occured. For example, a player may last 250 cycles of play, with a peak stake of 130. We don't know if that peak occurred once or 100 times out of that 250. Additionally, the length of the session has an upper bound on the number of cycles. This forces the distribution of values to be skewed away from the predictable distribution.

We will design a Statistics class with responsibility to retain and summarize a list of numbers and produce the average (also known as the mean) and standard deviation. The Simulator can then use this this Statistics class to get an average of the maximum stakes from the list of session-level measures. The Simulator can also apply this Statistics class to the list of session durations to see an average length of game play before going broke.

We can encapsulate this statistical processing in two ways: we could extend an existing class or we could delegate the statistical functions to a separate class. If we extend the library java.util.List, we can add the needed statistical summary features; given this new class, we can replace the original List of sample values with a StatisticalList that both saves the values and computes descriptive statistics. In addition to delegation, we have two choices for implementation of this extended version of List, giving us three alternative designs.

1. Extend LinkedList. In this case, we are simply adding two new methods to the existing LinkedList implementation. However, our new methods would not apply to ArrayList or Vector.
2. Extend AbstractList. However, in doing this we would need to provide the implementation details of the list structure itself. In effect, we would reimplement LinkedList or ArrayList.
3. Create a separate class that computes statistics on a List given as an argument to the methods of the statistical class. In this case, our statistical methods will work with any subclass that implements the interface List. This can be applied to any of LinkedList, ArrayList or Vector.

Alternative three — a separate statistical class — has the most reuse potential. We'll create a simple class with two methods: mean and stdev to compute the mean and standard deviation of a List of Integer objects. This can be used in a variety of contexts, and allows us the freedom to switch List implementation classes without any other changes.

Many times the outcome of a situation is difficult, maybe impossible, to predict. All we can say is that there is some range or distribution of possible outcomes. This is true for situations involving only inanimate objects, but is especially true for situations (like those you might find in an HCI environment) involving human beings. We might hope during these times to see some of the typical behaviors or events possible. This notion lies behind the statistical quantity of the *mean*.

It would also be nice to know something about the variety of events that are likely to occur. This corresponds to a quantity like *variance* or else *standard deviation*.

Another problem is that we can only make a finite number of measurements on the real world, called a *sample,* as we seek to gain information about it. It's possible that the sample we get may not actually represent what is typical in the real world. We would like to be able to get an idea of what level of *confidence* can we place on the ability of our measurements to represent what is really going on in the world.

When we need to compare two samples or a sample to some required value, we can use the *t*-test to determine the how *significant* our sample is. If we have sample data that falls into categories, the *chi-square* analysis helps us determine the significance.

Statistics Measures such as (univariate statistics) applied to datasets, and associated formulas for calculating the measure from a sample dataset in summation form (rather than integral form) where necessary. In some instances these formulas are adjusted to provide estimates of the population values rather than those obtained from the sample of data one is working on.

Many of the measures can be extended to two-dimensional forms in a very straightforward manner, and thus they provide the basis for numerous standard formulas in spatial statistics. For a number of univariate statistics (variance, skewness, kurtosis) we refer to the notion of (estimated) *moments* about the mean. These are computations of the form

$$\sum(x_i - \bar{x})^r, r = 1, 2, 3...$$

When $r = 1$ this summation will be 0, since this is just the difference of all values from the mean. For values of $r > 1$ the expression provides measures that are useful for describing the shape (spread, skewness, peakedness) of a distribution, and simple variations on the formula are used to define the correlation between two or more datasets (the *product moment* correlation). The term *moment* in this context comes from physics, i.e. like 'momentum' and 'moment of inertia', and in a spatial (2D) context provides the basis for the definition of a centroid — the centre of mass or centre of gravity of an object, such as a polygon.

STATISTICAL MEASURES

This table of measures has been divided into 9 subsections for ease of use. Each is provided with its own subheading:

- Counts and specific values
- Measures of centrality.
- Measures of spread.
- Measures of distribution shape.
- Measures of complexity and dimensionality.
- Common distributions.
- Data transforms and back transforms.
- Selected functions.
- Matrix expressions.

DEFINITION

Measures of central tendency, or "location", attempt to quantify what we mean when we think of as the "typical" or "average" score in a data set. The concept is extremely important and we encounter it frequently in daily life. For example, we often want to know before purchasing a car its average distance per litre of petrol.

Or before accepting a job, you might want to know what a typical salary is for people in that position so you will know whether or not you are going to be paid what you are worth. Or, if you are a smoker, you might often think about how many cigarettes you smoke "on average" per day. Statistics geared toward measuring central tendency all focus on this concept of "typical" or "average." As we will see, we often ask questions in psychological science revolving around how groups differ from each other "on average". Answers to such a question tell us a lot about the phenomenon or process we are studying.

MODE

By far the simplest, but also the least widely used, measure of central tendency is the mode. The mode in a distribution of data is simply the score that occurs most frequently. In the distribution of sexual partners data, the mode is "1" because it is the most frequently occurring score in the data set. If you have had only one sexual partner in the last year, it would be reasonable therefore to say that you are fairly typical of UNE students (or at least of those students who responded to the question).

Importantly, you cant necessarily claim that "most" UNE students had only one sexual partner last year. From the frequency distribution, notice that actually fewer than half of the respondents reported having only one sexual partner. So "most" students reported having something different to 1 sexual partner. Still, "1" was the most frequent single response to this question, and so it is the mode or modal response. In some cases, however, such a conclusion would be justified.

Recall that one way of describing a distribution is in terms of the number of modes in the data. A unimodal distribution has one mode. In contrast, a bimodal distribution has two. Now this might seem odd to you.

How can there be more than one "most frequently occurring" score in a data set? I suppose statisticians are a bit bizarre in this way. We would accept that a distribution is bimodal if it seems that more than one score or value "stands out" as occurring especially frequently in comparison to other values. But when the data are quantitative in nature, we also want to make sure that the two more frequently occurring scores are not too close to each other in value before we accept the distribution as one that could be described as "bimodal." So there is some subjectivity in the decision as to whether or not a distribution is best characterised as unimodal, bimodal, or multimodal.

MEDIAN

Technically, the median of a distribution is the value that cuts the distribution exactly in half, such that an equal number of scores are larger than that value as there are smaller than that value. The median is by definition what we call the 50th percentile. This is an ideal definition, but often distributions can be cut exactly in half in this way, but we still can define the median in the distribution. Distributions of qualitative data do not have a median.

The median is most easily computed by sorting the data in the data set from smallest to largest. The median is the "middle" score in the distribution. Suppose we have the following scores in a data set: 5, 7, 6, 1, 8. Sorting the data, we have: 1, 5, 6, 7, 8. The "middle score" is 6, so the median is 6. Half of the (remaining) scores are larger than 6 and half of the (remaining) scores are smaller than 6.

To derive the median, using the following rule. First, compute (n + 1)/2, where n is the number of data points. Here, there are 5, so n = 5. If (n + 1)/2 is an integer, the median is the value that is in the (n + 1)/2 location in the sorted distribution. Here, (n + 1)/2 = 6/2 or 3, which is an integer. So the median is the 3rd score in the sorted distribution, which is 6. If (n + 1)/2 is not an integer, then there is no "middle" score. In such a case, the median is defined as one half of the sum of the two data points that hold the two nearest locations to (n + 1)/2. For example, suppose the data are 1, 4, 6, 5, 8, 0. The sorted distribution is 0, 1, 4, 5, 6, 8. n = 6, and (n + 1)/2 = 7/2 = 3.5. This is not an integer. So the median is one half of the sum of the 3rd and 4th scores in the sorted distribution. The 3rd score is 4 and the firth score is 5. One half of 4 + 5 is 9/2 or 4.5. So the median is 4.5. Here, notice that half of the scores are above 4.5 and half are below. In this case, the ideal definition is satisfied. Also, notice that the median may not be an actual value in the data set. Indeed, the median may not even be a possible value.

One of the most common quantities used to summarize a set of data is its centre. The centre is a single value, chosen in such a way that it gives a reasonable approximation of normality. There are many ways to approximate the centre of a set of data. One of the most familiar and useful measures of centre is the mean, however, using only the mean to approximate normality can often be misleading.

To obtain a better understanding of what is considered normal, other measures of central tendency such as the median, the trimmed mean, and the trimean may be utilized in addition to the mean.

MEAN

The mean, or "average", is the most widely used measure of central tendency. The mean is defined technically as the sum of all the data scores divided by n (the number of scores in the distribution). In a sample, we often symbolise the mean with a letter with a line over it. If the letter is "X", then the mean is symbolised as $\bar{x}$, pronounced "X-bar." If we use the letter X to represent the variable being measured, then symbolically, the mean is defined as $\frac{\sum X}{n}$

For example, using the data from above, where the n = 5 values of X were 5, 7, 6, 1, and 8, the mean is (5 + 7 + 6 + 1 + 8) / 5 = 5.4. The mean number of sexual partners reported by UNE students who responded to the question is, from Figure 4.1, (1 + 0 + 2 + 4 +... + 0 + 6 + 2 + 2)/ 177 = 1.864. Note that this is higher than both the mode and the median. In a positively skewed distribution, the mean will be higher than the median because its value will be dragged in the direction of the tail. Similarly in a negatively skewed distribution, the mean will be dragged lower than the median because of the extra large values in the left-hand tail. Distributions of qualitative data do not have a mean.

Frequently an experiment will be performed several times under (assumed) identical conditions, resulting in what is referred to as a data set - several values that purport to measure the same thing. In this lesson we look at ways of characterizing the data set.

Perhaps the most common way in which we do this is by giving the mean and the standard deviation of the data. The mean is simply the arithmetic average of the data. To calculate the mean you simply add up all of the values in your data set and divide by the number of elements in the set. For example, suppose you run the 100 meter dash on eight different occasions, under identical conditions, and your times are 12.23, 12.14, 12.45, 12.18, 12.26, 12.51, 12.47 and 12.36 seconds.

You would find the mean by adding this series of numbers and dividing by eight.

Do this calculation, either by hand or using your calculator, and write down the value you obtain for the mean. You will submit this value to your laboratory instructor later. We can represent the mean mathematically by the formula

$$\text{mean} = \overline{X} = \frac{\sum_{i=1}^{n} X_i}{n}$$

where the x with the bar over it (read x-bar) is the mean, x_i represents the individual data points, and there are n such points.

VARIABILITY

Variability refers to how "spread out" a group of scores is. To see what we mean by spread out, consider graphs in Figure. These graphs represent the scores on two quizzes. The mean score for each quiz is 7.0. Despite the equality of means, you can see that the distributions are quite different. Specifically, the scores on Quiz 1 are more densely packed and those on Quiz 2 are more spread out. The differences among students was much greater on Quiz 2 than on Quiz 1.

Quix 1

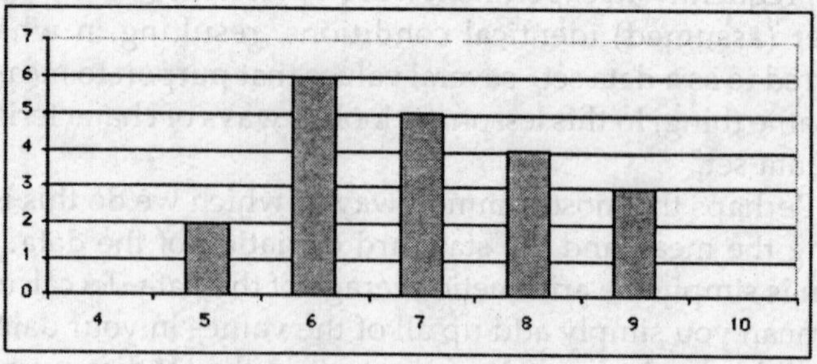

Fig. Bar charts of Two Quizzes.

Quiz 2

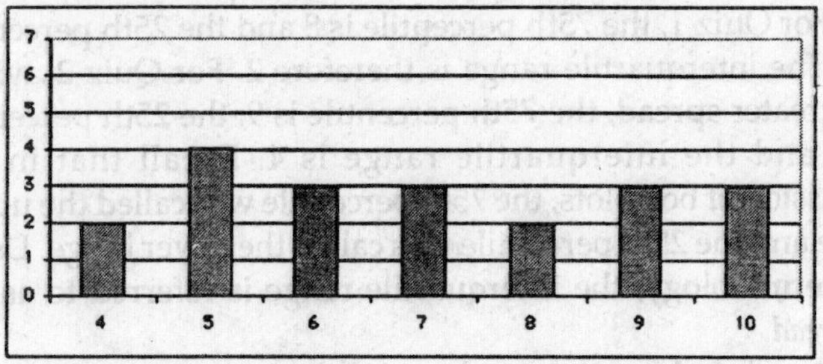

The terms variability, spread, and dispersion are synonyms, and refer to how spread out a distribution is. Just as in the section on central tendency we discussed measures of the centre of a distribution of scores, in this chapter we will discuss measures of the variability of a distribution. There are four frequently used measures of variability, the range: interquartile range, variance, and standard deviation. In the next few paragraphs, we will look at each of these four measures of variability in more detail.

RANGE

The range is the simplest measure of variability to calculate, and one you have probably encountered many times in your life. The range is simply the highest score minus the lowest score. Let's take a few examples. What is the range of the following group of numbers: 10, 2, 5, 6, 7, 3, 4? Well, the highest number is 10, and the lowest number is 2, so 10 - 2 = 8. The range is 8. Let's take another example. Here's a dataset with 10 numbers: 99, 45, 23, 67, 45, 91, 82, 78, 62, 51. What is the range? The highest number is 99 and the lowest number is 23, so 99 - 23 equals 76; the range is 76. Now consider the two quizzes shown in Figure. On Quiz 1, the lowest score is 5 and the highest score is 9. Therefore, the range is 4. The range on Quiz 2 was larger: the lowest score was 4 and the highest score was 10. Therefore the range is 6.

INTERQUARTILE RANGE

The *interquartile range* (IQR) is the range of the middle 50%

of the scores in a distribution. It is computed as follows:

IQR = 75th percentile - 25th percentile

For Quiz 1, the 75th percentile is 8 and the 25th percentile is 6. The interquartile range is therefore 2. For Quiz 2, which has greater spread, the 75th percentile is 9, the 25th percentile is 5, and the interquartile range is 4. Recall that in the discussion of box plots, the 75th percentile was called the upper hinge and the 25th percentile was called the lower hinge. Using this terminology, the interquartile range is referred to as the *H-spread*.

A related measure of variability is called the *semi-interquartile range*. The semi-interquartile range is defined simply as the interquartile range divided by 2. If a distribution is symmetric, the median plus or minus the semi-interquartile range contains half the scores in the distribution.

VARIANCE

Variability can also be defined in terms of how close the scores in the distribution are to the middle of the distribution. Using the mean as the measure of the middle of the distribution, the variance is defined as the average squared difference of the scores from the mean. The data from Quiz 1 are shown in table. The mean score is 7.0. Therefore, the column "Deviation from Mean" contains the score minus 7. The column "Squared Deviation" is simply the previous column squares.

One thing that is important to notice is that the mean deviation from the mean is 0. This will always be the case. The mean of the squared deviations is 1.5. Therefore, the variance is 1.5. Analogous calculations with Quiz 2 show that it's variance is 6.7. The formula for the variance is:

$$\sigma^2 = \frac{\sum (X - \mu)^2}{N}$$

where σ^2 is the variance, μ is the mean, and N is the number of numbers. For Quiz 1, $\mu = 7$ and N = 20.

If the variance in a sample is used to estimate the variance in a population, then the previous formula underestimates the variance and the following formula should be used:

$$s^2 = \frac{\sum (X - M)^2}{N - 1}$$

Table 1. Calculation of Variance for Quiz 1 Scores.

Scores	*Deviation from Mean*	*Squared Deviation*
9	2	4
9	2	4
9	2	4
8	1	1
8	1	1
8	1	1
8	1	1
7	0	0
7	0	0
7	0	0
7	0	0
7	0	0
6	-1	1
6	-1	1
6	-1	1
6	-1	1
6	-1	1
6	-1	1
5	-2	4
5	-2	4
7	0	1.5

where s^2 is the estimate of the variance and M is the sample mean. Note that M is the mean of a sample taken from a population with a mean of μ. Since, in practice, the variance is usually computed in a sample, this formula is most often used. The simulation "estimating variance" illustrates the bias in the formula with N in the denominator.

Let's take a concrete example. Assume the scores 1, 2, 4, and 5 were sampled from a larger population. To estimate the variance in the population you would compute s^2 as follows:

$M = (1 + 2 + 4 + 5)/4 = 12/4 = 3.$

$s^2 = [(1 - 3)^2 + (2 - 3)^2 + (4 - 3)^2 + (5 - 3)^2]/(4 - 1)$

$= (4 + 1 + 1 + 4)/3 = 10/3 = 3.333$

There are alternate formulas that can be easier to use if you are doing your calculations with a hand calculator:

$$\sigma^2 = \frac{\sum X^2 - \frac{\left(\sum X\right)^2}{N}}{N}$$

and

$$s^2 = \frac{\sum X^2 - \frac{\left(\sum X\right)^2}{N}}{N-1}$$

For this example,

$\Sigma X^2 = 1^2 + 2^2 + 4^2 + 5^2 = 46$

$(\Sigma X)^2 = (1 + 2 + 4 + 5)^2/N = 144/4 = 36$

$\sigma^2 = (46 - 36)/4 = 2.5$ and

$s^2 = (46 - 36)/3 = 3.333$ as with the other formula.

STANDARD DEVIATION

The *standard deviation* is simply the square root of the variance. This makes the standard deviations of the two quiz distributions 1.225 and 2.588. The standard deviation is an especially useful measure of variability when the distribution is normal or approximately normal because the proportion of the distribution within a given number of standard deviations from the mean can be calculated. For example, 68% of the distribution is within one standard deviation of the mean and approximately 95% of the distribution is within two standard deviations of the mean.

Therefore, if you had a normal distribution with a mean of 50 and a standard deviation of 10, then 68% of the distribution would be between 50 – 10 = 40 and 50 + 10 = 60. Similarly, about 95% of the distribution would be between 50 – 2 × 10 = 30 and 50 + 2 × 10 = 70. The symbol for the population standard deviation is σ; the symbol for an estimate computed in a sample is *s*. Figure shows two normal distributions.

Both distributions have means of 50. The blue distribution has a standard deviation of 5; the red distribution has a standard deviation of 10. For the blue distribution, 68% of the distribution is between 45 and 55; for the red distribution, 68% is between 40 and 60.

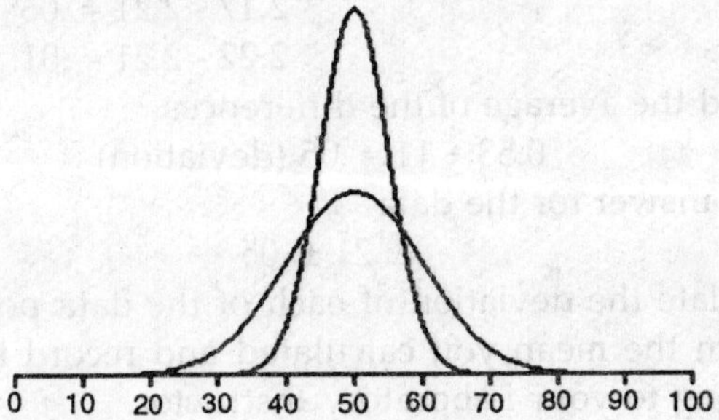

Fig. Normal Distributions with Standard Deviations of 5 and 10.

AVERAGE DEVIATION

The average deviation or the average absolute deviation is a measure of dispersion. It is the average of absolute deviations of the individual values from the median or from the mean.

CALCULATING AVERAGE DEVIATION

1. Find the average of your measurements.
2. Find the difference between the average and each of your measurements use absolute value.
3. Find the average of these differences. This will be your deviation.

Example:

In the data set

2.10	1. Find average	2. Find difference between
2.30	24.26 ÷ 11 = 2.21	average and each
2.22		measurement.
2.23		2.10 - 2.21 = .11
2.25		2.30 - 2.21 = .09

2.22	2.22 - 2.21 = .01
2.13	2.23 - 2.21 = .02
2.24	2.25 - 2.21 = .04
2.28	2.22 - 2.21 = .01
2.17	2.13 - 2.21 = .08
2.22	2.24 - 2.21 = .03
	2.28 - 2.21 = .07
	2.17 - 2.21 = .06
	2.22 - 2.21 = .01

3. Find the average of the differences

$$0.53 \div 11 = .05 \text{ (deviation)}$$

Final answer for the data

$$2.21 \pm .05$$

Calculate the deviation of each of the data points given above from the mean you calculated and record the results for reporting to your Laboratory Instructor.

Occasionally you will encounter the average deviation, given by the expression.

$$\text{average deviation} = \frac{\sum_{i=1}^{n} \left|(x_i - \overline{x})\right|}{n}$$

Calculate and report the average deviation for the data above. Although the average deviation is easy to calculate, it has no statistical significance. The form of the deviation that is statistically significant, and which we will use in the next lesson to predict the form of the distribution curve for a set of data, is the standard deviation.

You will encounter two similar, but slightly different, formulas for the standard deviation. The first one is known as the standard deviation of the population, and refers to the case when n is very large (or infinite).

$$\text{Standard deviation} = \sigma = \sqrt{\frac{\sum_{i=1}^{n} (x_i - \overline{x})^2}{n}}$$

For a small data set, such as the ones you usually have in

an experimental science, the standard deviation is approximated by what is referred to as the standard deviation for the sample, ususally represented by s to distinguish it from the population standard deviation σ

$$s = \sqrt{\frac{\sum_{i=1}^{n}(x_i - \bar{x})^2}{n-1}}$$

This is the form of the standard deviation that we will use. Calculate both expressions for your data set (and report them, naturally). What will happen to the difference between the two expressions as n increases? Why?

Now let's perform the calculations you have done above on a larger data set. When you click on the button labeled go, you will proceed to an Excel spreadsheet which shows the masses of a number of pre-1985 U.S. pennies. You should characterize that data set by the mean and explore several ways of expressing the deviations from the mean. In doing so, you will use the computational capabilities of Excel, rather than calculating by hand.

The spreadsheet will show the data only, and will have a number of other column headings. You need to fill out those other columns and to compute the mean, average deviation and standard deviation.

If you lose track of where you are while working on the spreadsheet you can always minimize it and look back at this page. When you are finished with your calculations, record your values for the mean, average deviation, maximum deviation and standard deviation.

You will enter these in the electronic form to send to your laboratory instructor. Before leaving this exercise, quit Excel, and answer no when asked if you wish to save any changes in the spreadsheet.

QUARTILE DEVIATION

The quartile deviation is also called semi-quartile range. It is defined as the amount of dispersion present in the middle of 50% of the values. The equation given by:

Where:

= the quartile deviation

= the first quartile

= the third quartile

Since the second quartile, is actually the median, then its formula is [...]

The quartile deviation is also called semi-quartile range. It is defined as the amount of dispersion present in the middle of 50% of the values. The equation given by:

$$Q.D. = (Q_3 - Q_1)/2$$

Where:

$Q.D.$ = the quartile deviation

Q_1 = the first quartile

Q_3 = the third quartile

Since the second quartile Q_2, is actually the median, then its formula is analogous to that for the median. This is also true with Q_1 and Q_3.

The first quartile Q_1 divides the distribution into a lower one-fourth and upper three fourths of the data while Q_3 divides the distribution into a lower three-fourths and upper one-fourth of the data. Since we are after the lower one-fourth of the distribution for computing, Q_1 then its formula will be

$$Q_1 = L[((N/4) - F_1)f_1]_i$$

Where:

Q_1 = the first quartile.

L = the lower limit of the first quartile class.

F_1 = the cumulative frequency just above the 1st quartile.

f_1 = the frequency of the 1st quartile class.

N = the total frequency.

i = the class interval size.

Relative to Q_3, we are after the value that separates the lower three-fourths of the data from the upper one-fourth. Hence, the formula for the third quartile will be:

$$Q_3 = L[((3N/4) - F_3)/f_3]_i$$

Where:

Q_3 = the third quartile.

L = the lower limit of the 3rd quartile class.

F_3 = the cumulative frequency just above the 3rd quartile class.

N = the total frequency.
i = the class interval size.

RANK AND CORRELATION

In the original feature-set of our dataset, system log i is represented as the message count vector $\vec{c_i}$ defined above. There are 15,000 message types in our dataset, hence this results in a 3,000 × 15,000 matrix. This matrix is very sparse; only about 0.6% of the entries are non-zero. The high dimensionality of the data and its sparseness make k-means clustering impractical for this representation.

Since our objective is message ranking, we propose a new feature construction scheme of the system-log dataset that measures the difference in the ranking of messages between system logs. Two known rank correlation measures can be used to achieve this: The Spearman rank correlation and Kendall's tau rank correlation.

Let $\vec{x}$ and $\vec{y}$ be vectors of dimension N. Let $\vec{r_x}$ and $\vec{r_y}$ be vectors of ranks for $\vec{x}$ and $\vec{y}$, i.e. $r_x[i] = k$ if $x[i]$ is the k'th largest number in $\vec{x}$, and similarly for r_y. The two correlation measures are defined as follows:

Definition: (Spearman Rank Correlation) Let $\vec{d} \stackrel{def}{=} \vec{r_x} - \vec{r_y}$.

The Spearman rank Correlation between $\vec{x}$ and $\vec{y}$ is defined by:

$$\rho(\vec{x}, \vec{y}) \stackrel{def}{=} 1 - \frac{6\|\vec{d}\|^2}{N(N^2 - 1)}$$

Definition. (Kendall's Tau Rank Correlation) Let $P(\vec{x}, \vec{y})$ be the number of pairs such that both $r_x[i] > r_x[j]$ and $r_y[i] > r_y[j]$. Kendall's tau rank correlation between $\vec{x}$ and $\vec{y}$ is defined by:

$$\tau(\vec{x}, \vec{y}) \stackrel{def}{=} \frac{4P(\vec{x}, \vec{y})}{N(N-1)} - 1$$

We first define a new *Spearman-based* feature-set. In this feature-set, system log i is represented by the vector$\left(\rho\left(\vec{c_i},\vec{c_1}\right),\ldots,\rho\left(\vec{c_i},\vec{c_k}\right)\right)$, where k is the number of samples in our dataset. A Kendall's-tau-based feature-set can be generated in an analogous way. The resulting matrix is a sample correlation matrix, and the new feature-set has k dimensions instead of the much larger n(the number of different message types in the dataset). It is generally expected that in a typical dataset, n would be much larger than k as it is in our own dataset, because of the diversity of possible messages in a computer system. It is interesting to note that using either the Spearman-based feature-set or the Kendall's-tau-based feature set generates a kernel similarity matrix for the original dataset. This opens the possibility of using these correlation measures in kernel-based algorithms. We prove that both sample correlation matrices are kernel matrices, using the fact that a kernel matrix is a Positive Semi-Definite (PSD) matrix. A matrix A is PSD if for any non-zero vector x, $x'Ax \geq 0$. We first prove that the Pearson Sample Correlation matrix is PSD, and then conclude that so are the Spearman rank correlation matrix and the Kendall's-tau sample correlation matrix.

Definition. (Pearson Sample Correlation) Let $\vec{x}$ and $\vec{y}$ be vectors of the same dimension. The Pearson correlation coefficient is defined by:

$$r\left(\vec{x},\vec{y}\right)=\frac{\operatorname{cov}\left(\vec{x},\vec{y}\right)}{\sqrt{\operatorname{var}\left(\vec{x}\right).\operatorname{var}\left(\vec{y}\right)}}$$

where *cov* is the sample covariance function and *var* is the sample variance function.

Theorem. A Pearson sample correlation matrix is PSD.

Proof. Let X be a matrix in which each row is a sample. Let S be a diagonal matrix such that entry (i, i) is the variance of row i in X. Assume, without loss of generality, that the mean of each sample in X is zero. Then the Pearson correlation matrix can be written in vector form as:

$$R = S^{-\frac{1}{2}} XX' S^{-\frac{1}{2}}$$

For any non-zero vector $\vec{x}$, the expression $\vec{x}R\vec{x}$ can be written as:

$$\vec{x}R\vec{x} = \vec{x}\left(S^{-\frac{1}{2}} XX' S'^{-\frac{1}{2}}\right)\vec{x} = \left(\vec{x}S^{-\frac{1}{2}} X\right)^2$$

The rightmost element is a square term, hence it is greater than or equal to zero. Therefore R is PSD.

Theorem. A Spearman rank correlation matrix is PSD.

Proof. Spearman correlation is Pearson correlation applied to ranks. Therefore, the Spearman rank correlation matrix is PSD.

Theorem. A Kendall's-tau correlation matrix is PSD.

Proof. For a vector $\vec{x}$ of dimension N, let $\overrightarrow{x_K}$ of dimension N^2 be defined by:

$$x_K[j + (i-1).N] = \begin{cases} 1 & r_x[i] > r_x[j] \\ 0 & \text{otherwise} \end{cases}$$

Then $P(\vec{x}, \vec{y}) = \sum_{k=1}^{N^2} x_K[k].y_k[k]$, and it can be easily verified that Kendall's tau correlation of $\vec{x}$ and $\vec{y}$ is the Pearson correlation of c.$\overrightarrow{x_K}$ and $c.\overrightarrow{y_K}$, for c a constant that depends on n. Hence, Kendall's tau correlation matrix is also a Pearson correlation matrix, and so it is PSD.

Spearman's Rank Correlation Coefficient - usually just called The Spearman Correlation, sometimes Spearman's Rank or Spearman's Rho - is a method of determining the similarity between two numeric sets (we also go over the Pearson and the Kendall). If you don't know what a correlation is, start with Statistics in Erlang part 5, which covers the basic idea of correlations. A good math-based explanation is available at David M Lane's Hyperstat.

In English, for two lists of length N, you take the square of the difference between each matched row in the two lists, sum them, multiply by six, and divide by N cubed minus N. This provides the rank correlation squared, which is over the interval [–1, 1]. However, with spearman you usually use the rank squared, so we leave it that way instead of providing the root; the tuple's atom label makes it clear that's happening.

Sorry again about the screwy formatting; I'm just getting things to fit on the blog. The stuff in the library is better formatted.

```
spearman_correlation(List1, List2) when
    is_list(List1), is_list(List2),
    length(List1) /= length(List2) -> {error, lists_must_be_
same_length};
spearman_correlation(List1, List2) when is_list(List1),
is_list(List2) ->
    {TR1,_} = lists:unzip(ordered_ranks_of(List1)),
    {TR2,_} = lists:unzip(ordered_ranks_of(List2)),
    Numerator = 6 * lists:sum([(D1-D2)*(D1-D2)
                          || {D1,D2} <- lists:zip(TR1,TR2)]),
    Denominator = math:pow(length(List1),3)-length(List1),
    {rsquared,1-(Numerator/Denominator)}.
    1> X = [50,175,270,375,425,580,710,790,890,980].
    [50,175,270,375,425,580,710,790,890,980]
    2> Y = [1.80,1.20,2.00,1.00,1.00,1.20,0.80,0.60,1.00,0.85].
    [1.80000, 1.20000, 2.00000, 1.00000, 1.00000,
     1.20000, 0.800000, 0.600000, 1.00000, 0.850000]
    3> scutil:spearman_correlation(X,Y).
    {rsquared, –0.730303}
```

Bibliography

Abramowitz, M. (ed.) (1964), *Handbook of Mathematical Functions with Formulas,* Washington DC, 1965.

Acton, F.S. (1990), *Numerical Methods that Usually Work,* Mathematical Association of America, Washington DC.

Arnold, V.I., Silverman, R.A. (translater) (1973), *Ordinary Differential Equations,* Cambridge MA.

Atkinson, K.E. (1993), *Elementary Numerical Analysis, 2nd ed.,* New York.

Birkhoff, G., Rota, G.C. (1989), *Ordinary Differential Equations, 4th ed.,* John Wiley, New York.

Blachman, N. (1999), *Mathematica : a Practical Approach, 2nd ed.,* (Upper Saddle River, N.J).

Borovkov, A.A. (1998), *Probability Theory,* (the Netherlands).

Boyce, W.E., DiPrima, R.C. (1997), *Elementary Differential Equations, 6th ed.,* (New York).

Bracewell, R.N. (1986), *The Fourier Transform and Its Applications, 2nd ed.,* (New York).

Brown, J.W., Churchill, R.V. (1993), *Fourier Series and Boundary Value Problems, 3rd ed.,* (New York).

Dahlquist, G., Bjorck, A. (1974), *Numerical Methods,* (Englewood Cliffs, NJ).

Davis, H.F. (1963), *Fourier Series and Orthogonal Functions,* (Boston).

Edwards, C.H., Penney, D.E. (1998), *Calculus with Analytic Geometry, 5th ed.*, (Upper Saddle River, N.J).

Franklin, J.N. (1968), *Matrix Theory*, (Englewood Cliffs, NJ).

Gerald, C.F. (1999), *Applied Numerical Analysis, 6th ed.*, (Cambridge, MA).

Golub, G.H. (1996), *Matrix Computations, 3rd ed.*, (Baltimore).

Index

A

B

C

D

E